The Broadview Guide to Grammar, Usage, and Punctuation

A Note on the Cover

For thousands of years humans have been likening the process of writing to the ways in which we interact with the land—ploughing and digging, sowing and reaping. In the early seventh century CE Isadore of Seville tells of how the Romans for their writing used styluses that were at first made of iron, later of bone, and quotes from a now-lost Roman play by the now-unknown playwright Atta: "we shall turn the ploughshare upon wax, and plough with a bone point." Around 1400 the German poet Johannes von Tepl begins his long poem *The Ploughman of Bohemia* with a reference to what he refers to as a well-known maxim of scribes: "the quill is my plough." In some sense the quill or pen is of course like a plough in that it digs into the writing surface. But the likeness is also a reminder that writing—delving into the language to find the right words and to arrange them in the right order—is hard work. That connection was famously recognized by Seamus Heaney in a 1964 poem likening writing to the digging that humans do with a plough or a spade—likening his father's digging in the earth to the digging Heaney himself does with his "squat pen."

Companion Website

Included in the purchase price of this book is free access to a passcode-protected website. Here you will find a wide range of exercises on English grammar and usage—many of them interactive, so that you can see immediately if you have answered correctly (and, if you haven't, discover where you have gone wrong). The site also makes available MLA, APA, Chicago, and CSE style guides.

For access to this website please visit

sites.broadviewpress.com/grammar

and enter the code

2r9vbur7

The Broadview Guide to Grammar, Usage, and Punctuation

The Mechanics of Writing

Doug Babington, Corey Frost, Don LePan,
Maureen Okun, Nora Ruddock, and Karen Weingarten

broadview press

BROADVIEW PRESS
Peterborough, Ontario, Canada

Founded in 1985, Broadview Press remains a wholly independent publishing house. Broadview's focus is on academic publishing; our titles are accessible to university and college students as well as scholars and general readers. With over 800 titles in print, Broadview has become a leading international publisher in the humanities, with world-wide distribution. Broadview is committed to environmentally responsible publishing and fair business practices.

Library and Archives Canada Cataloguing in Publication

Title: The Broadview guide to grammar, usage, and punctuation : the mechanics of writing / Doug Babington, Corey Frost, Don LePan, Maureen Okun, Nora Ruddock, and Karen Weingarten.
Other titles: Guide to grammar, usage, and punctuation : the mechanics of writing
Names: Babington, Doug, author. | Frost, Corey, author. | LePan, Don, 1954- author. | Okun, Maureen, 1961- author. | Ruddock, Nora, 1978- author. | Weingarten, Karen, 1980- author.
Description: Includes bibliographical references and index.
Identifiers: Canadiana (print) 20240299213 | Canadiana (ebook) 2024029923X | ISBN 9781554816774 (softcover) | ISBN 9781460408797 (EPUB) | ISBN 9781770489554 (PDF)
Subjects: LCSH: English language—Grammar—Handbooks, manuals, etc. | LCSH: English language—Usage—Handbooks, manuals, etc. | LCSH: English language—Punctuation—Handbooks, manuals, etc.
Classification: LCC PE1112 .B27 2024 | DDC 428.2—dc23

Broadview Press handles its own distribution in Canada and the United States:
PO Box 1243, Peterborough, Ontario K9J 7H5, Canada
555 Riverwalk Parkway, Tonawanda, NY 14150, USA
Tel: (705) 482-5915
email: customerservice@broadviewpress.com

For all territories outside Canada and the United States, distribution is handled by the Eurospan Group.

Broadview Press acknowledges the financial support of the Government of Canada for our publishing activities.

Cover Design: Lisa Brawn
Managing Editor: Tara Lowes
Design and Typesetting: Eileen Eckert and Jonathan Ranallo

Broadview Press® is the registered trademark of Broadview Press Inc.

PRINTED IN CANADA

CONTENTS

HOW TO USE THIS BOOK AND ITS COMPANION WEBSITE

For many years, the coverage of grammar and usage in *The Broadview Guide to Writing* has received particular praise. Now, for the first time, that material is made available in a stand-alone volume—*The Broadview Guide to Grammar, Usage, and Punctuation.*

We've built in a number of features that we hope will make the book easy for you to find your way around in:

- Page headers: Book sections are indicated throughout in the headers for each page.
- Marginal tabs: For convenience, sections are also indicated with colored tabs in the margin of each page—tabs that 'bleed' to the edge of the page to enhance visibility.
- Index: Go to the index at the back of the book to find the location within the body of the book for any topic, large or small.
- Table of contents: The detailed table of contents at the beginning of the book sets out sections, chapters, and topics within chapters.

Companion website: The purchase price of *The Broadview Guide to Grammar, Usage, and Punctuation* includes free access to the companion website, where you will find various sorts of material related to this book—including a wide range of interactive exercises, a guide to national variants (American usage compared to Canadian, British, and Australian), and extensive information on citation and documentation systems.

The website includes hundreds of exercises relating to almost every aspect of grammar, usage, and punctuation. Many of these are interactive; you can check immediately if you have answered correctly and—if you haven't—find an explanation. The companion website is located here: <https://sites.broadviewpress.com/grammar> With any of the interactive exercises, we recommend that you first read the introductory material—and/or the relevant material in the pages of *The Broadview Guide to Grammar, Usage, and Punctuation.* Then answer all the questions in the exercise; when you are done, click on the "Submit Quiz" button at the bottom. You will be given your score—told how many of the answers you gave are correct—and also given an explanation as to *why* the correct answer is correct (and the incorrect answers wrong).

There are also "Print" and "Email" options. If, for example, an instructor wants to see evidence that students have completed an assigned quiz, the instructor can ask the students to click on the "Email" button and email the results to the instructor—or ask the students to print out a completed quiz and hand in the hard copy.

This book does *not* provide certain features that you will find in most other writing guides: glossy paper that is both expensive and environmentally unfriendly, and highlighting in many different colors throughout the book. We have added one accent color, but we have no desire to add more—or to move away from our long-standing policy of using plain (and, as much as possible, recycled) paper stock. That's a good choice for the environment—and also one that helps us keep the price of this book at a reasonable level.

If you have questions or comments about *The Broadview Guide to Grammar, Usage, and Punctuation* (or suggestions as to what else we should consider including for future editions, whether on the companion website or in the book itself), we'd like to hear from you. Just email <customerservice@broadviewpress.com>. Thank you!

Acknowledgements: The authors gratefully acknowledge the assistance of those academics and students who have taken the time to comment and to offer suggestions on the grammar and usage sections of *The Broadview Guide to Writing* in its many editions, and also to respond to the publisher's queries as to the advisability of publishing the grammar and usage material as a stand-alone volume. We wish in particular to acknowledge the assistance provided by the following: Terri Baker, Mount Royal University; Louise Kane Bishop, Central Florida University; Ruth Bradley-St.-Cyr, University of Ottawa; Maria DiCenzo, Wilfrid Laurier University; Eileen Eckert; Dorrita Fong, Douglas College; Elisa Johnson, South Georgia State College; Stephen Latta; Jonathan Lavery, Wilfrid Laurier University; Ann Levey, University of Calgary; Kathryn MacLennan, University of Regina; Micaela Maftei, Camosun College; Robert M. Martin, Dalhousie University; Emily McGiffin, University of British Columbia; Angela Patton, Walsh College; Sarah Waisvisz, Carleton University; Kevin Whetter, Acadia University; Saihua Xia, Murray State University. Warm thanks to all of you!

WRITING MECHANICS

1 GRAMMAR

1.1 What Is Grammar?

What is grammar, and what is usage? Simply put, the first has to do with the structures into which words are put together in a language, and the ways in which the structures of the words themselves can signify their meaning. The second has to do with the myriad ways in which words are used within those structures.

There's no structural reason why we should use the word *careless* rather than the word *uncaring* if we are talking about someone being negligent or thoughtless, and use the word *uncaring* when we are talking about someone being insufficiently concerned about the feelings of others. It's simply a matter of the way in which English-speakers have grown accustomed to using the words over centuries. It's purely a matter of usage, in other words. But there is a structural reason why we say "he drove the car carelessly" and not "carelessly the car he drove." The normal structure of English places the grammatical subject of a sentence (in this case, the pronoun *he*) before the verb; grammatical objects (in this case, *the car*) are normally placed after the verb.

Different languages have different structures and different ways of indicating grammatical relationships. In languages which are heavily inflected, a word may very frequently have several different possible endings, with each of the endings indicating a different grammatical relationship. In a language such as English, on the other hand, grammatical relationships tend to be indicated rather less by the words themselves and rather more by the order in which words appear in a sentence.

That's not to say that English words never convey grammatical information in themselves. A great many English words do in fact have grammatical information embedded within them. The word *he*, for example, is a subject pronoun; it is used as a grammatical subject. If you are referring to the same person as the grammatical object of an action, the appropriate pronoun to use is *him*. (And if you want to indicate that the same person possesses something, you use the adjective *his* [e.g., *his car, his book*]). The form of a verb conveys grammatical information too; when we say "he **drove** the car carelessly," we are indicating that the action of driving occurred in the past. If we want to indicate that the action is occurring right now, or that it occurs on an ongoing basis, then we use different verb forms: "he **is driving** the car carelessly" or "he **drives** the car carelessly."

Those particular forms of the verb signify different tenses—the simple past tense (*drove*), the present continuous tense (*is driving*), and the simple present tense (*drives*). It's not of course necessary to know the rules and terminology of English grammar in order to use words correctly according to the conventions of English grammar. In acquiring standard English, most native English speakers learn to say and write the forms *drove* and *drives* and *is driving* correctly before they have learned about verb tenses. And they may well continue to use them correctly throughout life without ever learning what verb tenses are. In similar fashion, they are likely to learn at an unconscious level that a third-person singular present tense verb takes an *s*—to say and write *I drive* and *he drives* (not *I drives* and *he drive*)—before they know the terms "third-person" or "present tense" or "verb." But for anyone who aspires to speak and write truly well in formal contexts, who wants to be able to use the English language with precision and eloquence, it's immensely helpful to understand the basics of English grammar and usage.

1.2 Parts of Speech

The most basic building blocks of English grammar are the parts of speech; nouns, verbs, adjectives, adverbs, pronouns, prepositions, and conjunctions are the categories we'll use here. These labels designate the potential uses to which a word can be put, so in the dictionary you'll notice that each word has been given at least one of these labels. Sometimes a word can only belong to one category: between, for example, is always a preposition. Often, though, a word can have more than one meaning and be used as more than one part of speech. Take the word down, for example, which can be any of the following:

a noun ("The team scored on the first *down*."),
a verb ("I thirstily *downed* the whole bottle."),
an adjective ("He was feeling a little *down*."),
an adverb ("The airplane went *down*."), or
a preposition ("I walked *down* the street.").

Labeling a word as a part of speech tells us what kind of a word it is, but it doesn't tell us what function it might serve in a particular sentence—for that you need to understand the parts of a sentence. It's a bit hard, though, to define one without referring to the other, so if some of the terminology used below seems unfamiliar, the next section should provide clarity. As you read this introduction to grammar basics, you should also keep something important in mind: categories such as "verbs" and "nouns" are not naturally occurring phenomena with clearly defined characteristics like elements or species. Rather they are attempts to define certain features of language that usually act in certain ways, so that we can accurately describe the functioning of this infinitely complex and fascinating system we use to communicate. The upshot of this is that there are often disputes among reasonable people about how best to categorize these features of language. Some grammar guides say that articles are a distinct part of speech; for others, they are a subset of adjectives. For some there are four categories of pronouns; others count more. Don't get too bogged down in these details; grammarians are for the most part in agreement as to the core principles of English grammar—and as to the value for the student of learning these principles.

Nouns

Nouns are words that name people, things, places, or qualities.

Some examples:
girl, Wilma, surgeon, grandparents, Admiral Byrd (people);
spaghetti, hippo, atmosphere, word, motion, English (things);
hospital, bedroom, Zambia, Mt. Rushmore, Venus (places);
silence, intelligence, anger, height, loveliness (qualities)

Nouns can be used to fill the gaps in sentences like these:

I saw ________ at the market yesterday.
He dropped the ________ into the soup.
That is not the right _________ for the occasion!
We live in a __________ in the middle of ___________.
Has learning Italian taken a lot of _________?

Nouns can be either **countable** (e.g., *hat, street, clown*) or **uncountable** (e.g., *air, milk, knowledge*) and this affects how they are pluralized and combined with articles. We say, for example, *he's wearing a hat* or *he's wearing many hats*—because *hat* is a countable noun and can therefore be **singular** or **plural**. But we never say, *he's breathing an air* or *he's breathing many airs*—because *air* is uncountable, and so can't be pluralized. The correct forms would be *he's breathing air* or *he's breathing a lot of air.*

Nouns can also be either **common** nouns (e.g., *city*, *whale*, *toy*, *president*), which are not capitalized, or **proper** nouns, which refer to specific individual things or people (e.g., *Syracuse*, *Shamu*, *Frisbee*, *Obama*) and are capitalized.

Many nouns are **compound nouns**—combinations in which two or more words have been brought together in a single grammatical unit that acts as a noun (e.g., *office tower*, *public speaking*, *animal rights*, *soap opera*, *business partner*). Long established compounds often become new words, either with a hyphen (e.g., *meeting-room*) or without (e.g., *lawnmower*, *skyscraper*, *haircut*, *rainfall*, *girlfriend*, *software*). Notice that the meaning of the compound exists unto itself; the meaning of *greenhouse* (compound noun) is different from that of *green house* (adjective *green* plus noun *house*), and many people would not automatically class a *boyfriend* or a *girlfriend* as a type of *friend*. In some cases (e.g., *cultural genocide*), the precise meanings of compounds can be difficult to pin down—and can be subject to vigorous debate. For more on compound nouns see p. 144.

Verbs

Verbs are words that express actions or states of affairs. Most verbs can be conveniently thought of as "doing" words (e.g., *do*, *think*, *make*, *say*, *get*, *receive*, *munch*, *plummet*, *contemplate*), but several verbs do not fit into this **action verb** category. Indeed, the most common verb of all—*be*—expresses not an action but a state of affairs. It belongs to another category called **linking verbs**. Rather than expressing an action, a linking verb connects the subject to a noun, pronoun, or adjective that provides additional information about the subject.

Action verbs	**Linking verbs**
Tiger hit the ball.	The chances looked good.
Sara loves Silas.	Silas is her only love.
I felt the wind in my hair.	The wind felt cool.

Note that some verbs (like *feel*) can be either action or linking verbs.

Verbs sometimes change form depending on number, as nouns do: compare "the dog *barks*" (singular subject and verb) and "the dogs *bark*" (plural subject and verb). They can also change form depending on whether the subject is the speaker ("first person"), the addressee ("second person"), or someone else ('third person"). The verbs *am* (as in *I am*), *are* (as in *you are*), and *is* (as in *she is*) are the first person singular, second person singular, and third person singular forms of the verb *to be* in the present tense.

One thing that makes verbs different from other parts of speech is that they also change form depending on time frame; in other words, they have **tenses**. *I am*, *you are*, and *he is*, for example, are all present tense forms. Past tense forms of the verb *to be* include *I was*, *you were*, and *he was*. Some verb forms require **auxiliary verbs** (or "helping verbs") to indicate a tense, and auxiliary verbs are also used to form negatives or interrogatives. **Modal** auxiliaries are a small set of specialized words that don't change form but change the meaning of the verb they are placed in front of.

Tiger *is hitting* the ball. (auxiliary verb: *is*)
Tiger *has won* many championships. (auxiliary verb: *has*)
Tiger *does* not *play* baseball. (auxiliary verb: *does*)
Do you *know* what he plays? (auxiliary verb: *do*)
Can you *guess*? (modal auxiliary: *can*)
It *should be* obvious. (modal auxiliary: *should*)

The form of a **regular** verb follows rules that apply to all regular verbs, but **irregular** verbs don't follow the same rules and may have their own unique forms. In the present tense, the only verbs that have irregular written forms are *to be* and *to have*. However there is a long list of verbs that are irregular in the past tense, such as *drive* (*drove*), *sing* (*sang*), or *speak* (*spoke*).

See section 1.4 for a more complete discussion of verb tenses.

Adjectives

An adjective tells us something more about a person, thing, place, or quality that has been named by a noun. (In grammatical terms, adjectives are said to *describe* or *modify* nouns.) There are two classes: **descriptive adjectives**, like *yummy*, *huge*, *terrible*, or *purple*, are the most obvious kind; the other kind is **determiners**, which we'll address below. Here are some examples of descriptive adjectives:

The *small* boy lifted the *heavy* table.
A *revised* version will be sent to your *downtown* office.
Loud, *frenetic* music was emanating from the *open* window.

Notice that adjectives usually come before the nouns that they describe. This is not always the case, however; **predicate adjectives** come after the noun and after the verb *to be*:

That woman is particularly *careful* about money.
The exercise is too *difficult*.
My brothers and sisters are *dependable*.

Most adjectives (and most adverbs) have three forms—positive, comparative, and superlative. Use the comparative when referring to two, the superlative when referring to more than two.

Of the two cities, Pittsburgh is the more livable.
Of the three sisters, Tonderai is the most reliable.

Most comparative adjectives are formed with -er and -est endings (e.g., *clean*, *cleaner*, *cleanest*, *dark*, *darker*, *darkest*). For longer adjectives (and most adverbs), the comparative and superlative are formed using *more/less* for the comparative and *most/least* for the superlative (e.g., *more responsible/less responsible*, *most responsible/least responsible*; *more responsibly/less responsibly*, *most responsibly/least responsibly*).

A number of the most commonly used adjectives and adverbs are irregular in form:

Adjectives	**Adverbs**
good, better, best	well, better, best

[N.B. In limited contexts when physical health is being discussed, *well* is used as an adjective (e.g., she was very sick last month, but now she is almost well).]

bad, worse, worst	badly, worse, worst
far, farther, farthest (distance)	far, farther, farthest
far, further, furthest (amount, time)	far, further, furthest
little, less, least (amount)	little, less, least

[N.B. For countable amounts use few, fewer, fewest.]

some, more, most	some, more, most
many, more, most	many, more, most
much, more, most	much, more, most

See pages 179-80 for a discussion of terms considered not to admit of degrees (e.g., *unique*, *universal*, *perfect*, *complete*, *correct*). See 4.10 for a discussion of the error of using double comparatives or superlatives.

Determiners are categorized by come linguists as a type of adjective, by others as a separate part-of-speech category. They appear before nouns and act to specify rather than to describe. When we differentiate among *a cookie*, *one cookie*, *the cookie*, *this cookie*, and *that cookie*, we are using as determiners the words *a*, *the*, *one*, *this*, and *that*. (Note that if we also use a descriptive adjective, the determiner comes first, as in "the *scrumptious* cookie.")

A, *an*, and *the* are a sub-category of determiners known as **articles**. For native speakers, using articles is fairly intuitive—but explaining how to use them can be complicated, and they can cause problems for some non-native speakers. Generally speaking, the **indefinite article** (*a*, or *an* when used before a vowel) is used when the noun is a member of a general class, or its specificity has not yet been established. "Yesterday I met *a* poodle" doesn't tell us which poodle in particular. The **definite article** (*the*) most often indicates that the noun should be taken as specific, either because it is unique, or because its specificity has been previously established.

Yesterday I met *the* friendliest poodle ever.
(The noun is specific in that there can only be one friendliest poodle ever.)
Yesterday I met *the* poodle that Sara adopted.
(The noun is specific because of the extra information supplied after the noun.)

The choice of article is often context-dependent.

I looked out my window and saw *the* moon.
I looked up at the sky of the alien planet and saw *a* large reddish moon.

She had *a* conversation with *a* friend.
She had *the* conversation she needed to have with *the* friend she trusts the most.

Besides articles, the category of determiners includes **numbers** ("one cookie"), **quantifiers** ("some cookies"), **possessives** ("Sara's cookie"), and **demonstratives** ("that cookie").

Adverbs

Usually, an adverb tells us something more about an action or a state of affairs that has been expressed by a verb. Adverbs can also tell us something more about the state of affairs indicated by adjectives or, in some cases, by other adverbs. (In grammatical terms, adverbs are said to *describe* or *modify* verbs, adjectives, or other adverbs.) Many adverbs are easily recognized because they consist of an adjective (like *easy*) with the letters *ly* appended (*easily*), but be careful: some adverbs look the same as their adjective counterparts (like *far*). And some words that end in *ly* are not adverbs at all (like *early*). Here are a few examples, alongside adjectives for comparison:

Adjective	**Adverb**
careful	carefully
beautiful	beautifully
slow	slowly
fast	fast
good	well

The adverbs above are all used to tell us *how* an action is done, but adverbs can also tell us *when*, *where*, or *to what degree* something happens: *there*, *here*, *high*, *low*, *later*, *soon*, *often*, *occasionally*, and *entirely* are all adverbs. Words like *very*, *extremely*, or *somewhat* are adverbs that can be used to modify adjectives or other adverbs, and sometimes adverbs actually modify whole clauses or sentences:

If he walks *quickly*, he will arrive *soon*.

(The adverbs *quickly* and *soon* modify the verbs *walks* and *will arrive*.)

She looked *up* and she felt *very* happy.

(The adverb *up* modifies the verb *looked*, and the adverb *very* modifies the adjective *happy*.)

He was *quite* sure that things would not end *so* happily.

(The adverb *quite* modifies the adjective *sure*, and the adverb *so* modifies the adverb *happily*.)

The US administration has *usually* supported the British government. *Interestingly*, though, the administration has in this case not issued any comment on the British government's announcement.

(The adverb *usually* modifies the verb *supported*, and the adverb *interestingly* modifies the entire second sentence.)

Pronouns

Pronouns replace or stand for nouns. Instead of saying, "I saw Sara when Sara arrived," we can say, "I saw Sara when *she* arrived." *Sara* is now the pronoun's *antecedent*—the noun the pronoun refers back to.

There are several different classes of pronouns; here is a quick overview. Note that some pronouns can be used more than one way (e.g., *that* can be either a relative pronoun or a demonstrative pronoun). Help with common pronoun errors can be found on pages 124–32.

Personal pronouns refer to specific people or things, and they come in different forms depending on what role they play in a sentence (see 1.3 for more on parts of sentences) and whether they are singular or plural. **Subject pronouns** replace subjects—the doers of an action—and **object pronouns** replace objects—the recipients or targets of an action.

	singular	*plural*
Subject Pronouns:	I	we
	you	you
	he / she / it	they
Object Pronouns:	me	us
	you	you
	him / her / it	them

She loves Silas. (The pronoun is the subject.)
Silas loves *her*. (The pronoun is the object; *Silas* is the subject.)

There are also personal **interrogative pronouns**: *who* and *what* (subject) as well as *whom* and *what* (object).

Who loves Silas? *What* is her name?
Whom does Silas love? *What* do you think?

Personal pronouns also include the **possessive pronouns** *mine*, *ours*, *yours*, *his*, *hers*, and *theirs*, which generally stand for a noun phrase showing possession (*its* is only rarely used this way).

Is this cookie *yours*?
(The pronoun replaces "your cookie.")
He ate his cookie and Sara ate *hers*.
(The pronoun replaces "her cookie.")

Note the difference between *yours* and *your*. In the phrase "your book," *your* is a **possessive adjective** (as are *my*, *our*, *his*, *her*, *its*, *their*, and *whose*). Because these words are only used as modifiers for a noun (as in "your book"), they are technically adjectives, not pronouns.

Reflexive pronouns, which include *myself, yourself, himself, herself, itself, ourselves, yourselves,* and *themselves,* usually replace the object of some self-directed action.

Sara treated *herself* to a cookie.

(The pronoun replaces "Sara" as the object of a sentence in which Sara is also the subject.)

Whereas personal pronouns refer to a definite person, **indefinite pronouns**, such as *each, every, all, either, neither, one, another, much,* or *many* are used when the antecedent is indefinite (that is, it could be any or all of a number of possibilities).

Great cookies! Can I have *another*?

(The pronoun replaces "another cookie.")

These words may be used as pronouns or as adjectives.

All is good. (*All* is a pronoun.)
All cookies are good. (*All* is an adjective.)

There are four **demonstrative pronouns**: *this, that, these,* and *those.* They serve to point to something, and they can also be used as pronouns or adjectives (determiners).

This is Sara. *That* is Silas. She likes *these* cookies; he likes *those.*

Relative pronouns (*who, whom, whose, which,* and *that*) relate a clause to a noun that has been used earlier in the same sentence. Consider how repetitious these sentences sound: *I talked to a man. The man wore a red hat.* We could of course replace the second *man* with *he.* Even better, though, is to relate the second idea to the first by using a relative pronoun: *I talked to a man* who *wore a red hat.* This turns the second sentence into a **relative clause**. Relative clauses are usually placed near the part of the sentence they relate back to. Compare:

I found the cookie under the bed. I had lost the cookie a year ago.
I found the cookie that I had lost a year ago under the bed.

Try replacing the second noun in these pairs of sentences with a relative pronoun, so as to make only one sentence out of each pair:

I ate the cookies. Silas had made the cookies.

The Senator is on a trip to Asia. The trip was originally slated for last year.

Rhetoric refers to the art of persuasion using words. *Rhetoric* is derived from a Greek word meaning "speaker."

Prepositions

Prepositions are joining words, normally used before nouns or pronouns to create prepositional phrases, which can function to modify nouns or verbs. Here are some of the most common prepositions:

about	before	into	over
across	for	of	to
after	from	off	until
at	in	on	with

I will tell you *about* it *in* the morning.
Please try to arrive *before* eight o'clock.
He won't get *to* Edmonton *until* tomorrow.
I received a letter *from* my sister.

Conjunctions

Conjunctions and conjunctive adverbs are normally used to join words or groups of words together, and in particular to join clauses together. Conjunctions can be divided into three types: coordinating, subordinating, and correlative.

Coordinating conjunctions are words that indicate a connection between words or groups of words that form grammatical elements of the same type and rank. There are only seven such conjunctions in English: *and*, *but*, *for*, *nor*, *or*, *so*, *yet*. (Since there are so few of them, they can easily be memorized; some people use the acronym FANBOYS as a memory aid—For, And, Nor, But, Or, Yet, So). Coordinating conjunctions can indicate a connection between two or more nouns (*cars* ***or*** *trucks*); two or more verbs (*see, hear,* ***and*** *understand*); two or more adjectives (*sturdy* ***yet*** *flexible*); or two or more adverbs (*slowly* ***but*** *surely*). They can indicate a connection between phrases (*with patience* ***and*** *with understanding; in warm sunshine* ***or*** *in the midst of winter*). Perhaps most notably, coordinating conjunctions can be used to join two or more independent clauses within one sentence:

They arrived quite late, **and** they left very early.

The company wanted to increase its market share, **so** it lowered prices on all its products.

Everyone agreed that the statue was beautifully sculpted, **but** many felt the monument honored someone who did not deserve this sort of public commemoration.

(Note that when coordinating conjunctions are used to join independent clauses in this way, they are typically preceded by a comma.)

It's less widely known that coordinating conjunctions can also be used to indicate a connection between two independent clauses that form separate sentences; it would be grammatically correct to begin a new sentence with the coordinating conjunction in any of the three examples above. But, as a matter of style rather than of grammatical correctness, it may be particularly appropriate to start a new sentence with a coordinating conjunction in cases where a sentence would otherwise become quite long or syntactically complex:

In the face of growing competition, the company was nevertheless determined to increase its market share. **So** it lowered prices on all its products.

Everyone agreed that the statue was beautifully sculpted and that it depicted its subject very realistically. **But** many felt the monument honored someone who did not deserve this sort of public commemoration.

The above point deserves emphasis, particularly where the coordinating conjunctions *and* and *but* are concerned, since many students emerge from high school with the sense that it is wrong to start a new sentence with *and* or *but*. That's simply not the case; so long as they are used to begin a sentence that includes a subject and a verb, it is perfectly correct to use *and* or *but* to begin a sentence. The group of words *but not that way* cannot form a complete sentence; it lacks both a subject and a verb. The same is true of this group of words: *And now, the most anticipated film of the year.* But the following are both perfectly correct:

Authorities claimed that the armed forces had been restrained in dealing with the protest. But the video evidence tells a different story.

Dozens of films were postponed or canceled last month as a result of the pandemic. And now, the most anticipated film of the year has also been indefinitely postponed.

Here are a few more examples of the ways in which coordinating conjunctions can be used:

Carmen hated the movie, but we really liked it.

(The coordinating conjunction *but* joins two independent clauses. Note that it is preceded by a comma.)

His anxiety made him uncomfortable yet improved his playing.
(The coordinating conjunction *yet* joins two verb phrases.)

The action of the novel is fast-moving and intense.
(The coordinating conjunction *and* joins two adjectives that modify the same noun.)

Subordinating conjunctions are used to indicate a connection between dependent clauses and independent clauses; they indicate that the one is subordinate to the other (in other words, that it is of a lower grammatical rank). A dependent clause can provide information of various sorts about the action in an independent clause—when that action occurred, for example, or why it occurred, or where it occurred.

She left Minnesota and moved to the west coast **when her marriage collapsed.**

I will wash the floor **after I have done the dishes**.

The administration has set this deadline **because it needs to make a decision soon**.

Dependent clauses introduced by subordinating conjunctions can also provide information as to concessions being made with regard to the statement contained in the independent clause, or as to conditions being attached to the statement in the independent clause, or as to comparisons being made with the action named in the independent clause:

We are very confident of achieving success, **though we expect a struggle.**

I will tell her the news **if I see her**.

The Tigers have had an excellent season this year, **whereas they missed the playoffs last year.**

Notice that a dependent clause need not be shorter in length than an independent clause, and notice as well that a dependent clause need not follow the independent clause to which it relates:

After I have done the dishes, I will wash the floor.

Because the administration needs to make a decision soon, it has set this deadline.

If I see her, I will tell her the news.

Though we expect a struggle, we are very confident of achieving success.

English has many subordinating conjunctions; below is a list of some commonly used ones. (Note that some subordinating conjunctions are groups of words rather than single words.)

> after, although, as, as a result of, as long as, as soon as, as though, because, before, even if, even though, if, in order that, just as, provided that, since, so that, though, unless, until, whenever, whereas, while

Correlative conjunctions come in pairs and can join single words or word groups. Here are some examples:

both ... and,	neither ... nor,	so ... that
either ... or,	not only ... but also,	such ... as

Whatever is joined by correlative conjunctions must have the same grammatical structure, as in the examples below:

> That dishcloth is *both* smelly *and* unsanitary.
>
> (Two adjectives are joined—*smelly* and *unsanitary*.)
>
> *Neither* the dollar *nor* the economy will fare well if oil prices drop any lower.
>
> (Two noun phrases are joined—*the dollar* and *the economy*.)
>
> *Not only* is our candidate well educated *but* she is *also* personable.
>
> (Two clauses are joined—*our candidate is well educated* and *she is personable*. Note that when joining clauses, *not only* requires that the usual order of subject and verb in the following clause be reversed—and *but also* is split by the following clause's subject and verb.)

Conjunctive adverbs, as their name suggests, are adverbs that join word groups as well as modifying them. Conjunctive adverbs can join main clauses together or join a stand-alone main clause to a previous sentence; either way, and unlike other types of conjunctions, conjunctive adverbs need not appear exactly at the beginning of the word groups they join—but they are usually set off by commas. Here are some common conjunctive adverbs:

accordingly	alternatively	certainly
finally	furthermore	hence
however	indeed	in fact
likewise	meanwhile	moreover
nonetheless	otherwise	similarly

subsequently	that is	therefore
thus	unfortunately	

Miss Polly was busy hiding the silverware. *Meanwhile*, the Foley brothers arrived at the ranch.

(*Meanwhile* links the two sentences by indicating the time relationship between them.)

That new tablet is fantastic. No one, *however*, will want to pay such a high price for it.

(*However* signals a contrast between the two points made by the two sentences, and so is a transition joining them. Because it is embedded in its sentence, *however* is set apart with commas.)

They must have felt confident that their house would weather the hurricane. *Otherwise*, they would have evacuated when they heard the storm warnings.

(*Otherwise* links the two sentences by indicating that the second sentence is presenting an alternative scenario.)

The storm became much less intense as it approached the coast. *Therefore*, most people saw no reason for concern.

(*Therefore* links the two sentences, indicating that the information provided in the first sentence offers an explanation for people's lack of concern.)

Certain groups of words can also act as conjunctive adverbs. Here are some of the most commonly used:

as a result	at the same time	even so
for example	for instance	in addition
in conclusion	in other words	on the other hand

The storm became much less intense as it approached the coast. *As a result*, most people saw no reason for concern.

(Here the phrase *as a result* functions as a conjunctive adverb—functioning in the same way as *therefore* does above.)

Distinctions between grammatical categories such as coordinating conjunctions, subordinating conjunctions, and conjunctive adverbs are sometimes seen as the sorts of detail that students at the undergraduate level need not be bothered with. But understanding the differences can be a real help in learning to avoid incomplete sentences and run-on sentences in your writing. (More on this below, pages 22–31.)

1.3 Parts of Sentences

Sentences are the basic units of prose writing. They tell us about something happening or something existing or something exhibiting some quality. But what is a **sentence**? It could be defined as a set of words that contains at least one independent clause and conveys a complete thought. The problem with this definition, though, is likely obvious: what is an independent clause? And what is a complete thought? As in the last section, many of the terms we'll use in this section need to be defined with reference to each other.

A **clause** is a distinct group of words, such as "my new phone died suddenly," that includes both a subject and a predicate. A **phrase**, by comparison, is a group of words that either lacks a subject, such as "died suddenly," or lacks a predicate, such as "my new phone." An independent clause is one that can stand on its own as a complete sentence; a dependent clause, on the other hand, while it still has a subject and predicate, is not a complete sentence.

Independent clause	my phone died
Dependent clause	which I bought yesterday

Every sentence has at least one **independent clause**. (Where there is only one, it may also be referred to as the **main clause**.) Other clauses in the sentence that wouldn't be a sentence on their own are called **subordinate clauses** or **dependent clauses**.

A clause tells us about or refers to the actions of—or the existence of or the qualities of—some entity. That entity—a thing, a person, an idea—is the **subject**. The action or state or quality is described by the **predicate**. The core subject can usually be narrowed down to one word, which is always a noun or pronoun, but the complete subject may contain determiners and modifiers and other clauses and may even be a clause itself. The predicate always contains a verb, and may be as simple as that, but it can also contain verb modifiers, including other clauses.

My new phone died suddenly.

Phone is the core subject in this example. *My new phone* is the complete subject. The event described by the predicate is something that the phone did—it *died suddenly*. The predicate consists of a verb and an adverb that describe what the subject did and how.

> My new phone, which I bought yesterday, died suddenly.

Here the complete subject includes a subordinate clause (*which I bought yesterday*)—which has its own subject (*I*) and predicate (*bought yesterday*).

> My fantastic, expensive, next-gen, whip-smart smart phone is extinct.

Here the subject is a phrase consisting of a noun (*phone*) preceded by a string of modifiers (adjectives). The predicate is the linking verb *is* followed by a predicate adjective that describes the subject.

The next example is as simple as they come: a pronoun as subject and a predicate consisting of a one-word verb.

> It died.

A sentence that has just one main clause is called a **simple sentence**, while one that contains additional subordinate clauses is called a **complex sentence**. A sentence may also contain more than one main clause, joined by a coordinating conjunction or a semicolon, in which case it is a **compound sentence**. Sentences can be both complex and compound at once, as well.

Simple sentence	My new phone died suddenly.
Complex sentence	My new phone, which I bought yesterday, died suddenly.
Compound sentence	My new phone died and I was bereft.
Compound-complex sentence	My phone died and I was bereft, so I wept.

Types of Predicate

If you were paying close attention to the examples so far, you may have noticed that while subjects are always essentially a pronoun or noun plus modifiers, predicates can operate in several fairly distinct ways and can include other important parts—objects or complements. The most familiar predicate is the **intransitive verb**, as in "I wept." Predicates like these describe an action taken by the subject, and they can also include adverbial modifiers, as in "I wept like a baby."

Verbs can also be **transitive**, meaning that they describe an action that is done *to* something or someone. That something or someone is the **direct object**. This second type of predicate describes an action that the subject does to the object, as in "I threw the phone to the ground."

In this example the direct object is *phone*. Note that some verbs are always intransitive (such as *weep*), some are always or nearly always transitive (such as *throw*), and some can be either (such as *break*).

In addition to a direct object, some predicates include an **indirect object**—someone or something that the action is done *for*. In this case the predicate describes an action that the subject does to the direct object for the indirect object, as in "My mother bought me a new phone," where the subject is *mother*, the direct object is *phone*, and the indirect object is *me*. If a clause has an indirect object, it always has a direct object as well (and if there is only one object, it is always a direct object). Note, too, that instead of an indirect object, the same meaning can be conveyed with a prepositional phrase (a preposition, usually *to* or *for* in this case, plus a noun or pronoun), as in "My mother bought a new phone for me."

Those first three types of predicate all involve action verbs. In a clause like "my phone is extinct," however, the predicate is different in that it describes a state rather than an action. The verb here is *to be*, the most common of the **linking verbs**. Linking verbs don't describe actions, and they don't take objects; rather they describe states, and they take complements. Other linking verbs include *appear*, *become*, *feel*, *look*, *seem*, *sound*—if you can complete the predicate with an adjective, then the verb is a linking verb. There are three basic ways that a predicate with a linking verb can be completed:

- by an adjective (or adjectival phrase) that describes the subject, as in "my phone is extinct" (an **adjectival subject complement**);
- by a noun (or noun phrase) that describes the subject, as in "my phone was a dud" (a **nominal subject complement**); or
- by an adverb (or adverbial phrase), as in "my phone is there, on the ground" (an **adverbial complement**).

There is one more type of predicate that is a little bit rarer, though surely recognizable. Some transitive verbs take an **object complement** in addition to an object, as in "My mother called me irresponsible." In this example, *me* is the direct object, but the meaning is not complete without the adjective *irresponsible*, which is the object complement. Like subject complements, object complements can be adjectives (as in the above example) or nouns (as in "They elected her President"), but not adverbs. There are only a handful of verbs that work this way; other examples would be "Consider it done," or "It makes me happy."

Not every grammarian will agree with how this list is organized (one could argue that the three kinds of subject complement are three different types of predicate, for example), but they will all agree that it is comprehensive. To review, here are five example sentences illustrating the five predicate types we've outlined:

Intransitive	The professor reads in class.
Transitive with one object	The professor reads poems in class.
Transitive with two objects	The professor reads her students a poem in class.
Transitive with object complement	She declares the poem brilliant.
Linking with subject complement	The professor is an avid reader of poems.

Types of Clause

The two main types of clause—**independent** and **dependent** (also known as **main** and **subordinate**)—can be distinguished based on whether they form a complete sentence. There is a certain degree of circularity involved in this definition: a sentence contains an independent clause, while an independent clause is one that can form a sentence in itself. The difference is usually clear in practice, though. A complete sentence or independent clause—"My parrot has escaped again!"—should elicit a response of "oh, I see." An incomplete sentence or dependent clause, on the other hand—"The last time my parrot escaped"—will make one ask, "well, what about it?" Independent clauses are not introduced with conjunctions (though they may be joined by the coordinating conjunctions *and*, *but*, *or*, *nor*, *for*, *yet*, and *so*), so if a clause begins with a word such as *because*, *although*, or *if*, you can be confident it is a dependent clause. (See above under "Conjunctions" and below under "Complete and Incomplete Sentences" for much more on this subject.) Similarly, relative pronouns introduce dependent clauses—never main clauses.

She lives near Vancouver.
(One main clause forming a complete sentence.)

He danced in the street because he was feeling happy.
(Main clause: *He danced in the street*; subordinate clause: *because he was feeling happy.*)

Mavis has a cat who likes to drink from the kitchen faucet.
(Main clause: *Mavis has a cat*; subordinate clause: *who likes to drink from the kitchen faucet.*)

Dependent (or subordinate) clauses can also be classified into several different types, based on the function they serve in the sentence. **Adjectival clauses** (also called relative clauses) modify nouns or pronouns, as adjectives do. Adjectival clauses begin with relative pronouns such as *who*, *whom*, *whose*, *which*, and *that*.

The parrot *who escaped yesterday* is sitting on my car.

I don't really like the phone *that my mother bought for me.*

Adverbial clauses tell us more about the action of the verb—telling *how*, *when*, *why*, or *where* the action occurred.

The parrot escaped *because someone left the window open.*

When someone buys you a new phone, you can't complain.

Noun clauses act like a noun to form the subject or object of a sentence or the object of a preposition.

I'll never forget *what the parrot said as it left.*

My mother told me *that she expected me to pay her back.*

Subordinate clauses can also be divided into **finite** and **nonfinite** clauses, which is important when we look at the wide variety of clauses we commonly use. All of the clauses in the examples above are finite clauses, because they use verbs that match their subjects. Nonfinite clauses use verbs that don't change form to agree with their subjects—participles (*-ed* and *-ing* verb forms), infinitives (such as *to be*, *to go*), or gerunds (*-ing* forms used as nouns). Here are a few examples of nonfinite clauses:

My phone dying was the worst moment of my week.

The parrot flew into the sky, *its colorful plumage shining brightly.*

Would it be possible *to keep the window closed*?

Types of Phrase

Like clauses, phrases can serve different functions within a sentence. They can be labeled according to form or function.

A **noun phrase** contains a noun (or pronoun) and invariably functions in roles suited for nouns—as a subject or object or complement. It may also contain adjectives (determiners or modifiers) that tell us more about the noun.

a tan van	five cheese pizzas
my dearly-departed phone	everyone here

A **prepositional phrase** contains a preposition followed by a noun or pronoun or noun phrase, which is called the object of the preposition. It can function in various roles, modifying nouns or verbs.

My friend *with the poodle* came to visit.

The police called *during the night*.

He suggested that we go *to infinity and beyond*!

An **adjectival phrase** functions as an adjective (it modifies a noun or pronoun) and can have various forms—a string of adjectives, for example, or a prepositional phrase, or a non-finite verb phrase.

She is looking for someone who is *tall, dark, and handsome*.

This taco *from the truck on the corner* is excellent.

Have you seen a poodle *wearing a pink collar*?

An **adverbial phrase** functions as an adverb (it modifies a verb or adjective or adverb) and can also have various forms. There are two adverbial phrases in each of these example sentences.

On my thirteenth birthday my family went to an amusement park.

I can't see very well *with my left eye*.

The monster wandered *down the street* destroying buildings.

Distinguishing Phrases and Clauses

They were late *because of the weather*.

(*Because of the weather* is an adverbial *phrase*—not a clause, because it has no predicate.)

They were late because the weather was bad.

(*Because the weather was bad* is an adverbial *clause*—it has a subject [*the weather*] and a predicate [*was bad*].)

The man *at the corner* appeared to be upset.

(Adjectival *phrase*)

The man *who stood at the corner* appeared to be upset.

(Adjectival *clause*)

Parts of Speech and Parts of the Sentence

As practice in recognizing the parts of speech, label each of the words and phrases in this example. Then identify the parts of the sentence.

After the generous man with the big ears has bought presents, he will give them quickly to his friends.

Parts of speech:

after: *conjunction* the: *article* generous: ________

man: ________ with: ________ the: ________

big: ________ ears: ________ has bought: ________

presents: ________ he: ________ will give: ________

them: ________ quickly: ________ to: ________

his: ________ friends: ________

Parts of the sentence:

main clause: He will give them quickly to his friends.

subject: ________ verb: ________

direct object: ________ indirect object: ________

subordinate clause: After the generous man with the big ears has bought presents

core subject: ________ complete subject: ________

adjectival phrase: ____________ verb: ____________

direct object: ___________

Additional Material

A discussion of run-on sentences ("comma splices") and sentence fragments ("incomplete sentences") follows below (1.3.1).

For exercises on these topics go to **sites.broadviewpress.com/grammar**.

Click on **Exercises** and go to **1.3 "Parts of Sentences."**

1.3.1 Complete and Incomplete Sentences

What constitutes a complete or incomplete sentence? What constitutes a run-on sentence, or a sentence fragment?

An incomplete sentence (or sentence fragment) is a group of words that has been written as if it were a complete sentence, but that, as a matter of grammatical correctness, needs something else to make it complete. If you write "And in the morning" and put a period after what you have written, the sentence has been left incomplete. It's a sentence fragment, not a complete sentence. Your reader will be left wondering "And in the morning, what?" Similarly, the group of words "When the meeting ends" cannot form a complete sentence on its own; grammatically, it is structured as a dependent (or subordinate) clause. Like independent clauses, dependent clauses include both a subject and a verb. Unlike independent clauses, though, they begin with a subordinating word. Subordinating conjunctions such as *because*, *although*, and *when* may be used in this way, as can relative pronouns such as *that*, *which*, and *whose*. To turn a dependent clause into a complete sentence, one can either transform it into an independent clause ("The meeting will end tomorrow") or attach it to a separate, independent clause ("When the meeting ends tomorrow, we should have a comprehensive agreement").

Focusing on the word "fragment," some people imagine incomplete sentences to be always very short. That's not the case. The idea of a sentence fragment is a grammatical concept, unrelated to how many words there may be in a phrase or clause; whether a sentence is complete or not is a matter of grammatical correctness, not a matter of sentence length. The first (quite short) group of words below forms a complete sentence, while the much longer group of words that follows is a sentence fragment:

> Marina walked to the sea.
>
> While Marina was walking to the sea and thinking of her father.

To correct the mistake here, one can either remove the subordinating conjunction *while*—

> Marina was walking to the sea and thinking of her father.

Or add an independent clause—

> While Marina was walking to the sea and thinking of her father, she heard the sound of a wood thrush.

In similar fashion, the grammatical concept of a run-on sentence is just that—a grammatical concept. A run-on sentence need not be long. Here is a very short example of a comma splice (one form of run-on sentence):

Night fell, the moon rose.

To correct it, one can divide it into two sentences—

Night fell. The moon rose.

or connect the two parts with a coordinating conjunction—

Night fell, and the moon rose.

or use a semicolon rather than a comma to separate the independent clauses—

Night fell; the moon rose.

Let's look at four more examples:

Protests were widespread, but the authorities refused to back down.
(complete sentence—two independent clauses, joined by a coordinating conjunction [*but*])

Although protests were widespread, the authorities refused to back down.
(complete sentence—subordinate clause [introduced by the subordinating conjunction *although*], followed by a main [or independent] clause)

Protests were widespread, however the authorities refused to back down
(comma splice [a form of run-on sentence]. *However* is a conjunctive adverb; if it is used to join independent clauses, it must be preceded by a semicolon rather than a comma.)

The authorities refused to back down. Although protests were widespread.
(The second is an incomplete sentence—as a subordinating conjunction, *although* cannot introduce a clause that can stand independently as a complete sentence.)

Students often experience considerable frustration when faced with examples such as these. In all four cases the meaning is plain, yet—according to the conventional rules of English grammar and usage—only two of the four are correct. The distinctions among categories such as coordinating conjunctions, subordinating conjunctions, and coordinating adverbs—confusing enough in themselves—become

Online

If you have been under the impression that a run-on sentence is by definition a long sentence, a blog post entitled "The Long Sentence and the Freight Train" may be worth consulting. It provides an extended discussion of how the issues involved in writing run-on sentences differ from those involved in writing long sentences, and discusses long and run-on sentences not only in academic writing but also in fiction (a context in which it is quite acceptable to write long sentences that are grammatically incorrect). The post may be found online at **http://donlepan.blogspot.com/2015/08/the-long-sentence-and-freight-train.html**.

understandably more confusing when the words involved mean more or less the same thing. It may seem hard not to feel that the definitions of *complete sentence* and *incomplete sentence* are, to the extent that they rely on such distinctions, purely arbitrary. Such feelings are not unreasonable. Yet those distinctions matter in the academic world and in the world of work; if you are able to understand and follow the conventions of English grammar and usage in your writing, it is sure to be noted and appreciated by many of your instructors and co-workers.

The question of what constitutes a complete sentence, then, is a highly complicated one. It involves the structures of English grammar (1.2) and the conventions governing the use of various joining words (2.9), as well as the rules governing the use of periods, commas, and semicolons (3.1). For a full understanding, we recommend you read all these sections, in addition to the material below. We recommend as well that you complete all of the interactive exercises that are included in the 1.3 section of the companion website for this book.

• **run-on sentences**: A run-on sentence is a sentence that continues running on when, as a matter of grammatical correctness, it should be broken up into two or more sentences. Sometimes people use the expression *run-on sentence* loosely to refer to a sentence that is simply very long, regardless of whether or not it is grammatically correct. A well-constructed long sentence, though, can be an excellent means of expressing complex ideas; for the sake of clarity, then, it's important not to confuse the idea of a long sentence with the idea of a run-on sentence. The term *run-on sentence* should be used only when issues of grammatical correctness are involved.

One variety of run-on sentence (a **fused sentence**) occurs when independent clauses are not separated by any punctuation.

needs checking Early last Thursday we were walking in the woods it was a lovely morning.

revised Early last Thursday we were walking in the woods. It was a lovely morning.

A second (and more common) variety of run-on sentence occurs when a comma (rather than a period or a semicolon) is used between independent clauses, without the addition of any coordinating conjunction. This type of run-on sentence is called a **comma-splice**.

needs checking It was a lovely morning, we were walking in the woods.

revised It was a lovely morning. We were walking in the woods.

or It was a lovely morning, and we were walking in the woods.

In simple examples such as those above, the matter may seem straightforward. Sometimes, though, it is not so simple. The conventions of English dictate that only certain words may be used to join two independent clauses into one sentence. The seven coordinating conjunctions (*and, but, or, for, nor, so,* and *yet*) may be used to join independent clauses; other classes of joining words—notably, conjunctive adverbs—may not be used in the same way. Some of the words most commonly used as conjunctive adverbs are *also, besides, consequently, finally, hence, however, indeed, likewise, meanwhile, moreover, nevertheless, next, otherwise, still, then,* and *therefore.*[1]

When a coordinating conjunction is used to connect two independent clauses, then, you may combine them into a single sentence,

1 A cautionary note: Categorizing words by their part-of-speech function is not always easy, since some words can function in more than one way. Notably, several of the words listed here that can function as conjunctive adverbs can also act as ordinary adverbs or as adjectives. In the sentence *Finally, we must consider taking concrete action* the word "finally" functions as a conjunctive adverb, whereas in the sentence *He was finally ready* the word "finally" functions as an ordinary adverb modifying the adjective "ready." Similarly, in the sentence *Otherwise, thousands will die of starvation* the word "otherwise" functions as a conjunctive adverb, whereas in the sentence *She will respond quickly if she is not otherwise occupied* the word "otherwise" acts as an ordinary adverb modifying the adjective "occupied." Additional information on this topic (together with an interactive exercise) is included on the companion website.

with a comma separating the two clauses. But when a conjunctive adverb is used to indicate how the ideas of two independent clauses are connected to each other, you must use a period (or semicolon) to separate the ideas from each other. They should not be "spliced" together with a comma:

needs checking The temperature stayed below freezing, therefore the ice did not melt.

revised The temperature stayed below freezing. Therefore, the ice did not melt.

or The temperature stayed below freezing, so the ice did not melt.

(The word *therefore* is a conjunctive adverb, not a coordinating conjunction; it thus may not be used to join independent clauses. The word *so* is a coordinating conjunction, and may thus be used to join independent clauses—provided that a comma is used as well.)

needs checking You had better leave now, otherwise we'll call the police.

revised You had better leave now. Otherwise, we'll call the police.

or You had better leave now; otherwise, we'll call the police.

(The word *otherwise* is a conjunctive adverb, not a coordinating conjunction, and thus may not be used to join independent clauses.)

needs checking With the exception of identical twins no two people have exactly the same genetic makeup, hence it is impossible for two people to look exactly the same.

revised With the exception of identical twins no two people have exactly the same genetic makeup. Hence, it is impossible for two people to look exactly the same.

or With the exception of identical twins no two people have exactly the same genetic makeup; hence, it is impossible for two people to look exactly the same.

needs checking During the rainy season more water flows over Victoria Falls than over any other falls in the world, however several other falls are higher than Victoria.

revised During the rainy season more water flows over Victoria Falls than over any other falls in the world. However, several other falls are higher than Victoria.

or During the rainy season more water flows over Victoria Falls than over any other falls in the world; several other falls, however, are higher than Victoria.

needs checking Money was tight and jobs were scarce, therefore she decided to stay in a job she did not like.

revised Money was tight and jobs were scarce; therefore, she decided to stay in a job she did not like.

Notice in the above cases that one way to correct a comma splice is often to use a semicolon. Unlike a comma, a semicolon may be used as a connector between clauses. (The discussion of the semicolon below may be helpful in this connection.)

The most common culprit when it comes to run-on sentences may well be the word ***then***. The word *then* may act as an ordinary adverb or as a conjunctive adverb, but it can never act as a coordinating conjunction, and thus should not be used to join two clauses together into one sentence. *And then* may be used, or a semicolon, or a new sentence may be begun.

needs checking We applied the solution to the surface of the leaves then we made observations at half-hour intervals.

revised We applied the solution to the surface of the leaves. Then we made observations at half-hour intervals.

or We applied the solution to the surface of the leaves; then we made observations at half-hour intervals.

or We applied the solution to the surface of the leaves, and then we made observations at half-hour intervals.

needs checking Yugoslav troops began withdrawing, then the NATO bombing was suspended and the war in Kosovo ended.

revised Yugoslav troops began withdrawing. Then the NATO bombing was suspended and the war in Kosovo ended.

needs checking The pilot checked the speedometer and the altimeter, then she knew what to do.

revised The pilot checked the speedometer and the altimeter. Then she knew what to do.

or The pilot checked the speedometer and the altimeter; then she knew what to do.

or The pilot checked the speedometer and the altimeter, and then she knew what to do.

needs checking The Montreal Canadiens produced vital goals early in the game, then they wrapped their iron defense around the Calgary Flames.

revised The Montreal Canadiens produced vital goals early in the game, and then they wrapped their iron defense around the Calgary Flames.

or The Montreal Canadiens produced vital goals early in the game; then they wrapped their iron defense around the Calgary Flames.

and **and** ***but***: Almost every schoolchild is advised at some point that one should not begin a sentence with *and* or *but*. Many are taught to follow a more general rule—that one should not begin a sentence with any of the seven coordinating conjunctions (*and*, *but*, *for*, *nor*, *or*, *so*, *yet*). As we noted above in discussing coordinating conjunctions (pages 11–12), that advice is wrong, and that rule does not exist. It is perfectly correct to begin a sentence with *and* or *but* (or another of the coordinating conjunctions) so long as all the needed components of a complete sentence are present. Coordinating conjunctions may be used to join two independent clauses so as to make one sentence; they may also be used, however, as a pointer to the way in which the idea of one sentence connects to the idea of the previous one:

> Smith has written that Buckner's error led directly to Boston's World Series loss. **But that is not the way it happened.** Buckner's error was only one of several developments leading to Boston's loss in Game 6 of that series; the Red Sox still had to lose Game 7 to lose the series.

> Jones points out that the fact of the riot having broken out following the speech does not prove the speech caused the riot. **And he makes a fair point.** The order of events tells us nothing in itself; we have to look carefully at the content of the speech to understand the ways in which it was incendiary.

Notice that the bolded sentences above include both a subject ("that" in the "But" sentence, "he" in the "And" sentence) and a verb ("is" in the "But" sentence, "makes" in the "And" sentence). By way of contrast, consider the groups of words bolded below:

> Buckner's error occurred in the eighth inning. There was still the ninth inning to come. **And Game 7 the next day.**

> Ellis has said that he was willing to give Trump the benefit of the

doubt before the assault on the Capitol. **But not now.**

The first group of bolded words does not include a verb; it cannot be a complete sentence. And the second group of bolded words includes neither a subject nor a verb; clearly it cannot be a complete sentence either. Whether or not a group of words forms a complete sentence, once again, depends simply on whether or not the elements needed to make a complete sentence are present; the fact that the group of words begins with *and* or *but* is not relevant.

The same is true of the other five coordinating conjunctions. Coordinating conjunctions can join independent clauses within a sentence—or they can start a new sentence:

> Real Madrid might certainly win the cup, as might Barcelona**, or** it might be won by a team that no one is now expecting to have a serious chance. (correct—the coordinating conjunction *or* has been used to join two independent clauses)

> Real Madrid might certainly win the cup, as might Barcelona. **Or** it might be won by a team that no one is now expecting to have a serious chance. (correct—the coordinating conjunction *or* has been used to begin a new sentence)

> In the recent election, the Democrats won more votes than the other parties, **yet** they did not win the most seats. (correct—the coordinating conjunction *yet* has been used to join two independent clauses)

> In the recent election, the Democrats won more votes than the other parties. **Yet** they did not win the most seats. (correct—the coordinating conjunction *yet* has been used to begin a new sentence)

If there is no prohibition on beginning a sentence with coordinating conjunctions such as *and* or *but*, neither is there any prohibition, as a matter of grammatical correctness, on including *and* or *but* several times within a single sentence. As a matter of style, however, the appearance of more than one *and* or more than one *but* in a single sentence is often a signal that the ideas might better be rephrased.

needs checking Beaverbrook mobilized the resources of the country to serve the war effort overseas, and he later was knighted, and he is also well-known for creating a media empire.

(So far as the rules of grammar are concerned, this cannot be classed as a run-on sentence; it is perfectly correct grammatically. But as a matter of style, the repetitive structure leaves much to be desired.)

revised Beaverbrook mobilized the resources of the country to serve the war effort—an accomplishment for which he later was knighted. He is also well-known for creating a media empire.

or Beaverbrook, who had created a vast media empire before the war, then distinguished himself by mobilizing the resources of the country to serve the war effort. It was in recognition of this service that he was knighted.

or Beaverbrook, who had created a vast media empire before the war, then distinguished himself by mobilizing the resources of the country to serve the war effort; it was in recognition of this service that he was knighted.

- **sentence fragments (incomplete sentences)**: As we have seen, a grammatically complete sentence must include both a subject and a verb. A group of words such as *in a minute* or *from Pittsburgh to Philadelphia* includes neither subject nor verb; such groups of words are simply phrases. But nor can groups of words such as *which I find very useful* or *if we finish in time* be complete sentences; such groups of words do include both a subject and a verb, but they are dependent clauses (discussed above, pages 13 and 16–17). A grammatically complete sentence must always include at least one independent clause.

Some sorts of sentence fragments might be classed as "afterthought fragments"; the writer completes a sentence, and then adds an afterthought:

needs checking Unemployment was a serious problem in Britain in the early 1990s. In fact, throughout the world.

revised Unemployment was a serious problem in Britain in the early 1990s. In fact, it was a serious problem throughout the world.

or Unemployment was a serious problem in the early 1990s—not just in Britain but throughout the world.

needs checking In Nathaniel Hawthorne's story "Young Goodman Brown," the main character chooses not to trust the members of his own community but instead to presume them to be corrupted by sin. Although he has no way of knowing if they are truly corrupted or not.

revised In Nathaniel Hawthorne's story "Young Goodman Brown," the main character chooses not to trust the members of his own community but instead to presume them to be corrupted by sin, although he has no way of knowing if they are truly corrupted or not.

or In Nathaniel Hawthorne's story "Young Goodman Brown," the main character chooses not to trust the members of his own community. Instead, he presumes them to be corrupted by sin, although he has no way of knowing if they are truly corrupted or not.

needs checking When asked to propose an appropriate punishment after having been convicted by an Athenian jury for having committed impious acts, Socrates suggests that he be provided with free meals at public expense. An award that was typically given to Olympic champions.

revised When asked to propose an appropriate punishment after having been convicted by an Athenian jury of having committed impious acts, Socrates suggests that he be provided with free meals at public expense, an award that was typically given to Olympic champions.

or When asked to propose an appropriate punishment after having been convicted by an Athenian jury of having committed impious acts, Socrates suggests that he be provided with free meals at public expense—an award that was typically given to Olympic champions.

or Socrates is asked to propose an appropriate punishment after he has been convicted by an Athenian jury of having committed impious acts. He suggests that he be provided with free meals at public expense—an award that was typically given to Olympic champions.

Notice that in the last two cases, the "afterthought fragment" is preceded by quite a long sentence. It's easy to imagine the writer of such sentences thinking "I've made this sentence pretty long already; I had better stop, and start a new sentence with my next thought." As a matter of style, it's certainly a good thing to pay attention to sentence length—and to vary the lengths of your sentences. But as the last example in each group above illustrates, there are many ways to vary sentence length while still writing entirely in grammatically correct sentences.

We have seen that a sentence fragment need not be short. Indeed, writers can often be led into writing grammatically incomplete sentences by becoming tangled in their thoughts when attempting to write a long sentence. While "afterthought fragments" tend to be short follow-ups after a long sentence, "tangle-thought fragments" are typically themselves quite long:

needs checking In the event that interest rates remain low and the exchange rate remains favorable, companies that are contemplating export markets, so long as those markets are stable and the distribution channels are relatively efficient.

(For all its length, this sentence lacks an independent clause.)

revised In the event that interest rates remain low and the exchange rate remains favorable, companies can contemplate export markets with confidence, so long as those markets are stable and the distribution channels are relatively efficient.

or Interest rates may well remain low and the exchange rate favorable. In that case, companies can contemplate export markets with confidence—so long as those markets are stable and the distribution channels are relatively efficient.

needs checking While it is important to acknowledge the important role that Indigenous peoples have played within Canada, no less important, as a matter of historical accuracy as well as of fairness, acknowledging that national borders such as those separating Canada and the United States are, particularly in the case of Indigenous peoples, artificial borders.

revised While it is important to acknowledge the important role that Indigenous peoples have played within Canada, it is no less important, as a matter of historical accuracy as well as of fairness, to acknowledge that national borders such as those separating Canada and the United States are, particularly in the case of Indigenous peoples, artificial borders.

or While it is important to acknowledge the important role that Indigenous peoples have played within Canada, it is no less important to acknowledge that national borders such as those separating Canada and the United States are artificial borders. To recognize such artificiality is vitally important where Indigenous peoples are concerned; it's a matter of historical accuracy, and also a matter of fairness.

Here again we may notice that one can vary the length of one's sentences—and the order in which one's thoughts are presented—while being careful to write entirely in grammatically correct sentences.

because: As discussed above, many schoolchildren are given the erroneous impression that one should never begin a sentence with *and* or with *so*. So too with *because*—and the impression is erroneous here, too. The case of *because* is different from that of *and* and *so*, however. Whereas *and* and *so* are both coordinating conjunctions (see above, page 11), *because* is a subordinating conjunction (see above, page 13). A subordinating conjunction cannot be used to introduce an independent clause; subordinating conjunctions introduce dependent clauses. And as we have seen, a sentence with a dependent clause must also include an independent clause if the sentence is to be complete.

needs checking The government decided to shut down virtually everything. Because of the pandemic.

(*Because of the pandemic* is a phrase; it lacks both a subject and a verb.)

revised The government decided to shut down virtually everything because of the pandemic.

or Because of the pandemic, the government decided to shut down virtually everything.

needs checking In the early 1980s, Sandinista leaders told their people to be ready for war. Because the United States had been trying to destabilize Nicaragua.

(*Because the United States had been trying to destabilize Nicaragua* is a dependent clause.)

revised In the early 1980s, Sandinista leaders told their people to be ready for war, because the United States had been trying to destabilize Nicaragua.

or In the early 1980s, Sandinista leaders told their people to be ready for war; the United States had been trying to destabilize Nicaragua.

needs checking Because of the cold and wet weather, which affected the whole area. Many people were desperately trying to find more firewood.

revised Because of the cold and wet weather, which affected the whole area, many people were desperately trying to find more firewood.

or The cold and wet weather affected the whole area; many people were desperately trying to find more firewood.

Notice in the above examples that it does not matter whether the word *because* comes at the beginning or in the middle of the sentence; what is important is that the sentence has two parts. And notice too that using a semicolon to link two clauses where the meaning of the one follows from the meaning of the other can be an attractive alternative. (See also pages 16 and 13 regarding subordinate clauses and subordinating conjunctions, and pages 24 and 27–28 regarding use of the semicolon.)

• **complete sentences and sentence style**: Noticing how semicolons can be used effectively both to separate and to link the groups of words with which you express yourself points to an important fact about grammatical correctness. The goal of writing in a readable, engaging style and the goal of writing grammatically correct prose are two separate goals to strive for; while they may sometimes be interconnected, they may also sometimes exist in tension with each other. One of the reasons that schoolteachers have long advised students against beginning sentences with *and* or *so* or *because* is that doing so can have unfortunate consequences stylistically. This series of three sentences concerning *The Handmaid's Tale* is not incorrect grammatically—but nor does it constitute good writing:

needs checking Margaret Atwood's novel *The Handmaid's Tale* was first published in 1985. And it was made into a 1990 film. And in 2017 it became the basis for a successful television series.

revised Margaret Atwood's novel *The Handmaid's Tale*, which was first published in 1985, was made into a 1990 film, and in 2017 became the basis for a successful television series.

or Margaret Atwood's 1985 novel *The Handmaid's Tale* was made into a 1990 film; in 2017 the book became the basis for a successful television series.

Good writing, then, requires us to do more than make sure that all our sentences are grammatically correct. Here is a more extended example of a passage made up of grammatically correct complete sentences:

> The American Revolutionary War ended with the 1783 Treaty of Paris. Under its provisions, the "Northwest Territory" (much of modern-day Ohio and Indiana) was ceded by the British to the new American nation. The British were giving away what was not theirs to give. The British had previously agreed that most of this territory

> would be controlled by the Shawnee and other Indigenous groups. The 1783 treaty made no reference to these agreements. American settlers poured in to the Northwest Territory and started to farm and build homes on land that the Shawnee had long occupied. The Shawnee and other Indigenous groups tried to stop these encroachments. There were several battles. The Shawnee and their allies were defeated in 1794 at the Battle of Fallen Timbers by an American force led by "Mad Anthony" Wayne. Tecumseh, a Shawnee chief, became one of the most important figures in early nineteenth-century North American history. He was a young warrior when he participated in the Battle of Fallen Timbers. And then Tecumseh and the Shawnee ceded much of what is now Ohio to the Americans. In 1795 they signed the Treaty of Greenville. And then the Shawnee were forced to move west. They formed several new towns, the largest of them near the point where the Tippecanoe River meets the Wabash River. That is now part of western Indiana. By 1809 American settlers were encroaching on Shawnee settlements. Tecumseh formed a Confederation. He united various other Indigenous groups with the Shawnee. In 1811 he was away, trying to enlist more support. An American force led by William Henry Harrison defeated Shawnee forces near the mouth of the Tippecanoe River. It was called the Battle of Tippecanoe. Tecumseh then joined forces with the British (in what is now known as the War of 1812). And they won significant victories at Brownstown, Fort Detroit, and Fort Meigs. Tecumseh was defeated by Harrison and killed on October 5, 1813 (at Moraviantown, near present-day Chatham, Ontario) in the Battle of the Thames. Most of the Shawnee warriors surrendered. The dream of a Confederation of Indigenous peoples came to an end. The war ended. The Shawnee were forced to move farther west. The victories of the American army in battles such as Fallen Timbers and Tippecanoe were once seen as triumphs of the forces of civilization over those of savagery. Nowadays those battles are recognized as tragic episodes in a long narrative of aggression by settler colonial society against Indigenous peoples. The War of 1812 was once seen as a conflict between British and American forces that ended with no clear victor. Nowadays it is recognized as a three-way conflict. The Indigenous peoples of North America lost out.

This passage is written in grammatically correct English, but it lacks the sorts of links between clauses and sentences that help the reader to continually make connections. There are many ways in which such connections might be made. The rewrite below shows one way, with linking words (and/or semicolons) added, and with the material divided up into paragraphs.

> The American Revolutionary War ended with the 1783 Treaty of Paris. Under its provisions, the "Northwest Territory" (much of modern-day Ohio and Indiana) was ceded by the British to the new American nation. **But** the British were giving away what was not theirs to give**; they** had previously agreed that most of this territory would be controlled by the Shawnee and other Indigenous groups. The treaty**, however,** made no reference to these agreements.
>
> American settlers poured in to the Northwest Territory and started to farm and build homes on land that the Shawnee had long occupied. **As one might expect,** the Shawnee and other Indigenous groups tried to stop these encroachments**, and** there were several battles. The Shawnee and their allies were **finally** defeated in 1794 at the Battle of Fallen Timbers by an American force led by "Mad Anthony" Wayne.
>
> Tecumseh, a Shawnee chief who became one of the most important figures in early nineteenth-century North American history**,** was a young warrior when he participated in the Battle of Fallen Timbers. Tecumseh and the Shawnee were forced to cede much of what is now Ohio to the Americans **when** in 1795 they signed the treaty of Greenville.
>
> Forced to move west, the Shawnee **then** formed several new towns, the largest of them near the point where the Tippecanoe River meets the Wabash River in what is now western Indiana. By 1809, **however,** American settlers were **once more** encroaching on these new Shawnee settlements. Tecumseh formed a confederation**, uniting** various other Indigenous groups with the Shawnee. **But** in 1811, **while Tecumseh** was away trying to enlist more support, an American force led by William Henry Harrison defeated Shawnee forces near the mouth of the Tippecanoe River **in what became known as** the Battle of Tippecanoe. Tecumseh then joined forces with the British (in what is now known as the War of 1812). **Though** Tecumseh and his warriors won significant victories at Brownstown, Fort Detroit, and Fort Meigs**,** Tecumseh was **eventually** defeated by Harrison and killed on October 5, 1813 (at Moraviantown, near present-day Chatham, Ontario) in the Battle of the Thames. Most of the Shawnee warriors surrendered**, and** the dream of a Confederation of Indigenous peoples came to an end. **When** the war ended, the Shawnee were forced to move farther west.
>
> The battles of Fallen Timbers and Tippecanoe were once seen as triumphs of the forces of civilization over those of savagery. Nowadays**,**

> **however,** they are recognized as tragic episodes in a long narrative of aggression by settler colonial society against Indigenous peoples. The War of 1812 was once seen as a conflict between British and American forces that ended with no clear victor. Nowadays**, though,** it is recognized as a three-way conflict **in which** the Indigenous peoples of North America lost out.

Try rewriting the first passage in a different way yourself, breaking up and combining the material into complete sentences in different ways.

For more on how to make your writing clear and engaging in these sorts of ways, see 2.9 Joining Words and 1.6 Sentence Combining.

• **acceptable sentence fragments**: As the above example demonstrates, writing may be perfectly correct so far as the conventions of English grammar and usage are concerned, and nevertheless be in serious need of improvement: correctness is only one aspect of good writing. And sometimes, good writing may even include sentences that are grammatically incorrect. That is obviously the case with some works of fiction, in which an author may use stream-of-consciousness or other techniques in order to convey characters' thought processes to the reader. But it can also be true of essays and other forms of non-fiction. For skilled writers, the brevity of certain sorts of incomplete sentences may make for an effective means of emphasizing a point or of indicating a change of direction:

> In baseball, a lead of four runs going into the ninth inning is usually a safe lead. **Not this time.**
>
> Is the original film better than the re-make? **In every respect.**
>
> Ellis has said that he was willing to give Trump the benefit of the doubt before the assault on the Capitol. **But not now.**
>
> She wanted it to be a surprise. **A big surprise.**
>
> **A tumble on the basepaths by the Rays' best hitter, and two fielding errors by the Dodgers.** That was how Game 4 of the 2020 World Series ended.
>
> At the end of every day she felt tired. **Bone tired.**
>
> **Popular policies. A strong leader. An experienced staff.** All the ingredients for an election victory seemed to be in place.

Contexts in which such writing may be considered appropriate occur far more frequently in informal writing than in formal writing—and instructors at the post-secondary level often disagree as to when it is acceptable to deviate in this sort of way from grammatical conventions. For those reasons, students are well advised to consult their instructors before making a habit of intentionally writing sentence fragments in formal academic writing.

1.4 Verb Forms

The Infinitive

Although not properly speaking a verb tense, the infinitive is the starting point for building knowledge of verb tenses; the infinitive is the most basic form of the verb. Some examples of infinitives are *to go*, *to be*, *to do*, *to begin*, *to come*, *to investigate*. The infinitive form remains the same, of course, whether the action happens in the past, the present, or the future.

> **EAL**
>
> For particular problems with verbs faced by those whose native language is not English, see the EAL section later in the book (pages 280–89).

split infinitives: The most common mistake involving infinitives is undoubtedly the slang substitution of *and* for *to*, especially in the expression *try and do it* for *try to do it* (see page 205 for a fuller treatment). The great issue in this area among grammarians, however, is the split infinitive—the infinitive which has another word or words inserted between *to* and the verb:

needs checking The time has come to once again go to the polls. Economic conditions are likely to greatly influence the outcome, and the budget director has promised to forcefully speak out in defense of the government's fiscal record.

With re-united infinitives, the same passage looks like this:

revised The time has come to go once again to the polls. Economic conditions are likely to influence greatly the outcome, and the budget director has promised to speak out forcefully in defense of the government's fiscal record.

On what grounds can the second passage be considered better? It comes down to a matter of sound and rhythm. To most ears *to go once again* and *to speak out forcefully* are preferable to the split alternatives, but *to influence greatly* seems more awkward than *to greatly influence.* Happily, most authorities are now agreed that it is not a grievous sin to split an infinitive; Philip Howard, former editor of *The Times* of London, calls the split infinitive "the great shibboleth of English syntax," and even the traditionalist H.W. Fowler allows that while "the split infinitive is an ugly thing, we must warn the novice against the curious superstition that splitting or not splitting makes the difference between a good and a bad writer."

This is not to say that the splitting of infinitives should be encouraged. In many cases a split infinitive is a sign of wordiness; in cases such as the following it is better to drop the adverb entirely:

poor The chair said it was important to really investigate the matter thoroughly.

better The chair said it was important to investigate the matter thoroughly.

Like all verb forms, most infinitives have both an *active* and a *passive* voice. The active, which is more common, is used when the subject of the verb is doing the action, whereas the passive is used when the subject of the verb is receiving the action, or being acted on. *To do, to hit, to write* are examples of infinitives in the active voice, while *to be done, to be hit, to be written* are examples of infinitives in the passive voice.

On the Companion Website

Exercises on split infinitives may be found at **sites.broadviewpress.com/grammar**. Click on **Exercises** and go to **2.1 "Verbs and Verb Issues."**

The Simple Present

	singular	*plural*
1st person	I say	we say
2nd person	you say	you say
3rd person	he, she, it says	they say

subject–verb agreement: The simple present tense seems entirely straightforward, and usually it is. Most of us have no difficulty with the first person or the second person. But almost all of us occasionally have problems in writing the third person correctly. All too often the letter *s* at the end of the third person singular is left out. The simple rule to remember is that whenever you use a verb in the third person singular of the simple present tense, it must end in *s*:

needs checking He go to New York at least once a month.
revised He goes to New York at least once a month.

needs checking The litmus paper change immediately when the solution is mixed.
revised The litmus paper changes immediately when the solution is mixed.

(*Paper*, which is the subject, is an *it* and therefore third person singular.)

It is not particularly difficult to ensure that the subject agrees with the verb in the above examples, but even professional writers often have trouble with more complex sentences. Here are two common causes of subject–verb agreement errors:

(a) The subject and verb are separated by a long phrase or clause, especially when an intervening noun could be mistaken for the subject.

needs checking The state of Afghanistan's roads reflect the chaotic situation.
revised The state of Afghanistan's roads reflects the chaotic situation.

Here the writer has made the mental error of thinking of *roads* as the subject of the verb *reflect*, whereas in fact the subject is the singular noun *state*. *The state reflect* ... would immediately strike most people as wrong, but the intervening words have in this case caused grammatical confusion.

needs checking As the statement by Belgium's prime minister about his country's deficit and unemployment problems indicate, many nations are in the same shape, or worse.
revised As the statement by Belgium's prime minister about his country's deficit and unemployment problems indicates, many nations are in the same shape, or worse.

(The subject is the singular noun *statement*, so the verb must be *indicates* rather than *indicate.*)

needs checking Courses offered range from the history of the Greek and Roman world to the twenty-first century, and covers Britain, Europe, North America, Africa, and the Far East.

revised Courses offered range from the history of the Greek and Roman world to the twenty-first century, and cover Britain, Europe, North America, Africa, and the Far East.

Sometimes a long sentence can in itself throw off a writer's sense of subject–verb agreement, even if subject and verb are close together. In the following example the close proximity of the subject *simplifications* to the verb has not prevented error:

needs checking The decline in the quality of leadership is mirrored in the crude simplifications which characterizes the average person's view of the world.

revised The decline in the quality of leadership is mirrored in the crude simplifications which characterize the average person's view of the world.

(b) The error of using *there is* instead of *there are* when the subject is plural has become more and more frequent in writing as well as in speech. When these two expressions are used, remember that the subject comes after the verb; use *is* or *are* depending on whether the subject is singular or plural:

needs checking There's many more opportunities of that sort than there used to be.

revised There are many more opportunities of that sort than there used to be.

On the Companion Website

Exercises on subject–verb agreement may be found at **sites.broadviewpress.com/grammar**. Click on **Exercises** and go to **2.1 "Verbs and Verb Issues."**

historical present: To use the "historical present" is to use the present tense in a narrative set in the past. In many medieval histories the narrative alternates frequently between the present tense and the past tense, but from the sixteenth century until the late twentieth century most narratives of past action were recounted using the past tense. The historical present was used on a very selective basis by some historians and journalists (and by a few writers of fiction), the purpose being to lend a sense of immediacy to particular scenes that the writer wanted to express with memorable vividness. Here is an example, from Pierre Berton's work of popular history, *The Invasion of Canada*:

> [The British] are encouraged to strengthen their defences in Canada against possible invasion. This is Isaac Brock's doing.... The young lieutenant-colonel ... goes on to press for a better trained and expanded militia and for repairs to the fortress of Quebec. He does not easily get his way, but from this time on the prospect of an American invasion is never far from that determined and agile mind. When and if the Americans come, Isaac Brock intends to be ready.

In the twenty-first century the historical present has become much more commonly used in a wide variety of contexts. Many works of fiction are now written entirely in the present tense. Many works of history shift back and forth continually between the past tense and the historical present. Even newscasts now use the historical present frequently. As in earlier eras, the aim is presumably to impart a greater sense of immediacy and interest to what is being recounted. It is all too easy in such circumstances, however, to create a sense of confusion rather than a sense of immediacy in the reader's mind—particularly given that the present tense is often also used idiomatically to refer to future events (e.g., *We arrive at 9:00 in the morning* rather than *We will arrive at 9:00 in the morning*). It is essential, then, to pay careful attention to what tenses are being used.

needs checking Throughout the day, shells fall on the city. Dozens are killed. The President, however, refused to authorize a ceasefire. The Cabinet holds an emergency meeting tonight.

(The passage begins in the historical present, but then switches to the past tense. The fourth sentence shifts back to present tense—but it is not clear what time is being referred to. Is the emergency meeting also in the past [and the report being filed late at night]? If so, what was the outcome of the meeting? Or is the report being filed before "tonight"—in which case the emergency meeting is still in the future.)

revised Throughout the day, shells fell on the city. Dozens were killed. The President, however, refused to authorize a ceasefire. The Cabinet will hold an emergency meeting tonight.

or Throughout the day, shells fall on the city. Dozens are killed. The President, however, refuses to authorize a ceasefire. The Cabinet will hold an emergency meeting tonight.

The Simple Past

	singular	*plural*
1st person	I finished	we finished
2nd person	you finished	you finished
3rd person	he, she, it finished	they finished

irregular verbs: The occasional problems that crop up with the simple past tense usually involve irregular verbs—that is to say, verbs that do not follow a regular pattern in the formation of the simple past and other tenses. (See pages 89–96 for a fuller discussion and list.) One lesser-known past tense form is *might,* which, in addition to being a modal verb with the same meaning as *may* in the present tense, is also the past tense of *may*. More simply put, use *might* with past tense verbs, never *may*.

needs checking Bands such as U2 and Barenaked Ladies gained a foothold in North America through campus radio; without it they may not have broken through.

revised Bands such as U2 and Barenaked Ladies gained a foothold in North America through campus radio; without it they might not have broken through.

Two other verbs that often cause problems in the simple past are *lie* and *lay* (see also page 93). The difficulty many people have in keeping these straight is often ascribed to other factors, but is in part also attributable simply to the forms of the tenses; the past tense of *lie* is the same as the present tense of *lay*. Also, the past participle of *lie* is *lain*, not *laid*:

needs checking Many in our party have just laid down and rolled over; they cannot get over the fact that we have lost control of the legislature.

revised Many in our party have just lain down and rolled over; they cannot get over the fact that we have lost control of the legislature.

Given the difficulty of getting one's tongue round *lain down* rather than *laid down*, and the fact that almost anyone will know what meaning is intended with these words, many now feel that the distinctions are not worth troubling over in informal contexts. They remain important, however, in formal, written English.

habitual action: The simple past tense is often mistakenly used to express what is called habitual action—the way an action ordinarily, or habitually, occurs. The simple present tense should be used to name such action even if the main verb of the sentence is in the past or future tense:

needs checking The professor told us that Jupiter was the largest planet.
revised The professor told us that Jupiter is the largest planet.
(Jupiter has not stopped being the largest since he spoke.)

The Simple Future

	singular	*plural*
1st person	I will arrive	we will arrive
2nd person	you will arrive	you will arrive
3rd person	he, she, it will arrive	they will arrive

The Progressive (or Continuous) Aspect

The Present Progressive

	singular	*plural*
1st person	I am saying	we are saying
2nd person	you are saying	you are saying
3rd person	he, she, it are saying	they are saying

verbs not normally used in the continuous aspect: In English the progressive forms are not normally used with many verbs which have to do with feelings, emotions, or senses. Some of these verbs are *to see*, *to hear*, *to understand*, *to believe*, *to hope*, *to know*, *to think* (meaning *believe*), *to trust*, *to comprehend*, *to mean*, *to doubt*, *to suppose*, *to wish*, *to* *want, to love, to desire, to prefer, to dislike, to hate.*

needs checking	He is not understanding what I meant.
revised	He does not understand what I meant.

The Past Progressive

	singular	*plural*
1st person	I was leaving	we were leaving
2nd person	you were leaving	you were leaving
3rd person	he, she, it were leaving	they were leaving

The problems that sometimes occur with the past continuous are the same as those that occur with the present progressive (see above). Remember to avoid these forms when using verbs having to do with feelings, emotions, or senses (e.g., *see, hear, understand, believe, hope, know, think, trust, comprehend*) and when using the verb *to have* to mean *own, possess*, or *suffer from*:

needs checking	At that time he was believing that everything on earth was created within one week.
revised	At that time he believed that everything on earth was created within one week.

The Future Progressive

	singular	*plural*
1st person	I will be finding	we will be finding
2nd person	you will be finding	you will be finding
3rd person	he, she, it will be finding	they will be finding

The Perfect Aspect

As used to refer to the perfect verb forms, the word *perfect* means *completed*; as you might expect, then, the perfect tenses are often (though not always) used to express actions that have been completed. They are formed by combining some form of the verb *to have* with a past participle (e.g., *opened, finished, believed, done*).

The Present Perfect

	singular	*plural*
1st person	I have worked	we have worked
2nd person	you have worked	you have worked
3rd person	he, she, it has worked	they have worked

continuing past actions: One way in which this tense is used is to speak of past actions which may continue into the present, or be repeated in the present or future. In the sentence *Anne Carson has written a number of books*, for example, the form of the verb shows that she will probably write more; she has neither died nor given up writing.

Understanding this sort of thing is a simple enough practice in normal usage, but in the long sentences that often occur in academic writing, it is easy to become confused:

needs checking Since it called the First World Food Congress in 1963, the Food and Agriculture Organization has said clearly that the world, with the science and technology then known, had enough knowledge to ensure man's freedom from hunger. Successive world congresses and conferences have repeated this contention. (from a paper given by a distinguished professor at an academic conference)

Here the writer has evidently chosen the present perfect, thinking that he is referring to a situation which has continued on into the present. But when he refers to the science and technology then known and to successive world congresses and conferences, he has cut off the 1963 conference from any grammatical connection with the present. This is the sort of mistake that most writers can catch only during the revision process.

revised When it called the First World Food Congress in 1963, the Food and Agriculture Organization said clearly that the world, with the science and technology then known, had enough knowledge to ensure man's freedom from hunger. Successive world congresses and conferences have repeated this contention.

The Past Perfect

	singular	*plural*
1st person	I had believed	we had believed
2nd person	you had believed	you had believed
3rd person	he, she, it had believed	they had believed

Since the verb remains unchanged in all these forms, the past perfect is one of the easiest tenses to remember. What is difficult is learning how and when to use it. In English, however, there are quite definite rules about when the past perfect tense should be used. Its chief use is to show that one action in the past was completed before another action in the past began. Here are some examples:

> I told my parents what had happened.
>
> (The happening occurred before the telling.)
>
> By the time the group of tourists left Mozambique, they had formed a very favorable impression of the country.
>
> (The forming occurred before the leaving.)
>
> When he had gone I thought very seriously about what he had said.
>
> (Both the going and the saying occurred before the thinking.)

The usefulness of the past perfect tense can be clearly seen in passages in which the writer wishes to flashback, or move backwards in time. If you compare the following passages, you will see that the use of the past perfect tense in the second passage removes any confusion about the order in which the events happened. In the example below, when only the simple past tense is used, it sounds as if the dead snake is able to crawl:

needs checking The tail was still moving, but the snake itself was quite dead. It crawled out from the sewer and slowly moved across the pavement as I was turning the corner.

revised The tail was still moving, but the snake itself was quite dead. It had crawled out from the sewer and had slowly moved across the pavement as I had been turning the corner.

(In the second passage it is clear that the snake emerged *before* it died, and not afterwards.)

Perhaps the most common occasions in which we use the past perfect tense are when we are using indirect speech:

> She said that she had knocked on my door in the morning, but that there had been no answer.
>
> (The knocking happened before the saying.)
>
> The chair of the committee repeatedly asked the witness when the president had known of the diversion of funds.
>
> (The knowing happened before the asking.)

In a few cases it is possible to speak correctly of two actions which happened one after the other in the past by using the simple past tense for both actions. The use of the word *after*, for example, often makes it clear that the first action was completed before the other began.

past actions at different times, or over a prolonged period: Writers often neglect to use the past perfect to name the earlier action when they are speaking of two (or more) actions that happened at different times in the past:

needs checking He asked me if I talked to his secretary before coming to him.

revised He asked me if I had talked to his secretary before coming to him.

needs checking By the time the Allies decided to resist Hitler, the Nazis built up a huge military machine.

revised By the time the Allies decided to resist Hitler, the Nazis had built up a huge military machine.

needs checking Johnson's girlfriend, Marsha Dianne Blaylock, said she knew Williams since October 2013, when she and Johnson began their relationship.

revised Johnson's girlfriend, Marsha Dianne Blaylock, said she had known Williams since October 2013, when she and Johnson began their relationship.

(Note that like the present perfect, the past perfect is very frequently required with *since* or *for*.)

The past perfect is also used to indicate that a past action occurred over a prolonged period:

> In the early 1960s Sonny Bono was a disheveled pop singer and songwriter with hippie tendencies; by the time of his death in 1998 he had become a conservative Republican member of the House of Representatives.

needs checking In 1980, 10 percent of Chile's families did not have sufficient income to satisfy the minimum food requirements recommended by international organizations; in 2000 the figure grew to 32 percent.

revised In 1980, 10 percent of Chile's families did not have sufficient income to satisfy the minimum food requirements recommended by international organizations; by 2000 the figure had grown to 32 percent.

or ... in 2000 the figure was 32 percent.

(The original suggests that the figure had remained at 10 percent in every year from 1980 to 2000, and then jumped in the course of one year to 32 percent.)

The Future Perfect

	singular	*plural*
1st person	I will have gone	we will have gone
2nd person	you will have gone	you will have gone
3rd person	he, she, it will have gone	they will have gone

Conditional Constructions

	singular	*plural*
1st person	I would go	we would go
2nd person	you would go	you would go
3rd person	he, she, it would go	they would go

The above forms are used when we are speaking of actions that would or might happen if certain conditions were fulfilled. Here are some further examples:

If I wanted to go to Australia, I would have to fly.
If I drank a lot of gin, I would be very sick.
I would lend Joe the money he wants if I trusted him.
I might enjoy basketball more if I were taller.

Each of these sentences is made up of a main clause, in which a modal auxiliary verb (*would*, *might*) is used, and a subordinate clause beginning with *if*, with a verb in the same form as the simple past tense (*wanted*, *drank*, *trusted*, etc.). In all cases the action named in the *if* clause is considered by the speaker to be unlikely to happen, or quite impossible. The speaker does not really want to go to Australia; she is just speculating about what she would have to do if she did. Similarly the second speaker does not expect to drink a lot of gin; if he did, he would be sick, but he does not plan to. In the same way, the speaker of the third sentence does not trust Joe; he is speaking about what the situation would be if he did trust Joe. Situations like these which are not happening and which we do not expect to happen are called *hypothetical situations*: we speculate on what *would* or *might* happen *if* ... but we do not expect the *if* ... to come true.

If we think the *if*... is likely to come true, then we use the future tense instead of the conditional in the main clause, and the present tense in the subordinate *if* clause, as in these examples:

If I drink a lot of gin, I will be very sick.

(Here the speaker thinks that it is very possible or likely that he will drink a lot of gin.)

If I want to go to Australia, I will have to fly.

(Here the speaker thinks that she may really want to go.)

Notice the difference between the following two sentences:

If a socialist government is re-elected in Venezuela, the American administration will not be pleased.

(Here the writer thinks that it is quite possible or likely that the socialists will be re-elected.)

If a socialist government were re-elected in Venezuela, the American administration would not be pleased.

(Here the writer is assuming that the socialists probably will not be re-elected.)

On the Companion Website

Exercises on conditional sentences may be found at **sites.broadviewpress.com/grammar**.
Click on **Exercises** and go to
"Verbs and Verb Issues: Conditional Constructions."

choosing the right verb when writing about conditions: Some writers mistakenly use the auxiliary verb *would* in the *if*... clause when they are also using *would* in the main clause. Others use the present tense (instead of the past tense) in the *if*... clause when they are using *would* in the main clause. Both are incorrect.

needs checking If television networks would produce fewer series about violent crime, parents would allow their children to watch even more television than they do now.

revised If television networks produced fewer series about violent crime, parents would allow their children to watch even more television than they do now.

or If television networks were to produce fewer series about violent crime, parents would allow their children to watch even more television than they do now.

needs checking If I want to buy a car, I would look carefully at all the models available.

revised If I wanted to buy a car, I would look carefully at all the models available.

(The speaker does not want to buy a car.)

or If I want to buy a car, I will look carefully at all the models available.

(The speaker may really want to buy a car.)

Note that whenever one is referring to situations that are imagined, wished for, or in some other way contrary to fact, the subjunctive (typically, identical in form to that of the simple past tense) is used in the conditional *if*... clause. The subjunctive mood is explained in greater detail in the next section.

The Past Conditional

	singular	*plural*
1st person	I would have gone	we would have gone
2nd person	you would have gone	you would have gone
3rd person	he, she, it would have gone	they would have gone

This verb form is used in conditional sentences in which we are speaking of actions which never happened. It is used in the main clause, with the past tense in the subjunctive mood being used in the *if*... clause. Notice in the examples below that these past tense subjunctive forms are identical in form to the past perfect tense formations in the indicative mood.

If I had studied harder, I would have passed.

(meaning that in fact I did not study very hard, and did not pass)

If Kitchener had arrived at Khartoum a day earlier, he would have saved Gordon and the rest of the British garrison force.

(meaning that Kitchener did not come early enough, and was not able to prevent the 1885 massacre at Khartoum)

choosing the right verbs when writing about past conditions: Some people mistakenly use the past conditional in both clauses of sentences such as these; remember that the past conditional should be used only in the main clause:

needs checking If the *Titanic* would have carried more lifeboats, hundreds of lives would have been saved.

revised If the *Titanic* had carried more lifeboats, hundreds of lives would have been saved.

Other Verb Forms

The present perfect continuous tense—*I have been running, you have been working*, etc.

The past perfect continuous tense—*I had been looking, you had been following*, etc.

The future perfect continuous tense—*I will have been sleeping, they will have been studying*, etc.

The conditional continuous tense—*I would be bringing, she would be starting*, etc.

The past conditional continuous tense—*I would have been working, he would have been driving*, etc.

1.5 Mood and Voice

In grammatical terms, **mood** (sometimes called *mode* or *modality*) is not a measure of how grumpy or cheery a sentence is. Rather it reflects, essentially, how the speaker sees the relationship to reality of the states or events described by the verb: are they real, desired, or purely hypothetical? The tenses discussed in the previous section, and the vast majority of sentences we write, are all in the **indicative mood**; that is the way we express (or *indicate*) real—or really possible—actions.

It's easier to understand what the indicative mood is when we look at sentences that are not indicative. In English, there are two other moods that have distinct verb forms (though more moods may be expressed through the arrangement of the sentence). The **imperative mood** uses the simple form of a verb (e.g., *be, do, eat, come*) to express commands and instructions:

Follow the path to the right.
Come here immediately!

The mood that even many native English speakers find difficult to use correctly is the **subjunctive mood**. The subjunctive is used to denote actions or states that are wished for or imagined or otherwise not factual. It frequently appears in archaic expressions, such as "*Suffice* it to say..." or "*Be* that as it may...," where *suffice* and *be* are both in the subjunctive mood. In common English usage the indicative mood is now often employed where once the subjunctive was mandatory, but the subjunctive has by no means disappeared—and it is a frequent source of confusion for writers. Below are some examples of sentences that use the subjunctive:

The doctor advises that he *quit* smoking immediately.
(*Quit*, not the indicative form *quits*: here the doctor is not telling us that the patient is in fact stopping; he's conveying a strong suggestion.)

The judge insists that she *appear* in court for the trial.
(*Appear*, not *appears*: her presence in court is not a fact at this point but something expected to happen.)

In the above examples, the italicized verbs are both third person singular, which is the only form that differs between indicative and subjunctive in the present tense. If the verb were plural (or first or second person singular), the subjunctive form would be the same as the indicative:

The judge insists that we *appear* in court for the trial.

Since much of the time the subjunctive form is the same as the indicative form, we often use the subjunctive correctly without even thinking about it. This is true with unreal conditional sentences also, where the subjunctive form used is the same as the simple past form:

If I *had* a hammer, I'd hammer in the morning.
If we *went* to Iceland, would you go with us?

Until the second half of the twentieth century it was far more common than it is today to say *if we were to go* instead of *if we went*. Both forms are still acceptable, but the dominant form in formal writing as well as in conversation is the simple past tense. Where people used to say *If I were to send her something*, they would now typically say *If I sent her something.* Note that if the verb in the subjunctive is *to be* (which unlike other verbs has two simple past forms), the subjunctive form is always *were,* never *was.*

> If the verb *were* plural, the subjunctive form would be the same.
> If she *were* a man, she would have gotten the job.

It is perhaps tempting to say "if the verb *was* plural" or "if she *was* a man," but *was* is the simple past form: it indicates not a present hypothetical but a real situation in the past. "If she *was* a man, she would have gotten the job" suggests that she would be employed now if at some point in the past she actually *was* a man. As much as subjunctive forms play a smaller role in English than they used to, it is still important to use them correctly when called for. Given the difficulties involved, it may be worth spending some time on these.

Active and Passive Voice

As many authorities have pointed out, writers can often make their sentences less wordy and more effective by using the active voice rather than the passive:

needs checking The election was lost by the governor. (Passive—7 words)
revised The governor lost the election. (Active—5 words)

needs checking Union power was seen by them to have constrained the possibilities for full investment, and for achieving full employment.
revised The shareholders thought that union power had constrained the possibilities for full investment, and for achieving full employment.

It is too extreme, however, to conclude that the passive should be avoided wherever possible. Writers often want—for perfectly good reasons—to keep the focus of their writing on the recipient of an action rather than its agent. In such cases they are quite right to use the passive voice:

passive John Paul Getty III was released in Italy after a 2.8-million-dollar ransom had been paid.
active His kidnappers released John Paul Getty III in Italy after they had been paid a 2.8-million-dollar ransom.

If John Paul Getty III is the focus, it may be more appropriate to keep him as the subject of the sentence than to shift the focus to his kidnappers.

The passive is also sometimes useful as a means of dealing with issues of gender and usage. Compare, for example, the following sentences:

> If a writer uses vivid adjectives, his or her descriptive writing will carry greater force.
>
> If vivid adjectives are used, descriptive writing will carry greater force.

The passive-voice version allows the wordy *his or her* to disappear. Altering syntax in this sort of way can also help writers to write inclusive prose without resorting to awkward phrasing.

The vice associated with the use of passive voice, then, is not the passive *per se*, but the wordiness it sometimes gives rise to.

It has frequently been suggested that the passive voice also encourages vices more serious than wordiness. The most frequent reference point in such discussions is George Orwell's "Politics and the English Language," in which Orwell made "never use the passive where you can use the active" one of his six elementary rules of writing. In his essay Orwell persuasively suggests links between verbal subterfuge and political duplicity. Given this background, it is perhaps unsurprising that many have tended to conflate the use of a passive voice (in itself a matter purely of grammar and sentence construction) with the use in general of words to disguise agency—something that may be effected through a variety of verbal means. For example, the sentence *the police officer killed the protestor with a single baton blow to the head* is a simple sentence using the verb *to kill* in the active voice. One way to disguise agency here is to make *the protestor* the subject of the sentence and use the same verb in the passive voice. Such a construction readily allows for the omission of any mention of who wielded the baton: *the protestor was killed by a single baton blow to the head.* But one could also disguise agency with a sentence such as the following: *a blow to the head from a baton was the cause of the protestor's death.* In that case the change is not a matter of shifting from the active to the passive voice but of choosing a different verb.

As background here, it is essential to appreciate that the distinction between active and passive voice is not relevant to all verbs, but only to transitive verbs. You can hit someone or something, and someone or something can be hit by you; the active voice/passive voice distinction is certainly relevant to the verb *to hit.* But you cannot sleep someone or something, or be slept by someone or something; the active voice/passive voice distinction is not relevant to an intransitive verb such as *to sleep*. Nor is it relevant to that most common of verbs, the verb *to be*. In some cases, agency may be disguised by using either the active voice or the passive voice of a verb. Such, for example, is the case with the verb *to violate*, which may be used with the agent as the subject but may also be used with the action itself as the grammatical subject:

> The detention of the suspect without any charges violates her constitutional rights.
>
> The suspect's constitutional rights are violated by her detention without any charges.
>
> The prosecutor violated the defendant's constitutional rights by detaining her without laying any charges.

Agency is as much disguised in the first of these sentences as in the second, though the first is in the active voice, the second in the passive voice.

Let us look at another example of disguised agency. The sentence *I knocked that vase off the shelf* uses the past tense *knocked* in the active voice. Switching to the passive voice gives us *that vase was knocked off the shelf*, and of course allows for the option of omitting *by me*; this is one way of disguising agency. But if I wanted to disguise agency in such a situation I would be more likely to choose a different verb entirely, perhaps an intransitive verb such as *to fall* for which the active voice/passive voice distinction is not relevant: *that vase fell off the shelf.*

Many verbal stratagems that disguise agency use the pronoun *it* as the grammatical subject. If someone has just dumped a girlfriend or boyfriend, for example, the "dumper" is not always keen to say *I dumped her* or *I dumped him*. But nor is it likely that the speaker will shift to the passive voice and say *she was dumped by me/he was dumped by me*. Much more likely would be a shift to the use of *it* as the subject, together with intransitive verbs such as *to be* or *to work*: *it is over between us*, for example, or *it just didn't work out*.

It is important to recognize that there is nothing pernicious in itself in using the passive voice. In many cases, indeed, one may wish to use the passive voice in making political points of the sort that Orwell himself would approve of. Orwell himself does precisely this when he wishes to place appropriate emphasis on the recipient of an action—as in the following example, where he is emphasizing the experience of victims as well as the duplicity of language used to describe their suffering: "People are imprisoned for years without trial, or are shot in the back of the neck, or are sent to die of scurvy in Arctic lumber camps: this is called *elimination of unreliable elements.*"

The passive voice, then, is one means that *may* be used to disguise agency, and it is also a verbal construction that *may* involve awkwardness or unnecessary wordiness. If either is the case, it is often better to rephrase by using the active voice:

needs checking The ceremonial first pitch was thrown by the president. (Passive—9 words)

revised The president threw the ceremonial first pitch. (Active—7 words)

But again, the passive voice *per se* is not the problem.

active and passive voice in scientific writing: Discussions of impersonality and objectivity in scientific writing have also often been framed in terms of the question of whether to use the active or the passive voice. For most of the twentieth century, many instructors in the natural sciences tried to train students to use the passive voice[1]—to write things like "*It **was decided** that the experiment **would be conducted** in three stages*" and "*These results **will be discussed** from several perspectives*" in order to convey a more impersonal and objective tone. However, statements in the active voice such as "*We **conducted** the experiment in three stages*" and "*We **will discuss** these results from several perspectives*" are not any more or less objective. The reader of an article knows the researchers did the experiment, so using the passive voice does not change the degree of objectivity—though it may add unnecessary words.

Indeed, while instructors in the natural sciences encouraged the passive voice, in the second half of the twentieth century many academics in English studies were reluctant to acknowledge that it had much of a part to play in academic writing—even scientific writing. In the 1990s, Andrea Lunsford and Robert Connors were playing something of a pioneering role in their discipline when they put forward the following advice in their influential handbook: "Much scientific and technical writing uses the passive voice effectively to highlight

1 As Randy Moore and others have pointed out, nineteenth-century scientists used the active voice freely. The active voice and "first-person pronouns such as *I* and *we* began to disappear from scientific writing in the United States in the 1920s."

what is being studied rather than who is doing the studying." More than fifteen years later, a great many fellow writing studies scholars and composition teachers would give the same advice. Interestingly, just as handbook authors began to acknowledge that there could be a particular place for the passive voice in scientific writing, the scientific community began to swing around to the view that, much as the passive might sometimes have its place, the active voice should be the default writing choice. Here is Randy Moore, writing in *The American Biology Teacher* in 1991:

> The notion that passive voice ensures objectivity is ridiculous[; ...] objectivity has nothing to do with one's writing style or with personal pronouns. Objectivity in science results from the choice of subjects, facts that you choose to include or omit, sampling techniques, and how you state your conclusions. Scientific objectivity is a personal trait unrelated to writing.

The 1990s saw heated debates in the pages of certain scientific journals on the matter of whether the active or the passive should be the default. But in the end the decision was clear: the active voice was the best choice. Nearly every major scientific journal[1] now recommends that its authors use the active voice in most situations—and that they use the first person where appropriate as well. The various *Nature* journals, the *American Chemical Society Style Guide*, and the *American Society of Civil Engineers Style Guide* are representative. The following instructions are from their respective websites:

> *Nature* journals prefer authors to write in the active voice ("we performed the experiment ...") as experience has shown that readers find concepts and results to be conveyed more clearly if written directly. (*Nature*)
>
> Use the active voice when it is less wordy and more direct than the passive.... Use first person when it helps to keep your meaning clear and to express a purpose or a decision. (*ACS Style Guide*)
>
> Wherever possible, use active verbs that demonstrate what is being done and who is doing it....
>
> *Instead of:* Six possible causes of failure were identified in the

1 On his blog in 2012, Allen Downey conducted an informal survey and was able to identify only three exceptions: the *ICES Journal of Marine Science*, the *Journal of Animal Ecology*, and *Clinical Oncology and Cancer Research*.

forensic investigation.
Use: The forensic investigation identified six possible causes of failure. (*ASCE Style Guide*)

Though the active voice is better as a default choice, in some circumstances it can still be better to use the passive. Especially in scientific writing, the passive voice is useful in many ways, including as a way of shifting attention away from the researcher to the experiment itself. Indeed, the following examples show clearly the types of statements that make effective use of the passive:

- The cooling process was completed in approximately two hours.
- This compound is made up of three elements.
- Phenomena of this sort may be seen only during an eclipse.

Problems arise, however, when use of the passive reduces clarity or when the passive is used to disguise responsibility. Consider the following sentence in the passive voice, taken from the opening of a scientific article by Toby Knowles et al. from a 2007 PLOS ONE article entitled "Leg Disorders in Broiler Chickens": "Broiler chickens have been subjected to intense genetic selection." That is to say, they have been bred to grow so fast and become so heavy that they can barely walk. But this has not just happened; humans have done this to the birds, as part of a broad-based effort to generate more meat less expensively—too often, with little or no thought given to the birds themselves as sentient creatures. Here, the article's use of the passive voice de-emphasizes responsibility.

Yet the disguising or downplaying of agency—of just who is responsible for an action—is something that may be accomplished through a variety of verbal means. It need not be a matter of using the passive voice. Consider this example from another piece of scientific writing: Jeff Downing's "Non-invasive Assessment of Stress in Commercial Housing Systems": "hens need to deal with [challenges] in their environment.... In any flock there are likely to be some hens that perceive the challenges as more severe than others and have high corticosterone concentrations." In Downing's sentences, the hens are, in terms of grammatical voice, the active parties; they are the subjects of the verbs: "*hens* ***need***," "*hens* [...] ***perceive*** *the challenges*." But of course the controlling agents here in any sense other than a grammatical one are not the birds; it is humans who have subjected them to these "challenges"—if that euphemism is to be accepted. "Hardships," "privations," or "cruelties" are some of the other nouns that might be substituted for "challenges."

It would seem, then, that there is nothing pernicious in the passive voice itself. The passive voice is one means that *may* be used to disguise agency—and it is also a verbal construction that *may* involve unnecessary or inappropriate wordiness. If either is the case, it is often better to rephrase.

1.6 Sentence Combining: How to Build Sentences

As they become more and more skilled, writers become more adept at manipulating and varying the structures of their sentences. Such flexibility is a goal all serious writers should aspire to reach, and one of the best ways to achieve it is to engage in a process called sentence combining. As a means of helping students develop facility with more mature sentence structures, this technique goes back to the writing classrooms of the nineteenth century. But it wasn't until the 1960s that sentence combining gained a substantial following among writing teachers, largely because Noam Chomsky's new, highly influential linguistic theory, transformational-generative grammar, appeared to provide a theoretical rationale for this writing exercise. Subsequent research into the effectiveness of sentence combining in improving the fluency and maturity of developing writers' sentence structures gave the technique firm support. Since then, newer alternatives to and further development of Chomsky's grammar may also give some insight into the basis for the efficacy of sentence combining. But since it works, many are content to leave theoretical discussion to the specialists and simply take advantage of this useful practice.

In its most elementary practice, writers join two or more simple sentences, called "kernels," into a longer sentence or group of sentences. Kernels can be kept as they are and joined with conjunctions or conjunctive adverbs, or they can be embedded into other kernels, a process that often involves shortening the inserted structures. The corollary to combining short sentences is taking apart long sentences in order to examine how they were put together in the first place. Writers can analyze their own sentences in this way as well as those of other, admired authors, becoming conversant with the many options present whenever a writer considers how to express and even create a thought with words. Together, these combining and analyzing procedures are simple but effective. Writers who have mastered them are well on the way to acquiring the ability to write with stylistic fluency; such writers gain greater conscious control over and facility with their sentence structures and sentence variety, become better able to avoid problems like wordiness and repetition, and find elegance and strategic emphasis easier to achieve. Research into writing practices has shown that when unskilled writers revise a draft, they tend to focus exclusively on deleting and changing single words and phrases. What these basic writers often fail to do is reorder and add to their initial material; experienced writers, on the other hand, use all of these revision techniques, especially the latter two. Rewriting for them is an entire reworking and rethinking of their arguments. At the level of sentence style, then, inexperienced writers would do well to include in their studies practice in the reordering of sentences. The work of sentence combining, "de-combining," and recombining affords just such practice.

For many students, another plus of sentence combining and its offshoots is that they don't require an extensive knowledge of grammatical terminology. The exercises work on writers' intuitive understanding of language structures and help practitioners build an increased "feel" for them, which translates into yet another benefit: the ability to avoid certain kinds of grammatical sentence errors. For example, because some sentence combining exercises require kernels to be shortened and embedded as modifiers into other sentences, practice makes it easier to spot dangling constructions and other modifier errors (see as well the discussion on dangling constructions in 2.1, starting on page 83). Working with kernels, which are always short but full sentences, helps students internalize what constitutes a full sentence or main clause and so avoid sentence fragments, run-ons, and comma splices (see also section 1.3.1). Developing writers are also better able to recognize and write balanced, parallel structures after gaining greater awareness of sentence constituents.

A key ability of more experienced writers is reading well. Writers who are also good readers are able to see their own work as a reader would see it and allow that crucial insight to guide their revisions. Combining kernels and reconfiguring the results a few times gives writers more practice in reading at the level of the sentence, and because the process generates a variety of arrangements of the same words, students have an opportunity to compare them and decide which of the structures are most effective and why. It's important to note, though, that sentence combining alone cannot confer the ability to judge such matters well. Enthusiastic combining sessions can produce all manner of unfortunate sentences; an important complementary exercise is analysis both of sentences that work well and of ones that work less well. Those that work well may of course be used as models. Practice in analyzing the work of others also yields another benefit: greater ease in reading more sophisticated and difficult texts. Along the way, students can also examine the elements that make up an individual author's style. All told, diligent sentence "de-combining" and recombining leads to better reading skills, and better reading leads to better writing.

These exercises in sentence manipulation and analysis have been shown to be particularly useful for students who are learning to write in English as an additional language. The kernels and guidelines for combining them in various ways contain both explicit and implicit instructions on how English sentences are structured and on which words can combine with others in which ways. All of this information provides EAL students with useful models for their own writing.

Combining

Joining Kernels

One of the simplest ways to combine kernel sentences is to join them with a connecting word or phrase. Deciding on the best connector, of course, depends on the relationship among the kernels' ideas; see the section on joining words (pages 206–28) for advice on appropriate choices.

Consider the following kernels:

1) My ruse was sloppy.
2) My ruse deceived everyone.

Two noticeable features of a list of kernels are their choppiness of style and their tendency towards unnecessary repetition of words and phrases. Two of the tasks of sentence combining, consequently, are to create more fluent structures out of the kernel lists and to avoid wordiness. An obvious strategy in the case of the kernels above is to use a pronoun to replace one of the "my ruse" phrases. Joining the kernels will take care of the choppiness. Because the second kernel reverses the expectations raised by the first, a helpful joining word may be used to signal the contrast between the two. Here are some options for joining them.

A coordinating conjunction:

My ruse was sloppy, but it deceived everyone.

A subordinating conjunction (note that this conjunction does join the kernels despite its position before one of the kernels rather than between the two):

> Even though my ruse was sloppy, it deceived everyone.

A conjunctive adverb:

> My ruse was sloppy; nevertheless, it deceived everyone.

In some cases, word order can be rearranged somewhat, as in the following example that joins the kernels with the subordinating conjunction "though":

> Sloppy though my ruse was, it deceived everyone.

If a pair of kernels consists of linked or supporting ideas, several connecting words would be suitable (see, for examples, those listed on pages 212–15), but it might also be stylistically effective to join the kernels with only a mark of punctuation. This option makes for a punchier sentence that emphasizes the closeness of relationship between the joined ideas. Consider the following kernels:

1) My ruse was brilliant.
2) My ruse deceived everyone.

Joined with a conjunction, the kernels make a sentence that is satisfactory:

> My ruse was brilliant, and it deceived everyone.

Using only a semicolon as a connector, however, makes a more dramatic alternative:

> My ruse was brilliant; it deceived everyone.

Using a dash instead heightens the drama even further:

> My ruse was brilliant—it deceived everyone.

If one kernel illustrates, specifies, or provides an explanation for the other, a colon is an appropriate connector:

1) She had only one thing to say.
2) Don't touch the chocolate.

> She had only one thing to say: don't touch the chocolate.

Embedding Kernels

Structurally more complex sentences can be built by embedding one kernel within another. The embedded kernel can stay whole or substantially so, or parts of it can be deleted to create phrases and even single words for insertion into what then becomes the sentence's main kernel.

WHOLE CLAUSES EMBEDDED WITH PUNCTUATION

Certain marks of punctuation—paired dashes and parentheses, for example—allow for an entire kernel to be embedded in another unchanged.

1) The secret to Edith's success is her stubbornness.
2) The secret cannot be denied.

The secret to Edith's success—it cannot be denied—is her stubbornness.

1) She hung on to the bitter end.
2) She is so very stubborn.

She hung on (she is so very stubborn) to the bitter end.

RELATIVE CLAUSES

An embedded kernel left whole can also take the form of a relative clause, that is, an adjective clause introduced by a relative pronoun (see pages 8–10). Like other pronouns, relative pronouns eliminate some repetition of words or phrases by substituting for them. Below are examples of embedded relative clauses using the relative pronouns *that*, *who*, *which*, *where*, and *when*.

1) The music is the best music of all.
2) The music plays only in Kazuo's head.

The music that plays only in Kazuo's head is the best music of all.

Note that in the next two examples, which involve the relative pronoun *who*, the kernel that will become the relative clause in the combined sentence indicates which form, *who* or *whom*, the pronoun should take. In the first example, the pronoun takes the place of the kernel's subject and so takes the subject form, *who*. In the second, the pronoun takes the place of the kernel's object and so takes the object form, *whom*. Here is one instance of the ways in which sentence combining practice can help writers master some grammatical rules.

1) Lewis writes the best books.
2) Lewis is despicable.

Lewis, who is despicable, writes the best books.

1) Lewis writes the best books.
2) I despise Lewis.

Lewis, whom I despise, writes the best books.

1) Lewis is despised by all.
2) Lewis's books are the best.

Lewis, whose books are the best, is despised by all.

1) That book is everyone's favorite.
2) No one can understand that book.

That book, which no one can understand, is everyone's favorite.

1) Frieda's thoughts turned to evil at a precise moment.
2) No one knows the precise moment.

No one knows the precise moment when Frieda's thoughts turned to evil.

1) She left him in the attic.
2) No one ever goes to the attic.

She left him in the attic, where no one ever goes.

Abbreviated Kernels Joined as Absolute Phrases

Absolute phrases are shortened kernels that contain nouns and modifiers but no main verb. Absolutes often modify entire sentences and attach to them with commas.

1) Willard is an impatient man.
2) The experiment went badly.

Willard being an impatient man, the experiment went badly.

1) No one waited for the banana flambé.
2) The party was already wrecked by Shirley's antics.

The party already wrecked by Shirley's antics, no one waited for the banana flambé.

Abbreviated Kernels Embedded as Verb and Noun Phrases

Kernels can be abbreviated to phrases or even single words before being inserted into other kernels. When the ideas of paired kernels have an equal, independent status, they can be shortened to phrases and joined with coordinating conjunctions.

NOUN PHRASE

1) Dolores always cries while watching *Casablanca.*
2) Stan always cries while watching *Casablanca.*

Dolores and Stan always cry while watching *Casablanca.*

VERB PHRASE

1) Morton sang "Danny Boy."
2) Morton expected our applause.

Morton sang "Danny Boy" and expected our applause.

Abbreviated Kernels Embedded as Modifiers

Shortened kernels can also serve as various kinds of modifiers, including adjectives, adverbs, prepositional phrases, past and present participles, infinitive phrases, and appositives.

KERNELS EMBEDDED AS SINGLE-WORD ADJECTIVES

1) Herman's handshake was floppy.
2) Herman's handshake irritated his in-laws.

Herman's floppy handshake irritated his in-laws.

KERNELS EMBEDDED AS SINGLE-WORD ADVERBS

1) Souvankham was doubtful.
2) Souvankham frowned at the chocolate mousse bombe.

Souvankham frowned doubtfully at the chocolate mousse bombe.

KERNELS EMBEDDED AS PREPOSITIONAL PHRASES

1) The glove looked suspiciously familiar.
2) The glove was in the hallway.

The glove in the hallway looked suspiciously familiar.

1) Terrence threw Mabel's letter.
2) Mabel's letter landed on the fire.

Terrence threw Mabel's letter on the fire.

KERNELS EMBEDDED AS PRESENT PARTICIPLES

1) Walter paddled doggedly.
2) Walter finished another lap of the pool.

Paddling doggedly, Walter finished another lap of the pool.

KERNELS EMBEDDED AS PAST PARTICIPLES

1) Mei's insight was wrapped in obscurity.
2) Mei's insight went unnoticed.

Mei's insight, wrapped in obscurity, went unnoticed.

KERNELS EMBEDDED AS INFINITIVE PHRASES

1) They went home.
2) They reflected on their bad behavior.

They went home to reflect on their bad behavior.

KERNELS EMBEDDED AS APPOSITIVES

1) Amira is a wily tactician.
2) Amira always wins at checkers.

A wily tactician, Amira always wins at checkers.

Combining and Recombining

For building effective revision practices, exercises in recombining kernels work very well. The idea is to combine the same list of kernels into several combinations and compare the results. An important decision in any combination is which kernel will form the main clause or clauses of the sentence. The rule of thumb is that the main idea should rest in the main clause. Varying the way the kernels are combined can change the emphasis or even the fundamental idea of a sentence. Consider the following kernels:

1) I love halva.
2) I don't eat halva often.

The two could be given equivalent status and joined by a coordinating conjunction or conjunctive adverb into a sentence with two main clauses:

I love halva, but I don't eat it often.

I love halva; however, I don't eat it often.

In combinations such as this, notice that *but* must stay where it is, while *however* is able to move to a variety of spots in the sentence:

> I love halva; I don't, however, eat it often.
>
> I love halva; I don't eat it often, however.

Each option is subtly different from the others. Placed at the beginning of its clause, *however* signals an upcoming contrast right away, so readers anticipate some sort of reversal of the first idea. Placed after *I don't,* the transition word interrupts its clause and so emphasizes the idea of not doing something; the shift from the first clause's affirmative statement to the second's negative one is thus immediately more specific than the first sentence's broader signal of contrast. The third sentence delays the transition word until the very end, confronting the readers with a starker contrast between the affirmative and negative statements as their expectations after reading the first clause are suddenly reversed without notice.

Coordinating main clauses is not the only option for these kernels; one clause can be subordinated to the other for still different effects.

> Although I love halva, I don't eat it often.
>
> Although I don't eat it often, I love halva.

Each kernel becomes the sole main clause in each of the variations above. In the first, the emphasis is on not eating halva, while in the second, the focus is on loving it.

Embedding each kernel as a relative clause achieves a similar effect, but again, there are subtle differences:

> I love halva, which I don't eat often.
>
> I don't often eat halva, which I love.

There, the relative clauses feel more like wistful afterthoughts and less like blunt statements of fact (as in the sentences using *although*).

Here are still more variations with still different effects:

> I love but don't often eat halva.
>
> I don't often eat my beloved halva.
>
> Despite loving halva, I don't often eat it.
>
> Despite not often eating it, I love halva.

Depending on a writer's rhetorical purposes, any of these sentences would work well in a larger context. Sentence recombining helps writers see what options are available to them so that they can consider which would be preferable.

Combining Several Kernels into a Single Sentence

The next step after the simple combining of pairs of kernels is to work on joining three, four, and even more kernels. Consider the following list of kernels:

1) Clutter is far from causing certain things.
2) Clutter does not make the mind disorganized.
3) Clutter does not make the mind distracted.
4) Clutter does not make the mind distressed.
5) Clutter can foster thinking.
6) The thinking is creative.
7) Clutter can contain order.
8) The order is of a high degree.
9) The order is not visible to observation.
10) The observation is initial.
11) The observation is casual.

The more kernels in a list, the more options there are for combining them, and the more choices a writer must make. Not all possibilities are equally felicitous, however. It is very possible for an excited sentence combiner to produce questionable sentences. Here is one example:

> You might say that clutter makes the mind disorganized, that it makes the mind distracted, and that it makes the mind distressed, but clutter is far from having these effects; instead, it can foster thinking in a creative manner, and it can also contain a kind of order that is of a high degree but that is not visible to the first glance of the casual observer.

The sentence above is grammatically correct and makes some interesting substitutions and additions to the original list of kernels, but it is unnecessarily wordy and needn't be so long. The goal of sentence combining is never to write the longest, most complex sentence possible. Good writers vary their sentence lengths and recognize the rhetorical value of short, simple sentences for emphasis. For combining exercises involving more than two kernels, leaving one or more kernels uncombined is always an option. Other stylistic choices that such exercises call for are whether kernels should be joined or embedded, where embedded kernels should be placed within the finished sentence, whether transitions or conjunctions would be effective and which ones would work best, and, importantly, which kernel should become the main clause of a combined sentence. Some writers also find reading sentences out loud helpful, and many solicit the opinions of other readers. But particularly beneficial is taking the time to configure and then reconfigure a list of kernels, and then compare the results. Here are two more arrangements of the kernel list above:

> Clutter, far from making the mind disorganized, distracted, and distressed, can foster creative thinking and, moreover, contain a high degree of order not at first visible to casual observation.

> Clutter seems sure to make the mind disorganized, distracted, and distressed. Not so, however—it can actually foster creative thinking. Even more surprising, it can contain a high degree of order, which casual observation may not at first reveal.

Both of the recombinations above are less wordy than the first try and seem better for that reason. Which of the last two you prefer, however, will likely depend on what context you imagine the passages belonging to. The final combination includes more transitional words and so directs readers more strongly toward conclusions to be drawn from the claims it makes. It is also more casual in tone, largely because of phrases like *seems sure to*, and *not so*, and the use of a dash rather than, say, a semicolon. The middle combination is leaner and gives the impression of a less familiar, perhaps more professional voice behind the words.

"De-Combining" and Recombining

While combining kernels improves a writer's understanding of sentence structure, analyzing a complete sentence into its possible constituent kernels yields even more insights. The practice can clarify certain grammar problems (as in the relative clause examples above that use *who* and *whom*), helping writers to avoid them, and in the process, become better readers of their own work, an important skill that sets experienced writers apart from the less skilled. "De-combining" sentences can also help students become better able to read even difficult texts and more adept at grasping the components that make up the styles of a variety of writers and types of writing.

Help with Some Grammatical Errors: Two More Examples

Dangling Modifiers

Inexperienced writers sometimes dangle modifiers (see the section beginning on page 83 for more information on dangling constructions). Sentence combining can help writers recognize and so better avoid this common problem. Consider the following sentence:

> While watching an abominable film, even the popcorn tasted vile.

Dividing the sentence into kernels gives the following result:

1) The popcorn tasted vile.
2) _____ watched a film.
3) The film was abominable.

There is an obvious problem with kernel 2; it has no subject. That's what causes it to dangle when combined with the others. Embedded as a modifier, it attaches to the closest noun, *popcorn*, and creates the unintentionally amusing image of popcorn watching a film. Once the problem is clearly laid out in a kernel list, it's easy to see and to fix:

1) The popcorn tasted vile.
2) We watched a film.
3) The film was abominable.

> Because we were watching an abominable film, even the popcorn tasted vile.
> We were watching an abominable film; even the popcorn tasted vile.

Syntactic Ambiguity

Sometimes, unwanted ambiguity in a sentence comes from its syntax, or the arrangement of its words. The following is the title of an anthology of key philosophical texts:

> *Enduring Issues in Philosophy*

The title is not an entire sentence, but there are nonetheless abbreviated kernels underlying it. Analyzing the title shows that it has two possible underlying groups of kernels:

1) Philosophy has issues.
2) The issues have endured.

1) Philosophy has issues.
2) People can endure the issues.

It's doubtful that the publisher of that book intends us to read the second possible meaning of the title, but that reading is nonetheless available. An unambiguous title would combine one of the pairs of kernels above, presumably the first. Here are two possible reconfigurations:

> *Some Enduring Issues in Philosophy*
> *Philosophy's Enduring Issues*

Help with Reading Challenging Texts

Often, students have difficulty reading the work of authors from earlier eras simply because the language has changed considerably in the interval. Some of the challenge comes from changes in vocabulary, of course, for which the best remedy is to consult a good dictionary or glossary of words from the period. But some confusion can result from unfamiliar sentence structure, too; careful analysis of some sample sentences into their constituent kernels will, with practice, help students raise their literacy skills to the point where such texts no longer pose a problem. Look, for example, at the following passage from Thomas Hobbes's *Leviathan*:

> A LAW OF NATURE (*lex naturalis*) is a precept or general rule, found out by reason, by which a man is forbidden to do that which is destructive of his life, or taketh away the means of preserving the same, and to omit that by which he thinketh it may be best preserved.

Here is a possible division of this sentence into kernels:

1) The Latin for "law of nature" is *lex naturalis*.
2) A law of nature is a precept.
3) A law of nature is a general rule.
4) A law of nature is found out by reason.
5) A law of nature forbids a man to do certain things.
6) Some things are destructive of the man's life.
7) Some things take away means.
8) The means are for preserving his life.
9) A law of nature forbids the man to omit certain things.
10) Some things preserve the man's life.
11) The man thinks this.

Recombining these kernels into more contemporary language and, for better understanding, expanding them somewhat can help elucidate Hobbes's meaning.

> A law of nature, which in Latin is called a *lex naturalis*, is a precept or general rule. This kind of law can be discovered by reasoning; that is, the law does not need to be revealed to us by any other agent. A law of nature forbids a person[1] to do anything that would destroy his life or that would take away the means by which he preserves his life. A law of nature also obliges a person to follow any course of action that he thinks will help preserve his life.

The result is perhaps a little more cumbersome than it need be, but it is clear, and the point of this exercise in any case is to understand a challenging passage rather than offer a rewrite of it to a reader.

Here is another example, this time a passage from Sonnet 116 by William Shakespeare.

> Let me not to the marriage of true minds
> Admit impediments. Love is not love
> Which alters when it alteration finds,
> Or bends with the remover to remove.
> O, no, it is an ever-fixèd mark
> That looks on tempests and is never shaken;
> It is the star to every wandering bark,
> Whose worth's unknown, although his height be taken.

Part of our potential puzzlement on reading this passage comes again from unfamiliar vocabulary (for example, *remove* means *leave*, not *take away*, and *bark* is a noun meaning *ship*), but the glosses that are now almost always published with Shakespeare's work can help with that. Beyond gaining experience with his words and terms, readers of Shakespeare must gain skill interpreting the structures of his lines of verse. An important first step is to realize that a line does not necessarily constitute a sentence; the periods in the passage above show that it consists of three sentences divided over eight lines. Here is a list of kernels generated from the passage above, with more modern expressions substituted as needed. For ease of analysis, the kernels are grouped according to the sentences they make up, and the kernel that underlies each sentence's main clause or clauses is underlined:

---

1 In working through the meaning of a passage such as this, we may also need to ask whether the writer intended words such as man to apply only to males, or to all humans. In this case context makes clear that Hobbes intended the latter.

Sentence One

1) Do not let me allow certain things.
2) The things are impediments.
3) The impediments interfere with a marriage.
4) The marriage is between minds.
5) The minds are true.

Sentence Two

1) Certain things can seem like love.
2) These things are not love.
3) One thing changes under a certain circumstance.
4) This thing finds a change (in the one loved).
5) Another thing changes (*bends*) under a certain circumstance.
6) The loved one (*the remover*) goes away.
7) This thing departs (*removes*).

Sentence Three

1) Love is not this thing.
2) Love is a landmark that never moves or changes.
3) The landmark looks at tempests.
4) The landmark is not shaken.
5) Love is a star.
6) The star guides ships.
7) The ships are off course.
8) The star has a worth.
9) The worth is unknown.
10) The star has a height (above the horizon).
11) The height has been measured.

Note that some of the kernels include understood elements that don't appear in the original but that must nonetheless be included in the kernels in order to make them complete. Consider the clause *when it alteration finds*; in order to understand the point of this clause, we need to answer the question *alteration in what*? The line does not directly say what it is that alters, but the context of the rest of the poem, with its focus on the properties of true love, strongly suggests that this hypothetical alteration is in the object of such love.

Once the kernels are carefully written, recombining them yields a paraphrase of the passage. The meaning of much poetic language lies condensed in the structures of its words; the rendering below of the ideas of this sonnet includes an interpretive expansion of the metaphors used in the poem.

> Do not let me allow impediments to the marriage of minds that are true to one another. Some things can seem like love, but they are not love. For example, if a supposed lover changes his or her attitude when there is a change in the loved one, it is not love. Similarly, when a supposed lover stops loving if the beloved is gone, it is not love. Love is like an unchanging landmark at sea. Such a landmark is witness to tempests, but storms cannot move or change it. Likewise, love does not change or fall if there is any upheaval in its circumstances. Love is like a guiding star that helps every ship that's gone off course find its way. Such a star has a worth so great that it cannot be known, even if its physical height above the horizon has been measured. Likewise, the worth of love is too great to know, even if love's more mundane details can be described.

The process of analysis again helps to clarify the original meaning and points to the places where material must be added to or expanded on in order to facilitate this illumination. The subsequent recombination of the kernels is thus an exercise in careful interpretation of what rests within the poetic language. The paraphrase is again ungraceful, and because it provides a single reading with little possibility of variation in its own interpretation, it paints a unidimensional picture of a deeply textured original. But all that just serves to highlight the beauty and mastery of the sonnet, in which multiple meanings are folded into musical lines.

Gaining Awareness of Writing Style

A particular benefit of sentence "de-combining" comes from analyzing the work of admired writers. A close look at their sentences reveals sentence strategies that less experienced writers can use as models for their own writing. It may also serve to illuminate the characteristics of a given writer's style or the characteristics of a particular genre of writing.

Below is a passage from "The Art and Craft of Memoir," by Lewis Thomas, a non-fiction writer justly praised for his prose style:

> I am a member of a fragile species, still new to the earth, the youngest creatures of any scale, here only a few moments as evolutionary time is measured, a juvenile species, a child of a species. We are only

tentatively set in place, error-prone, at risk of fumbling, in real danger at the moment of leaving behind only a thin layer of our fossils, radioactive at that.

Here is a list of kernels generated from the passage by Thomas. Again, the kernels are grouped according to the sentences they are part of, with the main clause kernels underlined:

Sentence One

1) <u>I am a member of a species</u>.
2) The species is fragile.
3) The species is new to the earth.
4) The species consists of creatures.
5) The creatures are the youngest.
6) All creatures are ranked on many scales.
7) The creatures are here over moments.
8) The moments are few.
9) The moments are measured.
10) The measurement is of evolutionary time.
11) The species is juvenile.
12) The species is a child.

Sentence Two

1) <u>We are set in place</u>.
2) The setting is temporary.
3) We are error-prone.
4) We are at risk.
5) The risk is of fumbling.
6) We are in danger.
7) The danger is real.
8) The danger is now.
9) The danger is of leaving a residue.
10) The residue is the only one.
11) The residue is a layer.
12) The layer is of fossils.
13) The layer is thin.
14) The fossils are radioactive.

The list of kernels makes some aspects of Thomas's style jump out. Both of the two sentences that make up the passage start with a main clause made up of a whole kernel without any kind of transition leading in to it. Each of the sentence-opening kernels has another kernel embedded in it as a single-word modifier: *fragile* and *tentatively*. A series of abbreviated kernels acting as modifiers then follows each main clause. In the first sentence, if we consider the first three phrases following the main clause, *still new to the earth*, *the youngest creatures of any scale*, and *here only a few moments as evolutionary time is measured*, we can see that they are progressively more complex—each contains more embedded kernels than the last. The final two phrases of sentence one, *a juvenile species* and *a child of a species*, are then again made up of simple abbreviated kernels.

The pattern of the second sentence is similar, though not exactly the same. Set off by commas after the main clause are three phrases that are again progressively more complex: *error-prone*, *at risk of fumbling*, and *in real danger at the moment of leaving behind only a thin layer of our fossils*. The sentence then ends with one simple abbreviated kernel: *radioactive*. The two sentences together, then, create a pleasing symmetry that is varied just enough to keep it from being rigid. Another graceful touch is the pairing of a whole kernel with a list of abbreviated kernels in each sentence. Within the lists themselves, the movement in the modifying phrases toward greater complexity gives each sentence a momentum that is softly slowed with the simple closing kernels. In all, these structural elements contribute to the elegance of the passage.

Here, from Ursula K. Le Guin's novel *Lavinia*, is a passage of fictional prose that reveals the author's skill in crafting language. The speaker is Lavinia, a young woman. Her future husband, Aeneas, is looking with his people for a new homeland and has just arrived in her country.

> And in the twilight of morning of the next day, alone, kneeling in the mud by Tiber, I saw the great ships turn from the sea and come into the river. I saw my husband stand on the high stern of the first ship, though he did not see me. He gazed up the dark river, praying, dreaming. He did not see the deaths that lay before him, all along the river, all the way to Rome.

This passage can be "de-combined" into kernels as follows (the italicized kernel of sentence two is a full but subordinate clause):

Sentence One

1) It was twilight.
2) It was morning.

3) It was the next day.
4) I was alone.
5) I was kneeling in the mud.
6) The mud was by the Tiber.
7) I saw ships.
8) The ships were great.
9) The ships turned from the sea.
10) The ships came into the river.

Sentence Two

1) I saw my husband.
2) My husband stood on the stern.
3) The stern was of the first ship.
4) The stern was high.
5) *My husband did not see me.*

Sentence Three

1) My husband gazed up the river.
2) The river was dark.
3) My husband was praying.
4) My husband was dreaming.

Sentence Four

1) My husband did not see the deaths.
2) The deaths lay before him.
3) The deaths lay all along the river.
4) The deaths lay all the way to Rome.

Kernel analysis shows that Le Guin's passage also has an overall symmetry, though again it is not strict. The passage pulls the reader along from sentence to sentence with a pattern in which structures are mirrored by what follows next across sentence boundaries. After opening with six abbreviated kernels, the first sentence consists of one main clause, *I saw the great ships*, with three kernels embedded in it. The very next clause at the start of sentence two, *I saw my husband stand*, also contains three shortened kernels serving as modifiers. In structure (as well as wording), it closely repeats the pattern of the first sentence's main clause: *I saw the great ships turn* and *I saw my husband stand* echo one another substantially, and both are similarly followed by a short series of abbreviated kernels.

The next full clause is the second, subordinate clause of the second sentence, *he did not see me*. This clause, again a whole kernel, is itself echoed, though again not rigidly, by the next clause, which opens sentence three: *He gazed up the dark river*. This clause also consists of an unshortened kernel, though it has one embedded modifier. Attached to the end of this clause are two kernels abbreviated into a pair of present participles, *praying* and *dreaming*. That structure is loosely repeated in the next sentence, which features a whole kernel, *He did not see the deaths*, with one embedment (the relative clause *that lay before him*), to which are attached a pair of kernels shortened into two prepositional phrases, *all along the river* and *all the way to Rome*.

All of these echoed structures are contained within a whole that has its own mirror symmetry: the passage begins with six abbreviated kernels leading into a main clause, and ends with a main clause leading to three abbreviated kernels. These strings of shortened kernels slow the reader's progress, creating a heightened anticipation at the start of the passage and a sense of ending and inevitability at the close. In addition, the four kernels that are left whole are similar in wording and thematically linked; *I saw*, *I saw*, *He gazed*, and *He did not see* are all about seeing and not seeing, key themes in the novel as a whole. That these clauses have little or nothing embedded directly within them makes them stand out, startling and grave; the important themes they embody are thus highlighted and reinforced.

As the structure of such samples suggests, an almost but not quite exact symmetry is a common feature of powerful prose—both fictional and non-fictional.

Finally, consider the opening to the play *Glengarry Glen Ross* by David Mamet. The speaker is Shelly Levene, a real estate salesman in imminent danger of losing his job; he is addressing John Williamson, his supervisor:

> **Levene:** John ... John ... John. Okay. John. John. Look: *(Pause.)* The Glengarry Highland's leads, you're sending Roma out. Fine. He's a good man. We know what he is. He's fine. All I'm saying, you look at the *board*, he's throwing ... wait, wait, wait, he's throwing them *away*, he's throwing the leads away. All that I'm saying, that you're wasting leads. I don't want to tell you your *job*. All that I'm saying, things get *set*, I know they do, you get a certain *mindset*.... A guy gets a reputation. We know how this ... all I'm saying, put a *closer* on the job. There's more than one man for the ... Put a ... wait a second, put a *proven man out* ...

A possible breakdown of the passage into kernels is as follows:

1) John, listen. (uttered four times)
2) John, look.
3) You are sending Roma out.
4) Roma (is to do something).
5) Roma (will close) the Glengarry Highland leads.
6) That is fine.
7) Roma is a good man.
8) We know Roma.
9) Roma is (a certain kind of salesman).
10) Roma is fine.
11) I am saying only one thing.
12) Look at the board.
13) Roma is throwing the leads away. (uttered three times)
14) John, wait. (uttered three times)
15) I am saying only one thing.
16) You are wasting leads.
17) I don't want to tell you something.
18) Your job (is a certain thing).
19) I am saying only one thing.
20) Things get set.
21) I know they do.
22) You get a mindset.
23) The mindset is a certain kind.
24) A guy gets a reputation.
25) We know something.
26) This happens (in a certain way).
27) I am only saying one thing.
28) Put a closer on the job.
29) More than one man is suitable.
30) The suitability is for the (job).
31) Put a (closer on the job).
32) John, wait a second.
33) Put a man out.
34) The man is proven.

The kernel list makes several remarkable features of the passage immediately apparent. Four kernels (1, 11, 13, and 14) are repeated several times, with three of the repetitions (all but kernel 11) occurring in sequence. Other kernels are close but not exact repetitions: *Roma is a good man* and *Roma is fine*, and *put a closer on the job* and *put a proven man out*, for example. Very few kernels are embedded into others; in fact, almost all of the passage's sentences either consist of single, unembellished kernels or are a string of simple kernels. Some of the kernels as represented in the passage are incomplete: for example, *John* for *John, listen to me*; *all I'm saying* for *I'm only saying one thing*; and *The Glengarry Highland's leads, you're sending Roma out*, with the connection between the two elements left unspoken. Several of the kernels are also conceptually incomplete: how do things get set, and what are those things? What sort of mindset does one get about what? What kind of reputation does a guy get, and how?

These arresting features create some important effects. With its many broken and repeated kernels, the passage closely mimics spontaneous speech and implies non-verbal responses by Williamson to which Levene subsequently reacts. Both stylistic effects are common to drama, particularly modern drama. The choppy strings of simple and incomplete kernels also help establish Levene's emotional agitation. But the structure of the passage has thematic significance, as well. Throughout the play, salesmen use words to manipulate one another and their clients ruthlessly; what is implied by and left out of the utterances creates a subtext that has a crucial importance to the circumstances of each man. Unspoken completions to fragmented kernels imply a shared understanding and friendly intimacy, neither of which may actually exist. But their apparent existence is all that matters. Levene is clearly trying hard to play this game well, to maneuver Williamson into giving him a break. The gradual deterioration of the speech graphically illustrates Levene's growing desperation as he feels his skill at closing a "sale" slip away.

With great skill, Mamet has built word structures that fulfill a writing purpose quite different from Le Guin's.

2 USAGE

2.1 Verb Issues

Dangling Constructions

An error made frequently by writers at all levels of ability—including holders of graduate degrees in English—is allowing large chunks of sentences to "dangle," with no grammatical connection to the word or words they are intended to relate to. For that reason several pages are devoted here to that problem.

2 Usage

> **On the Companion Website**
>
> In *The Broadview Guide* we group together under the heading **dangling constructions** types of error that in many other texts are treated as separate categories. Information on the complex taxonomy of *dangling modifers, misplaced modifiers*, and *squinting modifiers* is provided alongside a range of relevant exercises at **sites.broadviewpress.com/grammar**. Click on **Exercises** and go to **2.1**.

Dangling Participles and Infinitives

A present participle is an *-ing* word (*going, thinking*, etc.). When combined with a form of the verb *to be*, participles form part of a finite verb. They can also be used in a number of ways on their own (as non-finite verbs), however:

The president felt that visiting China would be unwise at that time.
(Here *visiting China* acts as a noun phrase.)

Having taken into account the various reports, the committee decided to delay the project for a year.
(Here *having taken into account the various reports* acts as an adjectival phrase modifying the noun *committee.*)

dangling present participles or participial phrases: The danger of dangling occurs with sentences such as the second example above. If the writer does not take care that the participial phrase refers to the subject of the main clause, some absurd sentences can result:

needs checking Waiting for a bus, a brick fell on my head.
(Bricks do not normally wait for buses.)

revised While I was waiting for a bus, a brick fell on my head.

needs checking Leaving the room, the lights must be turned off.
(Lights do not normally leave the room.)

revised When you leave the room you must turn off the lights.

In sentences such as these the amusing error is relatively easy to notice; it can be much more difficult with longer and more complex sentences. Even seasoned writers and public speakers can easily find themselves using dangling constructions. Here, for example, is what one prominent politician said as he contemplated the prospect of resigning his position: "Although still hypothetical, I would be better able to devote myself to my family." What he meant to say, of course, was that the prospect of his resignation was hypothetical—not that *he* was hypothetical.

Experienced writers are especially alert to this pitfall if they begin a sentence with a participle or participial phrase that describes a mental operation; they are wary of beginning by *considering*, *believing*, *taking into account*, *remembering*, *turning for a moment*, or *regarding*:

needs checking Believing that he had done no wrong, the fact of being accused of dishonesty infuriated the company's CEO.

revised Believing that he had done no wrong, the company's CEO was infuriated at being accused of dishonesty.

or The company's CEO was infuriated at being accused of dishonesty; he believed he had done no wrong.

needs checking Considering all the above-mentioned studies, the evidence shows conclusively that smoking can cause cancer.

revised Considering all the above-mentioned studies, we conclude that smoking causes cancer.

better These studies show conclusively that smoking can cause cancer.

needs checking Turning for a moment to the thorny question of Joyce's style, the stream of consciousness technique realistically depicts the workings of the human mind.

revised Turning for a moment to the thorny question of Joyce's style, we may observe that his stream of consciousness technique realistically depicts the workings of the human mind.

better Joyce's style does not make *Ulysses* easy to read, but his stream of consciousness technique realistically depicts the workings of the human mind.

needs checking Taking into account the uncertainty as to the initial temperature of the beaker, the results are not conclusive.

revised Taking into account the uncertainty as to the initial temperature of the beaker necessitates that the results be deemed inconclusive.

better Since the initial temperature of the beaker was not recorded, the results are inconclusive.

Notice that in each of the above cases the best way to eliminate the problem is to dispense with the participial phrase entirely. More often than not one's writing is improved by using active verbs rather than participial phrases. Many people seem to feel that writing which is filled with participial phrases somehow sounds more important; in fact, such phrases tend to obscure the writer's meaning under unnecessary padding. This is true even when the participles are not dangling:

needs checking Another characteristic having a significant impact on animal populations is the extreme diurnal temperature range on the desert surface.

(Can a characteristic have an impact? A small point is here buried in a morass of meaningless abstraction.)

better The extreme diurnal temperature range on the desert surface also affects animal populations.

needs checking Referring generally to the social stratification systems of the city as a whole, we can see clearly that types of accommodation, varying throughout in accordance with income levels and other socio-economic factors, display an extraordinary diversity.

(Is there anything either clear or extraordinary about this?)

better In this city rich people and poor people live in different neighborhoods, and rich people live in larger houses than poor people.

By cutting out the padding in this way the writer may occasionally find to his surprise that instead of saying something rather weighty and important as he had thought he was doing, he is in fact saying little or nothing. But he should not be discouraged if this happens; the same is true for all writers.

dangling past participles (e.g., *considered*, *developed*, *regarded*): The same sorts of problems that occur with present participles occur frequently with past participles as well:

needs checking Considered from a cost point of view, Combarp Capital Corporation could not really afford to purchase Skinflint Securities.

(Combarp is not being considered; the purchase is.)

poor Considered from the point of view of cost, the purchase of Skinflint Securities was not a wise move by Combarp Capital Corporation.

better Combarp Capital Corporation could not really afford to buy Skinflint Securities.

needs checking Once regarded as daringly modern in its portrayal of fashionable *fin de siècle* decadence, Wilde draws on traditional patterns to create a powerful new Gothic tale. (*The Cambridge Guide to Literature in English*)

(The novel is an *it*; Oscar Wilde was a *he*.)

revised *The Picture of Dorian Gray* was once regarded as daringly modern in its portrayal of fashionable *fin de siècle* decadence. In the novel Wilde draws on traditional patterns to create a powerful new Gothic tale.

needs checking Used with frequency, a man will feel refreshed and rejuvenated. (aftershave advertisement)

revised Used with frequency, this product will help a man feel refreshed and rejuvenated.

dangling infinitive phrases:

needs checking To conclude this essay, the French Revolution was a product of many interacting causes.

(The French Revolution concluded no essays.)

poor To conclude this essay, I would like to say that the French Revolution was a product of many causes.

better The explanations given for the French Revolution, then, are not mutually exclusive; it was a product of many interacting causes.

(A good writer does not normally need to tell her readers that she is concluding an essay; they can see the space at the bottom of the page. A little word such as *then*, set off by commas, is more than enough to signal that this is a summing-up.)

needs checking To receive a complimentary copy, the business reply card should be returned before June 30.

(The card will not receive anything.)

revised To receive a complimentary copy, you should return the business reply card before June 30.

needs checking To appreciate the full significance of the Camp David Accords, a range of factors needs to be considered.

(A factor cannot appreciate.)

poor To appreciate the full significance of the Camp David Accords, we need to consider many things.

better The Camp David Accords were important in many ways.

dangling gerund or prepositional phrases:

needs checking In reviewing the evidence, one point stands out plainly.

(A point cannot review evidence.)

poor In reviewing the evidence, we can see one point standing out plainly.

better One point stands out plainly from this evidence.

needs checking When analyzing the figures, ways to achieve substantial savings can be discerned.

(The ways cannot analyze.)

poor When we analyze the figures we can see ways to achieve substantial savings.

better The figures suggest that we can greatly reduce our expenses.

Other sorts of phrases can be caught dangling too. But almost all writers are capable of attaching them properly if they re-read and revise their work carefully.

needs checking On behalf of city council and the people of Duluth, it gives me great pleasure to welcome you to our city. (from an announcement by the mayor)

(The mayor, not a faceless *it*, is acting on behalf of the others.)

revised On behalf of city council and the people of Duluth, I am pleased to welcome you to our city.

needs checking By adding more component parts to the prototype, this would cause an increase in the price of the product.

revised By adding more component parts to the prototype, we force an increase in the price of the product.

or Adding more component parts to the prototype makes it necessary to increase the price of the product.

A dangling modifier is not always cause for confusion, but don't assume that your intended meaning will be clear to your reader. "One morning I shot an elephant in my pajamas," said the comedian Groucho Marx. You might think the meaning is obvious, until he says the punch-line: "How he got into my pajamas I'll never know."

Sequence of Tenses

If the main verb of a sentence is in the past tense, other verbs must also express a past viewpoint (except when a general truth is being expressed). Some writers have trouble keeping the verb tenses they use in agreement, particularly when indirect speech is involved, or when a quotation is incorporated into a sentence.

agreement of tenses in indirect speech—past plus subjunctive:

needs checking He said that he will fix the engine before the end of the year.

revised He said that he would fix the engine before the end of the year.

(*He said that he will fix the engine* implies that the fixing has not yet occurred but may still occur.)

agreement of tenses in indirect speech—past plus past perfect:

needs checking He claimed that he smoked drugs many years earlier, but that he never inhaled.

revised He claimed that he had smoked drugs many years earlier, but that he had never inhaled.

agreement of tenses—quoted material:

needs checking Prime Minister Ardern admitted that "such a policy is not without its drawbacks."

(The past tense *admitted* and the present tense *is* do not agree.)

There are two ways of dealing with a difficulty such as this:

(a) Change the sentence so as to set off the quotation without using the connecting word *that*. Usually this can be done with a colon. In this case the tense you use does not have to agree with the tense used in the quotation. The words before the colon, though, must be able to act as a complete sentence in themselves.

(b) Use only that part of the quotation that can be used in agreement with the tense of the main verb:

revised Prime Minister Ardern did not claim perfection: "such a policy is not without its drawbacks," she admitted.

or Prime Minister Ardern admitted that such a policy was "not without its drawbacks."

Here are some other examples:

needs checking Churchill promised that "we shall fight on the beaches, ... we shall fight in the fields and in the streets, we shall fight in the hills; we shall never surrender."

(This suggests that you, the writer, will be among those fighting.)

revised Churchill made the following promise: "We shall fight on the beaches, ... we shall fight in the fields and in the streets, we shall fight in the hills; we shall never surrender."

(Notice that the word *that* is now removed.)

or Churchill promised that the British people would "fight on the beaches, ... in the fields and in the streets, ... in the hills," and that they would "never surrender."

On the Companion Website

Exercises on sequence of tenses may be found at **sites.broadviewpress.com/grammar**. Click on **Exercises** and go to **"Verbs and Verb Issues."**

Irregular or Difficult Verbs

The majority of verbs in English follow a regular pattern—*I open* in the simple present tense, *I opened* in the simple past tense, *I have opened* in the present perfect tense, and so forth. However, most of the more frequently used verbs are in some way or another irregular. To pick an obvious example, we say *I went* instead of *I goed*, and *I have gone* instead of *I have goed*. What follows is a list of the main irregular or difficult verbs in English. The past participle (column 3) is used in tenses such as the present perfect (e.g., *I have grown*, *he has found*) and the past perfect (*I had grown*, *I had found*).

The verbs that most frequently cause problems are given special treatment in the following list:

(Note: In both regular and irregular verbs, the present tense is formed by using the infinitive without the preposition *to*.)

Present & Infinitive	*Simple Past*	*Past Participle*
arise	arose	arisen

check A problem had arose even before the discussion began.
revised A problem had arisen even before the discussion began.

awake	awoke	awoken/woken
	(passive: *was awakened*)	
be	was/were	been
bear	bore	borne

check It was heartbreaking for her to lose the child after having bore it for so long.
revised It was heartbreaking for her to lose the child after having borne it for so long.

beat	beat	beaten

check The Yankees were badly beat by the Blue Jays.
revised The Yankees were badly beaten by the Blue Jays.

become	became	become
begin	began	begun

check He had already began treatment when I met him.
revised He had already begun treatment when I met him.

bend	bent	bent
bite	bit	bitten
bleed	bled	bled
blow	blew	blown
break	broke	broken
bring	brought	brought
build	built	built
burn	burned/burnt	burned/burnt
burst	burst	burst

check The pipes bursted while we were on holiday.
revised The pipes burst while we were on holiday.

buy	bought	bought
can	could	been able
catch	caught	caught

Present & Infinitive	*Simple Past*	*Past Participle*
choose	chose	chosen

check In 1999 East Timor choose to become a nation.
revised In 1999 East Timor chose to become a nation.

cling	clung	clung
come	came	come
cost	cost	cost
dig	dug	dug
dive	dived/dove	dived

less accepted He dove into the shallow water.
more formal He dived into the shallow water.

do	did	done
drag	dragged	dragged

check The newspapers drug up a lot of scandal about her.
revised The newspapers dragged up a lot of scandal about her.

draw	drew	drawn
dream	dreamed/dreamt	dreamed/dreamt
drink	drank	drunk

check He has drank more than is good for him.
revised He has drunk more than is good for him.

drive	drove	driven
eat	ate	eaten
fall	fell	fallen
feel	felt	felt
fight	fought	fought
find	found	found
fit	fit	fitted
flee	fled	fled
fling	flung	flung

check George flinged his plate across the room.
revised George flung his plate across the room.

fly	flew	flown
forbid	forbade	forbidden

	Present & Infinitive	*Simple Past*	*Past Participle*
check	Yesterday he forbid us to climb the fence.		
revised	Yesterday he forbade us to climb the fence.		
	forecast	forecast	forecast
check	The weather office has forecasted more rain.		
revised	The weather office has forecast more rain.		
	forget	forgot	forgotten
	forgive	forgave	forgiven
	freeze	froze	frozen
	get	got	got
	give	gave	given
	go	went	gone
	grind	ground	ground
	(e.g., *I have ground the coffee.*)		
	grow	grew	grown
	hang	hanged/hung	hanged/hung

Note: *Hanged* is used only when referring to a person being killed by hanging. Say *The criminal has been hanged*, but *We have hung the picture on the wall*:

check	No one has been publicly hung in Canada since 1962.		
revised	No one has been publicly hanged in Canada since 1962.		
	have	had	had
	hear	heard	heard
	hide	hid	hidden
	hit	hit	hit
	hold	held	held
	hurt	hurt	hurt
	keep	kept	kept

On the Companion Website

Exercises on irregular or difficult verbs may be found at **sites.broadviewpress.com/grammar**. Click on **Exercises** and go to **"Verbs and Verb Issues."**

2 Usage

Present & Infinitive	*Simple Past*	*Past Participle*
kneel	knelt	knelt
know	knew	known
lay	laid	laid

(Note: Although many authorities feel that the distinction is not worth troubling over in informal English, formal English still distinguishes between *lay* and *lie*; you *lay* something on a table, and a hen *lays* eggs, but you *lie* down to sleep. In other words, *lie* is an intransitive verb; it should not be followed by a direct object. *Lay*, by contrast, is transitive.)

check That old thing has been laying around for years.
revised That old thing has been lying around for years.

lead	led	led
lean	leaned/leant	leaned/leant
leap	leaped/leapt	leaped/leapt
learn	learned/learnt	learned/learnt
leave	left	left
lend	lent	lent
let	let	let
lie	lay	lain

check He asked if I would like to lay down and rest.
revised He asked if I would like to lie down and rest.

light	lighted/lit	lighted/lit
lose	lost	lost
make	made	made
may	might	
mean	meant	meant
meet	met	met
must	had to	had to
pay	paid	paid
plead	pleaded/pled	pleaded/pled

(Note: The growing use of *pled* rather than *pleaded* irks some traditionalists, but it is difficult to see why *pleaded* should not follow *leaded* to the grave where the latter was long ago led. If you are trying to please a traditionalist professor, it is probably still best to avoid *pled*. Otherwise, use consistently whichever of the two you prefer.)

	Present & Infinitive	*Simple Past*	*Past Participle*

accepted He had pled guilty to the same offence previously.
accepted He had pleaded guilty to the same offence previously.

prove	proved	proven

check We have proved the hypothesis to be correct.
revised We have proven the hypothesis to be correct.

put	put	put
read	read	read
ride	rode	ridden

check The actor had never rode a horse before.
revised The actor had never ridden a horse before.

ring	rang	rung

check I rung the bell three times, but no one answered.
revised I rang the bell three times, but no one answered.

rise	rose	risen
run	ran	run
saw	sawed	sawed/sawn
say	said	said
see	saw	seen
seek	sought	sought
sell	sold	sold
sew	sewed	sewed/sewn
shake	shook	shaken
shall	should	
shine	shone	shone

check The moon shined almost as brightly as the sun.
revised The moon shone almost as brightly as the sun.

(Note: *Shined* is the accepted formation of the simple past tense where the verb is transitive. Thus we say *she shined her shoes.*)

shoot	shot	shot
show	showed	showed/shown
shrink	shrank	shrunk

check The government's majority shrunk in the election.
revised The government's majority shrank in the election.

Present & Infinitive	*Simple Past*	*Past Participle*
shut	shut	shut
sing	sang	sung
sink	sank	sunk

check The *Edmund Fitzgerald* sunk on Lake Superior.
revised The *Edmund Fitzgerald* sank on Lake Superior.

sit	sat	sat
sleep	slept	slept
slide	slid	slid
smell	smelled/smelt	smelled/smelt
sow	sowed	sowed/sown
speak	spoke	spoken
speed	speeded/sped	speeded/sped
spell	spelled/spelt	spelled/spelt
spend	spent	spent
spill	spilled/spilt	spilled/spilt
spin	spun	spun
spit	spat	spat
split	split	split
spread	spread	spread
spring	sprang	sprung

check The soldiers hurriedly sprung to their feet.
revised The soldiers hurriedly sprang to their feet.

stand	stood	stood
steal	stole	stolen
stick	stuck	stuck
sting	stung	stung
strike	struck	struck
swear	swore	sworn
sweep	swept	swept
swim	swam	swum

check Pictures were taken while the royal couple swum in what they thought was a private cove.
revised Pictures were taken while the royal couple swam in what they had thought was a private cove.

Present & Infinitive	*Simple Past*	*Past Participle*
swing	swung	swung
take	took	taken
teach	taught	taught
tear	tore	torn
tell	told	told
think	thought	thought
throw	threw	thrown
tread	trod	trodden/trod
understand	understood	understood
wake	woke	woken
wear	wore	worn
weep	wept	wept
win	won	won
wind	wound	wound
wring	wrung	wrung
(e.g., *She wrings out her clothes if they are wet.*)		
write	wrote	written

Infinitives, Gerunds, Objects: "To Be or Not To Be?"

gerunds and prepositions: Gerunds have the form of verbs but act as nouns, and as such they do not necessarily require any preposition to introduce them. In particular, when a gerund does not relate to a preceding verb, it should not be accompanied by a preposition. Nor does it require a pronoun to stand in for it as the subject of a verb:

needs checking With using coal-fired generators, it is bad for the environment.

revised Using coal-fired generators is bad for the environment.

When a gerund follows a verb, however, it often must be introduced by a preposition—and unfortunately, there are no rules governing when this happens, or which preposition should be used. More broadly, there are no rules in English to explain why some words must be followed by an infinitive (*to go*, *to do*, *to be*, etc.), while others must be followed by a preposition plus a gerund (*of going*, *in doing*, etc.), and still others by a direct object. Following are some of the words with which difficulties of this sort most often arise:

• **accept something** (not *accept to do something*): It needs a direct object.

needs checking	The committee accepted to try to improve the quality of the postal service.
revised	The committee accepted the task of trying to improve the postal service.
or	The committee agreed to try to improve the postal service.

• **accuse someone of doing something** (not *to do*)

needs checking	Klaus Barbie was accused to have killed thousands of innocent civilians in WW II.
revised	Klaus Barbie was accused of having killed thousands of innocent civilians in WW II.

• **appreciate something**: When used to mean *be grateful*, this verb requires a direct object.

needs checking	I would appreciate if you could respond quickly.
revised	I would appreciate it if you could respond quickly.
or	I would appreciate a quick response.

(The verb *appreciate* without an object means *increase in value.*)

• **assist in doing something** (not *to do*)

needs checking	He assisted me to solve the problem.
revised	He assisted me in solving the problem.
or	He helped me to solve the problem.

• **capable of doing something** (not *to do*)

needs checking	He is capable to run 1500 metres in under four minutes.
revised	He is capable of running 1500 metres in under four minutes.
or	He is able to run 1500 metres in under four minutes.

• **confident of doing something** (not *to do*)

needs checking	She is confident to be able to finish the job before dusk.
revised	She is confident of being able to finish the job before dusk.
or	She is confident that she will finish the job before dusk.

• **consider something or someone to be something** or **consider it something** (not *as something*)

needs checking	According to a recent policy paper, the party now considers a guaranteed annual income as a good idea.

revised According to a recent policy paper, the party now considers a guaranteed annual income to be a good idea.

or According to a recent policy paper, the party now regards a guaranteed annual income as a good idea.

• **discourage someone from doing something** (not *to do*)

needs checking The new Immigration Act is intended to discourage people to enter the country illegally.

revised The new Immigration Act is intended to discourage people from entering the country illegally.

• **forbid someone to do something** (not *from doing*)

needs checking The witnesses were forbidden from leaving the scene of the crime until the police had completed their preliminary investigation.

revised The witnesses were forbidden to leave the scene of the crime until the police had completed their preliminary investigation.

EAL

For particular problems with infinitives, gerunds, and objects faced by those whose native language is not English, see Section 4.

• **insist on doing something** or **insist that something be done** (but not *insist to do*)

needs checking The customer has insisted to wait in the front office until she receives a refund.

revised The customer has insisted on waiting in the front office until she receives a refund.

• **intention**: *Have an intention of doing something* but *someone's intention is/was to do something*

needs checking Hitler had no intention to keep his word.

revised Hitler had no intention of keeping his word.

or Hitler did not intend to keep his word.

or Hitler's intention was to break the treaty.

- **justified in doing something** (not *to do something*)

needs checking He is not justified to make these allegations.
revised He is not justified in making these allegations.

- **look forward to doing something** (not *to do something*)

needs checking I am looking forward to receive your reply.
revised I am looking forward to receiving your reply.

- **opposed to doing something** (not *to do something*)

needs checking He was opposed to set up a dictatorship.
revised He was opposed to setting up a dictatorship.
or He was opposed to the idea of setting up a dictatorship.

- **organize something** (not *to do something*)

needs checking We organized to meet at ten the next morning.
revised We organized a meeting for ten the next morning.
or We arranged to meet at ten the next morning.

- **persist in doing something** (not *to do something*)

needs checking Despite international disapproval, the Reagan administration persisted to help the rebels in Nicaragua.
revised Despite international disapproval, the Reagan administration persisted in helping the rebels in Nicaragua.

- **plan to do** (not *on doing*)

needs checking They planned on closing the factory in Kingston.
revised They planned to close the factory in Kingston.

- **prohibit someone from doing something** (not *to do*)

needs checking Members of the public were prohibited to feed the animals.
revised Members of the public were prohibited from feeding the animals.

- **regarded as** (not *regarded to be*)

needs checking He is commonly regarded to be one of the country's best musicians.
revised He is commonly regarded as one of the country's best musicians.
or He is commonly thought to be one of the country's best musicians.

- **responsible for doing** (not *to do*)

needs checking Mr. Dumphy is responsible to market the full line of the company's pharmaceutical products.
revised Mr. Dumphy is responsible for marketing the full line of the company's pharmaceutical products.

- **sacrifice something** (not *to do*): The use of *sacrifice* without a direct object may have crept into the language through the use of the verb as a baseball term (*Tatis sacrificed in the ninth to bring home Machado*).

needs checking He sacrificed to work in an isolated community with no electricity or running water.
revised He sacrificed himself to work in an isolated community with no electricity or running water.
or He sacrificed a good deal; the isolated community he now works in has no electricity or running water.

- **seem to be** (not *as if*)

needs checking The patient seemed as if he was in shock.
revised The patient seemed to be in shock.

(Exception: When the subject is *it*, *seem* can be followed by *as* [e.g., *It seemed as if he was sick, so we called the doctor*].)

- **suspect someone of doing something** (not *to do*)

needs checking She suspected him to have committed adultery.
revised She suspected him of committing adultery.
or She suspected that he had committed adultery.

- **tendency to do something** (not *of doing*)

needs checking Some Buick engines have a tendency of over-revving.
revised Some Buick engines have a tendency to over-rev.
or Some Buick engines have a habit of over-revving.

The Text in the Present Tense

Learning to envision arguments about texts can be challenging; so too can learning how to phrase those arguments in ways that will be clear and persuasive to readers. This section discusses a common problem that arises in writing about literary and other texts at the level of sentence structure.

All academic subject areas have specialized vocabulary and conventions. One sort of convention that can take some getting used to is the way in which verb tenses are used. The past tense is, of course, normally used to name actions that happened in the past. But when one is writing about what is written in a work of literature (or, in some cases, about what is written in other sorts of texts), convention decrees that we use the simple present tense.

needs checking Romeo fell in love with Juliet as soon as he saw her.

revised Romeo falls in love with Juliet as soon as he sees her.

needs checking In her short stories, Alice Munro explored both the outer and the inner worlds of small town life.

revised In her short stories, Alice Munro explores both the outer and the inner worlds of small town life.

If literature in its historical context is being discussed, however, the simple past tense is usually the best choice:

needs checking Shakespeare writes *Romeo and Juliet* when he was about thirty years of age.

revised Shakespeare wrote *Romeo and Juliet* when he was about thirty years of age.

needs checking Alice Munro wins the 2013 Nobel Prize in Literature for mastery of the contemporary short story.

revised Alice Munro won the 2013 Nobel Prize in Literature for mastery of the contemporary short story.

In similar fashion, if you are writing about how a philosophical text speaks to us today, the present tense is the one to use:

needs checking Many sections of Plato's lesser-known works remain relevant to socio-economic debates today. In *Laws*, for example, Plato argued that those in the wealthiest class in society should be no more than four times richer than those in the poorest class.

revised Many sections of Plato's lesser-known works remain relevant to socio-economic debates today. In *Laws*, for example, Plato argues that those in the wealthiest class in society should be no more than four times richer than those in the poorest class.

If you are discussing the same text in its historical context, however, the past tense is usually more appropriate.

needs checking Whereas Plato argues that those in the wealthiest class in society should be no more than four times richer than those in the poorest class, his views do not greatly influence his contemporaries; the socioeconomic structure of ancient Greek society remains highly unequal, with the wealthiest hundreds of times richer than the average citizen.

revised Whereas Plato argued that those in the wealthiest class in society should be no more than four times richer than those in the poorest class, his views did not greatly influence his contemporaries; the socioeconomic structure of ancient Greek society remained highly unequal, with the wealthiest hundreds of times richer than the average citizen.

In some circumstances either the past or the present tense may be possible in a sentence, depending on the context:

correct In her early work Munro often explored themes relating to adolescence.

[appropriate if the focus is on historical developments relating to the author]

also correct In her early work Munro often explores themes relating to adolescence.

[appropriate if the focus is on the work itself]

Often in an essay about literature or philosophy the context may require shifting back and forth between past and present tenses. In the following passage, for example, the present tense is used except for the sentence that recounts the historical fact of Eliot refusing permission:

> T.S. Eliot's most notorious anti-Semitic remark is the opinion he expresses in *After Strange Gods* that in "the society that we desire," "any large number of free-thinking Jews" would be "undesirable" (64). Tellingly, Eliot never allowed *After Strange Gods* to be reprinted. But his anti-Semitism emerges repeatedly in his poetry as well. In "Gerontion," for example, he describes....

In such cases even experienced writers have to think carefully during the revision process about the most appropriate tense for each verb. Note in the following example the change in verb tense from *was* to *is*:

needs checking In *The Two Gentlemen of Verona* Shakespeare exhibited a degree and a variety of technical accomplishment unprecedented in the English drama. He still had much to learn as a dramatist and as a poet; in its wit or its power to move us emotionally *The Two Gentlemen of Verona* was at an enormous remove from the great works of a few years later. But already, in 1592, Shakespeare had mastered all the basic techniques of plot construction that were to sustain the structures of the great plays.

revised In *The Two Gentlemen of Verona* Shakespeare exhibits a degree and a variety of technical accomplishment unprecedented in the English drama. He still had much to learn as a dramatist and as a poet; in its wit or its power to move us emotionally *The Two Gentlemen of Verona* is at an enormous remove from the great works of a few years later. But already, in 1592, Shakespeare had mastered all the basic techniques of plot construction that were to sustain the structures of the great plays.

The same principles that are used in writing about literature also apply to writing about texts in many other disciplines. (Disciplines that follow APA style are the exception, preferring the past tense or the present perfect tense in such situations.) Generally, when you are treating the ideas you are discussing as "live" ideas, not just historical artifacts, it makes sense to use the present tense:

needs checking In an important recent book, Niall Ferguson surveyed the history of the decline of empires, and predicted that during the course of the twenty-first century China will replace the United States as the world's leading power.

revised In an important recent book, Niall Ferguson surveys the history of the decline of empires, and predicts that during the course of the twenty-first century China will replace the United States as the world's leading power.

needs checking In their recent paper Smith and Johnson suggested that parental influence is more important than that of peers, even for adolescents. This essay will examine these claims and assess their validity.

revised In their recent paper Smith and Johnson suggest that parental influence is more important than that of peers, even for adolescents. This essay will examine these claims and assess their validity.

In many disciplines, particularly in the sciences, it is also common to use the present perfect tense when discussing relevant recent research:

Although research has often found the attitude-to-behavior connec-

> tion to be quite weak, the behavior-to-attitude link has been shown to be quite strong. As Festinger (2008) and Kiesler, Nisbet, and Zanna (2006) have demonstrated, an asymmetry exists between the two possible directions. As Acheson (2009) has put it, "we are ... very good at finding reasons for what we do, but not very good at doing what we find reasons for" (25).

It is important to remember that the use of the present tense in such contexts is not dependent on how recently the ideas being discussed were first put forward; the key thing is whether or not you are discussing them as live ideas today. You may use the present tense when discussing a paper written six months ago—but you may also use the present tense when discussing a text dating from twenty-four centuries ago. Just as you may say when writing about literature that Shakespeare *explores* the potentially corrosive effects of ambition, so too you may say that Aristotle *approaches* ethical questions with an emphasis on individual virtue, and that Marx *values* highly the economic contribution of labor—even though these writers are themselves long dead. As with the text of a story or poem, the writings of dead thinkers may be discussed as embodying live thoughts—ideas that may be of interest and relevance.

needs checking Piketty argued that capitalism tends to produce ever-greater levels of inequality.

revised Piketty argues that capitalism tends to produce ever-greater levels of inequality.

(The arguments of economist Thomas Piketty remain "live ideas," widely debated.)

Conversely, if the ideas you are discussing are being considered historically, rather than as of current relevance, you should not use the present tense. A scientific theory that has been refuted is more likely to be written about as history than as a "live idea."

needs checking In several articles the renowned astronomer Fred Hoyle advances arguments against the big bang theory of the origin of the universe. Hoyle suggests that the universe perpetually regenerates itself.

(Hoyle's arguments have now been refuted.)

revised In several articles the renowned astronomer Fred Hoyle advanced arguments against the big bang theory of the origin of the universe. Hoyle suggested that the universe perpetually regenerates itself.

As is the case with writing about literature, academic writing in disciplines such as history or philosophy or political science may often look at a text *both* from a historical perspective *and* from the perspective of the live ideas that are put forward within it. In such circumstances the writer needs to be prepared to shift verb tenses depending on the context.

needs checking In *An Introduction to the Principles of Morals and Legislation*, Jeremy Bentham asked what question should be foremost in our minds as we considered how to treat non-human animals: "The question is not, Can they reason?, nor Can they talk? but, Can they suffer? Why should the law refuse its protection to any sensitive being?"

revised In *An Introduction to the Principles of Morals and Legislation*, Jeremy Bentham asks what question should be foremost in our minds as we consider how to treat non-human animals: "The question is not, Can they reason?, nor Can they talk? but, Can they suffer? Why should the law refuse its protection to any sensitive being?"

If one is writing about literature the writing will usually be in the *present* tense, but the quotations one wishes to use are likely to be in the *past* tense. Often it is thus necessary, if you are incorporating a quotation into a sentence, to rephrase and/or adjust the length of the quotation in order to preserve grammatical consistency. If a quotation is set apart from the body of your own writing, on the other hand, you do not need to (and should not) rephrase.

needs checking Emma Bovary lives largely through memory and fantasy. She daydreams frequently, and, as she reads, "the memory of the Vicomte kept her happy."

(The past tense *kept* is inconsistent with the present tense *reads* and *daydreams*.)

revised Emma Bovary lives largely through memory and fantasy. She daydreams frequently, and, as she reads, the "memory of the Vicomte [keeps] her happy."

or Emma Bovary lives largely through memory and fantasy. She daydreams frequently, and blends fact and fiction in her imaginings: "Always, as she read, the memory of the Vicomte kept her happy. She established a connection between him and the characters of her favorite fiction."

Additional Material Online

Exercises on choosing the correct tense when writing about literature and about other academic subjects may be found at **sites.broadviewpress.com/grammar**. Click on **Exercises** and go to **"Verbs and Verb Issues: Combining Verb Tenses When Writing about Texts."**

2.2 Preposition Issues

The prepositions used in English often make little or no sense. Why are "inferior *to*" and "worse *than*" correct (and "inferior *than*" and "worse *to*" incorrect)? There is no good reason for such distinctions, but over the centuries certain prepositions have come to be accepted as going together with certain verbs, nouns, etc. There are no rules to help one learn the combinations; here are some of the ones that most commonly cause difficulty:

• **advocate; advocate for**: The verb *advocate* (when used to mean *strongly recommend*, *argue for*, *lobby for*, especially with regard to political matters) was until recently considered a transitive verb; one advocated reform, not advocated for reform. In the twenty-first century it has become much more common to use *advocate for* rather than *advocate*. There is no good reason to resist this change; either can be considered correct.

correct Environmental groups are advocating new regulations to cover methane emissions.

also correct Environmental groups are advocating for new regulations to cover methane emissions.

• **agree with someone, with what someone says; agree to do something, to something; agree on a plan, proposal, etc.**

needs checking The union representatives did not agree with the proposed wage increase.

revised The union representatives did not agree to the proposed wage increase.

or The union representatives did not agree with management about the proposed wage increase.

• angry with someone; angry at or about something

needs checking He was angry at me for failing to keep our appointment.
revised He was angry with me for failing to keep our appointment.

• annoyed with someone; annoyed by something

needs checking The professor is often annoyed with the attitude of the class.
revised The professor is often annoyed by the attitude of the class.
or The professor is often annoyed with the class.

• appeal to someone for something

needs checking The governor appealed for the residents to help.
revised The governor appealed to the residents for help.

• approve; approve of: When the verb *approve* is used with *of* (and without a direct object), it means *have a good opinion of.* In this sense the verb is frequently used where issues of right and wrong are concerned (e.g., *I don't approve of allowing children to run wild like that*). When the verb *approve* is used with a direct object (e.g., *approve a proposal, approve the application*), it typically refers to formal administrative or bureaucratic procedures.

needs checking The issue of new shares was formally approved of by the Board of Directors at their August 28 meeting.
revised The issue of new shares was formally approved by the Board of Directors at their August 28 meeting.

• argue with someone about something

needs checking They argued against each other for half an hour.
revised They argued with each other about the merit of exams.

• arrive in a place, at a place (not *arrive a place*, except *arrive home*). Airlines have led the way in using both *arrive* and *depart* without prepositions. In formal writing one should still say *arrive in* or *arrive at*, and *depart from*.

needs checking He won't join the team until tomorrow night when they arrive San Diego.
revised He won't join the team until tomorrow night when they arrive in San Diego.

• attach two or more things (not *attach together*)

needs checking The conjoined twins were attached together at the hip.
revised The conjoined twins were attached at the hip.

• **based on; based off of**: A novel or a play or a film may be based *on* another work; it is never based *off of* another work.

needs checking The film *Clueless* is based off of a novel by Jane Austen.
revised The film *Clueless* is based on a novel by Jane Austen.

• **borrow something from someone**

needs checking I borrowed him a pair of trousers.
revised I borrowed a pair of trousers from him.

• **cancel something** (not *cancel out*, except when the verb is used to mean *counterbalance* or *neutralize*)

needs checking She canceled out all her appointments.
revised She canceled all her appointments.
or After playing hockey, he ate a huge snack that canceled out the calorie loss of the exercise.

• **care about something** (meaning *to think it worthwhile or important to you*)

needs checking George does not care for what happens to his sister.
revised George does not care what happens to his sister.
or George does not care about what happens to his sister.

• **center: centered on something** (not *around something*; for one thing to be centered around another is physically impossible)

needs checking The novel is centered around the conflict between British imperialism and Native aspirations.
revised The novel centers on the conflict between British imperialism and Native aspirations.

• **chase someone or something away for doing something**: Despite the way the word is used in baseball slang, in formal writing the verb *chase* with no preposition means *run after*, not *send away*.

On the Companion Website

Exercises on preposition problems may be found at **sites.broadviewpress.com/grammar**. Click on **Exercises** and go to **"Parts of Speech."**

informal Starting pitcher José Fernandez was chased in the fifth inning.

more formal Starting pitcher José Fernandez was pulled from the game in the fifth inning.

- **collide with something** (not *against something*)

needs checking The bus left the road and collided against a tree.
revised The bus left the road and collided with a tree.

- **compare to, compare with**: To compare something *to* something else is to liken it, especially when speaking metaphorically (e.g., *Shall I compare thee to a summer's day?*). To compare something *with* something else is to judge how the two are similar or different (*If you compare one brand with another you will notice little difference*). In informal writing it is now considered acceptable to use *compare to* and *compare with* interchangeably, but in formal academic writing it is best to use *compare with* when noting differences.

needs checking The First World War was a small conflict compared to the Second World War, but it changed humanity even more profoundly.
revised The First World War was a small conflict compared with the Second World War, but it changed humanity even more profoundly.

- **concerned with something** (meaning *having some connection with it, having something to do with it*) and **concerned about something** (meaning *being interested in it or worried about it*)

needs checking The inspector is very concerned with the level of pollution in this river.
revised The inspector is very concerned about the level of pollution in this river.

- **conform to** (not *with*)

needs checking The building does not conform with current standards.
revised The building does not conform to current standards.
or The contractors did not comply with current standards.

- **connect two things, connect one thing with another** (not *connect up with*)

needs checking As soon as he connects up these wires, the system should work.
revised As soon as he connects these wires, the system should work.

- **conscious of something** (not *that*)

needs checking	He was not conscious that he had done anything wrong.
revised	He was not conscious of having done anything wrong.

(Note: Unlike *conscious*, *aware* can be used with *of* or with a *that* clause.)

• **consist in/consist of**: *Consist in* means *to exist in*, *to have as the essential feature*; *consist of* means *to be made up of*.

needs checking	Success consists of hard work. (i.e., *The essence of success is hard work.*)
revised	Success consists in hard work.
needs checking	The US Congress consists in two houses—the House of Representatives and the Senate.
revised	The US Congress consists of two houses—the House of Representatives and the Senate.

• **consult someone** (not *consult with someone*). Unlike the verbs *talk* and *speak*, the verb *consult* does not need *to* or *with*.

needs checking	She will have to consult with a lawyer before giving us an answer.
revised	She will have to consult a lawyer before giving us an answer.
or	She will have to talk to a lawyer before giving us an answer.

• **continue something, with something, to a place** (not *continue on*)

needs checking	We were told to continue on with our work.
revised	We were told to continue with our work.

• **convenient for someone, for a purpose; convenient to a place**

needs checking	This house is very convenient to me; it is only a short walk to work.
revised	This house is very convenient for me; it is only a short walk to work.

• **cooperate with someone** (not *cooperate together*)

needs checking	Countries should cooperate together to break down trade barriers.
revised	Countries should cooperate with one another to break down trade barriers.

• **correspond to** (*be in agreement with*); **correspond with** (*exchange letters with*) *needs checking* The fingerprints at the scene of the crime corresponded with those of the suspect.

revised The fingerprints at the scene of the crime corresponded to those of the suspect.

• **couple of things, times, people, etc.**: In some informal contexts the omission of the word *of* in the expression *a couple of* is now considered acceptable, but in formal writing *of* should be included.

needs checking The body had been partially hidden under a pier on Lake Union, a couple hundred feet from the Aurora Avenue Bridge.

revised The body had been partially hidden under a pier on Lake Union, a couple of hundred feet from the Aurora Avenue Bridge.

or The body had been partially hidden under a pier on Lake Union, approximately two hundred feet from the Aurora Avenue Bridge.

(In formal writing it is better to use *two* than *a couple of*.)

• **criticism of something or somebody** (not *against*)

needs checking His criticisms against her were completely unfounded.

revised His criticisms of her were completely unfounded.

• **depart from a place**: See also **arrive** (above).

needs checking One woman was heard saying to a friend as they departed Wrigley Field....

revised One woman was heard saying to a friend as they departed from Wrigley Field....

or One woman was heard saying to a friend as they left Wrigley Field....

• **die of a disease, of old age; die from injuries, wounds**

needs checking My grandfather died from cancer when he was only forty-two years old.

revised My grandfather died of cancer when he was only forty-two years old.

• **different from, to, than**: *Different to* and *different from* are both accepted British usage; *different from* is the preferred form in the US and Canada. (*Different than* is a common alternative in certain contexts in the United States, but in formal writing *different from* is the more widely accepted of the two.)

UK	These results are different to those we obtained when we did the same experiment yesterday.
North America	These results are different from those we obtained when we did the same experiment yesterday.

• **discuss something** (not *discuss about something*; no preposition is needed)

needs checking	They discussed about what to do to ease tensions in the Middle East.
revised	They discussed what to do to ease tensions in the Middle East.

• **divide something** (no preposition necessary)

needs checking	Lear wants to divide up his kingdom among his three daughters.
revised	Lear wants to divide his kingdom among his three daughters.

• **do something for someone** (meaning *something that will help*); **do something to someone** (meaning *something that will hurt*)

needs checking	Norman Bethune did a lot to the people of China.
revised	Norman Bethune did a lot for the people of China.

• **end: at the end of something; in the end**: *In the end* is used when the writer does not say which end he means, but leaves this to be understood by the reader. *At the end of* is used when the writer mentions the end he is referring to.

needs checking	In the end of *Things Fall Apart*, we both admire and pity Okonkwo.
revised	At the end of *Things Fall Apart*, we both admire and pity Okonkwo.
or	In the end, we both admire and pity Okonkwo.

• **end at a place** (not *end up at*)

needs checking	We do not want to end up at the same place we started from.
revised	We do not want to end at the same place we started from.

• **fight someone or with someone** (not *against*; *fight* means *struggle against*, so to add *against* is redundant)

needs checking They fought against each other for almost an hour.
revised They fought with each other for almost an hour.
or They fought each other for almost an hour.

• **frightened by something** (when it has just frightened you); **frightened of something** (when talking about a constant condition)

needs checking He was suddenly frightened of the sound of a door slamming.
revised He was suddenly frightened by the sound of a door slamming.

• **graduate from a school**: In informal usage some people drop the preposition, but in formal writing *graduate from* remains standard usage.

needs checking He graduated Harvard in 2019.
revised He graduated from Harvard in 2019.

• **help doing**, as in *be unable to refrain from doing* (not *help from doing*)

needs checking She could not help from agreeing to his suggestion.
revised She could not help agreeing to his suggestion.

• **hurry** (not *hurry up*)

needs checking She told me to hurry up if I didn't want to miss the train.
revised She told me to hurry if I didn't want to miss the train.

• **in/into/throughout/within**: Whereas *in* typically indicates a particular location, *into* implies motion, and *throughout* implies omnipresence. *Within* and *in* are not interchangeable; *within* should be used only in certain contexts involving extent, duration, or enclosure.

needs checking Within the prologue to the play, the chorus addresses the audience directly.
revised In the prologue to the play, the chorus addresses the audience directly.

Note as well that *in to* should not always be converted to *into*; often the word *in* goes together with a previous verb rather than with *to*.

needs checking The authorities keep giving into her demands.
revised The authorities keep giving in to her demands.

• **independent of something or someone** (not *from*)

needs checking I would like to live entirely independent from my parents.
revised I would like to live entirely independent of my parents.

• **inferior to someone or something** (not *than*)

needs checking Many people think that margarine is inferior than butter.
revised Many people think that margarine is inferior to butter.
(*Inferior* and *superior* are the only two comparative adjectives which are not followed by *than*.)

• **inside or outside something** (not *of something*)

needs checking Within thirty minutes a green scum had formed inside of the beaker.
revised Within thirty minutes a green scum had formed inside the beaker.

• **interested in something, in doing something** (not *to*)

needs checking She is very interested to find out more about plant genetics.
revised She is very interested in finding out more about plant genetics.

• **investigate something** (not *investigate about* or *into something*)

needs checking The police are investigating into the murder in London last week.
revised The police are investigating the murder in London last week.

• **join someone** (not *join up with*)

needs checking Conrad Black joined up with his brother Montagu in making the proposal to buy the company.
revised Conrad Black joined his brother Montagu in making the proposal to buy the company.

• **jump** (not *jump up*)

needs checking Unemployment has jumped up to record levels recently.
revised Unemployment has jumped to record levels recently.

• **lift something** (not *lift up*)

needs checking I twisted my back as I was lifting up the box.
revised I twisted my back as I was lifting the box.

• **lower something** (not *lower down something*)

needs checking They lowered the coffin down into the grave.
revised They lowered the coffin into the grave.

• **meet/meet with**: *Meet with* in the sense of *attend a meeting with* is a recent addition to the language. If one is referring to a less formal or less prolonged encounter, however, there is no need for the preposition.

needs checking Stanley finally met with Livingstone near the shores of Lake Tanganyika.
revised Stanley finally met Livingstone near the shores of Lake Tanganyika.
(The meaning here is *came face to face with for the first time.*)

• **mercy: have mercy on someone; show mercy to or towards someone**

needs checking We should all have mercy for anyone who is suffering.
revised We should all have mercy on anyone who is suffering.

• **near something** (not *near to something*)

needs checking The village of Battle is very near to the place where the Battle of Hastings was fought in 1066.
revised The village of Battle is very near the place where the Battle of Hastings was fought in 1066.

• **object to something** (not *against*)

needs checking Some people have objected against being required to wear a seat belt.
revised Some people have objected to being required to wear a seat belt.

• **off something** (not *off of*)

needs checking The man stepped off of the platform into the path of the moving train.
revised The man stepped off the platform into the path of the moving train.

• **opposite**: When used as a noun, *opposite* is followed by *of*; when used as an adjective, it is followed by *to* or *from*, or by no preposition.

needs checking His conclusion was the opposite to mine.
(Here, *opposite* is a noun.)
revised His conclusion was the opposite of mine.
or His conclusion was opposite to mine.
(Here, *opposite* is an adjective.)

• partake of something; participate in something

needs checking They have refused to partake in a new round of talks on the subject of free trade.
revised They have refused to participate in a new round of talks on the subject of free trade.
or They have refused to partake of a new round of talks on the subject of free trade.

• pass away (as a euphemism for *die*): When someone says "he passed," it can mean "he passed his examination," "he passed on the betting in a round of poker," or a number of other things. There are so many meanings of the verb *pass* that, in the interests of clarity as well as directness, it makes sense to choose *pass away* rather than *pass* if you want to use a euphemism for *die*.

needs checking I heard yesterday that his sister has passed.
revised I heard yesterday that his sister has passed away.
or I heard yesterday that his sister has died.

• prefer one thing or person to another (not *more than another*)

needs checking They both prefer tennis more than golf.
revised They both prefer tennis to golf.

• protest something (not *protest against*). *To protest* means *to argue against*; the preposition is redundant.

needs checking The demonstrators were protesting against the government's decision to allow missile testing.
revised The demonstrators were protesting the government's decision to allow missile testing.

• refer to something (not *refer back to something*)

needs checking If you are confused, refer back to the diagram on page 24.
revised If you are confused, refer to the diagram on page 24.

• regard/regards: with regard to something; as regards something

needs checking I am writing in regards to the balance owing on your account.
fair I am writing with regard to the balance owing on your account.
better I am writing about the balance owing on your account.

(Note that *in regard to*, *with regard to*, and *as regards* may often be used interchangeably [*in regard to the issue you have raised, with regard to the issue you have raised, as regards the issue you have raised*]. All tend towards wordiness, however; usually there is a better way.)

- **rejoice at something** (not *for something*)

needs checking He rejoiced for his good fortune when he won the lottery.
revised He rejoiced at his good fortune when he won the lottery.

- **repeat something** (not *repeat again*)

needs checking If you miss an answer you must repeat the whole exercise again.
revised If you miss an answer you must repeat the whole exercise.

- **request something or request that something be done** (but not *request for something* unless one is using the noun—*a request for something*)

needs checking He has requested for two more men to help him.
revised He has requested two more men to help him.
or He has put in a request for two more men to help him.

- **retroactive to a date** (not *from*)

needs checking The tax changes are retroactive from July 1.
revised The tax changes are retroactive to July 1.

- **return to a place** (not *return back*)

needs checking He wanted to return back to the city as soon as possible.
revised He wanted to return to the city as soon as possible.

- **seek something or someone** (not *seek for something*)

needs checking She suggested that we seek for help from the police.
revised She suggested that we seek help from the police.

- **sight: in sight** (*near enough to be seen*); **out of sight** (*too far away to be seen*); **on sight** (*immediately after being seen*)

needs checking The general ordered that deserters be shot in sight.
revised The general ordered that deserters be shot on sight.

- **speak to someone** (when one speaker is giving information to a listener); **speak with someone** (when the two are having a discussion)

needs checking She spoke harshly with the secretary about his spelling mistakes.
revised She spoke harshly to the secretary about his spelling mistakes.

- **suffer from something** (not *with*)

needs checking He told me that he was suffering with the flu.
revised He told me that he was suffering from the flu.

- **superior to someone or something** (not *than someone or something*)

needs checking The advertisements claim that this detergent is superior than the others.
revised The advertisements claim that this detergent is superior to the others.

- **type of person or thing**

needs checking This type carburetor is no longer produced.
revised This type of carburetor is no longer produced.

- **underneath something** (not *underneath of*)

needs checking When we looked underneath of the table, we found what we had been looking for.
revised When we looked underneath the table, we found what we had been looking for.

- **until a time or an event** (not *up until*)

needs checking From 1942 up until 1967 the National Hockey League was made up of only six teams.
revised From 1942 until 1967 the National Hockey League was made up of only six teams.

- **warn someone of a danger, against doing something** (*not about something or to do something*)

needs checking She warned me about the danger involved in the expedition.
revised She warned me of the danger involved in the expedition.

- **worry about something** (not *at something* or *for something*)

needs checking He is always worried at what will happen if he loses his job.
revised He is always worried about what will happen if he loses his job.

prepositions in pairs or lists: If a sentence includes two or more nouns or verbs that take different prepositions, make sure to include all the necessary words:

needs checking The fire was widely reported in the newspapers and television.

revised The fire was widely reported in the newspapers and on television.

ending a sentence with a preposition: Students are still sometimes taught that it is awkward or incorrect to end a sentence with a preposition. It's true that in some cases ending with a preposition makes for awkward English—but in some cases the reverse is also true. It's more awkward to say *It's the first driveway on the right that you should turn at* (with the preposition at the end) than it is to say *You should turn at the first driveway on the right* (with the preposition coming earlier). But *That is the film of which I am thinking* (with the preposition in the middle of the sentence) is obviously more awkward than *That is the film I'm thinking of* (with the preposition at the end). So to those who still suggest that sentences should not end with prepositions, we say *Of what are you thinking?*

2.3 Noun and Pronoun Issues

2.3.1 Nouns

unusual nouns: A number of nouns are unusual in the way that either the singular or the plural is formed. Here is a list of some that frequently cause mistakes. The most troublesome—as well as a few pronouns that cause similar difficulties—are also given individual entries below:

appendix	appendices
attorney general	attorneys general
bacterium	bacteria
basis	bases
court martial	courts martial
crisis	crises
criterion	criteria
curriculum	curricula
datum	data
daylight-saving time	[no plural]
ellipsis	ellipses
emphasis	emphases
erratum	errata
father-in-law	fathers-in-law

focus	foci
index	indexes or indices
matrix	matrixes or matrices
medium	media
millennium	millennia
nucleus	nuclei
parenthesis	parentheses
referendum	referenda or referendums
runner-up	runners-up
stratum	strata
symposium	symposia
synthesis	syntheses
thesis	theses

• **accommodation**: When used to mean "a place to stay," the noun *accommodation* has, in British and Canadian usage, traditionally been regarded as uncountable; the singular form is used, even if one is speaking of finding rooms for a large group of people (e.g., "I was able to find accommodation for all twenty of us"). American usage has generally accepted the use of the plural in such circumstances, however. And the plural has also come to be accepted throughout North America if one is using the noun to refer to arrangements made to take account of exceptional circumstances (e.g., "The test is to be completed within two hours—though accommodations may be made for students with disabilities").

• **bacteria**: A plural word; the singular is *bacterium.*

needs checking There were many bacterias in the moldy bread.
revised There were a lot of bacteria in the moldy bread.

• **behavior**: Although social scientists speak of *a behavior* or of *behaviors* in technical writing, in other disciplines and in conversational English the word is uncountable (i.e., it cannot form a plural or be used with the indefinite article). Say *types of behavior*, not *behaviors*:

needs checking He has a good behavior.
revised His behavior is good.
or He behaves well.

• **between/among and singular/plural nouns**: It is often supposed that *between* should always be used for two, *among* for more than two. As the *Oxford English Dictionary* points out, however, "in all senses *between* has been, from its earliest appearance, extended to more than two." Perhaps the most important difference is that *between* suggests a relationship of things or people to each other as individuals, whereas *among* suggests a relationship that is collective and vague. Thus we say *the ball fell among the hollyhocks* where we are expressing the relationship of the ball to many flowers collectively, and where the precise location of the ball is unspecified. But we should not say, as we watch a baseball game, *the ball fell among the three fielders*; here we know the precise location of the ball and are expressing the relationship between it and the three individuals.

- **brain**: One person can have only one brain. The use of the plural to refer to the brain of one person (e.g., *He blew his brains out*) is slang, and should not be used in formal written work.

needs checking He used his brains to solve the problem.
revised He used his brain to solve the problem.

- **children**: Be careful when forming the possessive; the apostrophe should come before the *s*.

needs checking All the childrens' toys had been put away.
revised All the children's toys had been put away.

- **confusion**: Uncountable—we do not normally speak of *a confusion* or of *confusions*.

needs checking The misunderstanding about his time of arrival caused a confusion.
revised The misunderstanding about his time of arrival caused confusion.

- **criteria**: Plural; the singular is *criterion*.

needs checking The chief criteria on which an essay should be judged is whether or not it communicates clearly.
revised The chief criterion on which an essay should be judged is whether or not it communicates clearly.

EAL

For particular problems with nouns faced by those whose native language is not English, see Section 4.

• **damage**: In its usual meaning, this noun has no plural, since it is uncountable. We speak of *damage*, not *a damage*, and of *a lot of damage*, not *many damages*. The word *damages* means *money paid to cover the cost of any damage one has caused.*

needs checking	The crash caused many damages to his car, but he was unhurt.
revised	The crash caused a lot of damage to his car, but he was unhurt.

• **data**: Like *bacteria*, *media*, and *phenomena*, the noun *data* originated as a Latin plural (the rarely used singular form is *datum*). But usage is changing; even *The Economist* now accepts the singular data in most circumstances.

correct	These data prove that the lake is badly polluted.
also acceptable	This data proves that the lake is badly polluted.

• **government**: A singular noun.

needs checking	The government are intending to build a new terminal at this airport before 2030.
revised	The government is intending to build a new terminal at this airport before 2030.

• **graffiti**: A plural noun; the singular form is *graffito*.

needs checking	Graffiti covers most of the subway cars in the city.
revised	Graffiti cover most of the subway cars in the city.

• **media**: In most cases this noun should be treated as plural; the singular is *medium*.

needs checking	The media usually assumes that the audience has a very short attention span.
revised	The media usually assume that the audience has a very short attention span.

Many authorities now regard it as acceptable in *some* contexts to use media as a collective noun—in other words, as a noun that can take a singular verb. That is particularly the case with the phrase *social media*. In some contexts, the phrase *social media* is clearly plural and countable:

needs checking	Social media such as Facebook, Instagram, and Snapchat plays an important role in modern life.
revised	Social media such as Facebook, Instagram, and Snapchat play an important role in modern life.

In other contexts, though, *social media* can function either as a plural noun or as a non-count, collective noun. Most authorities now consider both of the following to be correct:

> Social media were what I relied on during the pandemic.
> Social media was what I relied on during the pandemic.

• **money**: Some people seem to think that *monies* has a more official ring to it than *money* when they are talking of business affairs, but there is no sound reason for using this plural form in good English.

needs checking The mayor has promised to provide some monies for this project.

revised The mayor has promised to provide some money for this project.

• **news**: Despite the *s*, this is a singular collective noun. Make sure to use a singular verb with it.

needs checking Today's news of troubles in the Middle East are very disturbing.

revised Today's news of troubles in the Middle East is very disturbing.

• **phenomena**: Plural; the singular is *phenomenon*.

needs checking The great popularity of disco music was a short-lived phenomena.

revised The great popularity of disco music was a short-lived phenomenon.

• **police**: A plural noun. Be sure to use a plural verb with it.

needs checking The police is investigating the case, and hope to make an arrest soon.

revised The police are investigating the case, and hope to make an arrest soon.

On the Companion Website

Exercises on singular and plural nouns and pronouns may be found at **sites.broadviewpress.com/grammar**. Click on **Exercises** and go to **"Parts of Speech."**

2.3.2 Pronouns: *Who Cares about Whom?*

Those unfamiliar with the territory may wish to refer to the section on pronouns in section 1.2.

• **any/anyone/anybody/each/either/every/neither/no one/nobody/someone/somebody**: Grammatically, all these indefinite pronouns[1] are singular. For a long while this fact led many grammarians to fret that many common sentences in which indefinite pronouns were used were incorrect. If pronouns should always match their subjects in number, then the plural pronoun *they*, these grammarians argued, could not be used with a singular subject. In their view, such common constructions as the following were grammatically incorrect:

> Anyone may visit when they like.
> No one likes to leave a place they have grown fond of.
> Each person applying for the job must fill out a form before they can be granted an interview.
> Some careless person has forgotten to turn off the stove; they should be more careful.
> Every gardener should wait until the frost risk has passed to plant their seeds outdoors.

By the late twentieth century, everyone realized that the pronoun *he* could not reasonably be used to represent everyone. As alternatives, *he or she* and *he/she* for a time became widely used. But such constructions are no longer recommended. For one thing, *he/she* and *he or she* are undeniably awkward ("anyone may visit when he or she likes" is quite a mouthful). Just as importantly, they are not inclusive—such constructions leave out nonbinary people. It's therefore now broadly agreed that using *they* with singular pronouns of this sort—as has always been commonplace in spoken English, and as many respected authors have done, from Chaucer and Shakespeare on down—should be regarded as entirely acceptable.

There are, however, some holdouts; some instructors may still insist that any pronoun must match its subject in number. If that's the case with any of your instructors, you can still avoid biased language by rewriting the sentence.

---

1 Note that some of these words can function either as pronouns or as adjectives. If we say "each person deserves respect" or "I don't want any dessert," *each* and *any* are adjectives modifying, respectively, the nouns *person* and *dessert*. But if we say "Each deserves respect" or "I don't want any," *each* and *any* become pronouns.

2 Usage

instead of Every gardener should wait until the frost risk has passed to plant their seeds outdoors.
revised Every gardener should wait until the frost risk has passed to plant seeds outdoors.
or Gardeners should wait until the frost risk has passed to plant their seeds outdoors.

For reference, here is a list of common indefinite pronouns:

always plural: *both, many*

always singular: *another, anybody, anyone, anything, each, either, every, everybody, everyone, everything, neither, nobody, no one, nothing, one, somebody, someone, something*

singular or plural, depending on the context: *all, any, more, most, none, some*

• **both/all**: Use *both* to refer to two, and *all* to refer to more than two.

needs checking Harris and Waluchow were the chief speakers in the debate yesterday. They all spoke very well.
revised Harris and Waluchow were the chief speakers in the debate yesterday. They both spoke very well.

• **each other/one another**: Use *each other* for two, *one another* for more than two:

needs checking The three brothers always tell stories to each other before going to sleep.
revised The three brothers always tell stories to one another before going to sleep.
needs checking The two men had long since begun to get on one another's nerves. (Alan Moorehead, *The White Nile*)
revised The two men had long since begun to get on each other's nerves.

• **either/any; neither/none**: Use *either* and *neither* for two, *any* and *none* for more than two:

needs checking Shirley has six sisters, but she hasn't seen either of them since Christmas.
revised Shirley has six sisters, but she hasn't seen any of them since Christmas.

• **extra pronoun**: It is easy to add an extra pronoun, particularly if the subject of the sentence is separated from the verb by a long adjectival clause:

needs checking The countries which Hitler wanted to conquer in the late 1930s they were too weak to resist him.

revised The countries which Hitler wanted to conquer in the late 1930s were too weak to resist him.

needs checking The line that is longest in a right-angled triangle it is called the hypotenuse.

revised The line that is longest in a right-angled triangle is called the hypotenuse.

• **first person**: In formal writing it is customary to use *I* and *me* infrequently or not at all. The object of a formal piece of writing is normally to present an argument, and writers realize that they can best argue their case by presenting evidence rather than by stating that such and such is what they think. Thus many teachers advise their students always to avoid using the first person singular (*I* and *me*) in their writing.

This guideline should not be regarded as a firm and fast rule. George Orwell, often praised as the finest essayist of the last century, uses *I* and *me* frequently. As the following example illustrates, however, he employs the first person to guide the reader through his argument, not to make the points in the argument:

> If one gets rid of these habits one can think more clearly, and to think more clearly is a necessary first step towards political regeneration: so that the fight against bad English is not frivolous and is not the exclusive concern of professional writers. I will come back to this presently, and I hope that by that time the meaning of what I have said will become clearer. ("Politics and the English Language")

Phrases such as *I think* and *I feel*, on the other hand, will not help you convince the reader of the strength of your main points.

needs checking Many authorities assume inflation to be a cause of high interest rates, but I think that high interest rates are a cause of inflation. This essay will prove my argument through numerous examples.

revised Many authorities assume inflation to be a cause of high interest rates; in fact, high interest rates are often a cause of inflation. Let us take the years 1978 to 1983 in the US as an example.

• **I/me/myself**: Perhaps as a result of slang use of *me* as a subject pronoun (*Me and him got together for a few beers last night*), the impression seems to have lodged in many minds that the distinction between *I* and *me* is one of degree of politeness or formality. It's not; the distinction is simply between subject pronoun (*I*) and object pronoun (*me*).

needs checking	There is no disagreement between you and I.
revised	There is no disagreement between you and me.

(Both *you* and *I* are here objects of a preposition—*between*. *Between you and I* is no more correct than is *I threw the ball at he*.)

Many are also sometimes uncertain as to how *myself* should be used. One way is as a reflexive pronoun used as a direct or indirect object (*I hurt myself*; *I talk to myself*). Another is as an intensifier, to point up a contrast or add emphasis (*Someone from our company will attend, but I won't be there myself*). Note that *myself* is used in conjunction with another first person pronoun, however, not in place of *I* or *me*.

needs checking	There was no need to consult Carol and myself about this.
revised	There was no need to consult Carol and me about this.

On the Companion Website

Exercises on pronoun problems may be found at **sites.broadviewpress.com/grammar**. Click on **Exercises** and go to **"Parts of Speech."**

• **gender issues and pronoun issues (see also above, "any/anyone" etc.)**: Many nonbinary or otherwise gender-nonconforming people use pronouns other than, or in addition to, *he* or *she*. The most common of these is the singular *they*, but many other pronouns exist, and some people use more than one set of pronouns (e.g., one person might be accurately described by *he* or *they*, while another might be accurately described by *she* or *he*). Regardless of the specifics, whenever someone tells you what pronouns should be used to refer to them, it is important to respect their wishes and use these pronouns. The pronouns *she* and *he* are fine to use if you know that the person you are discussing in your writing is a man or a woman; if you don't know, you are better off using the singular *they*. Because trans people often need to specify their pronouns in social and professional situations, it is now widely recommended that everyone do so (e.g., by specifying your pronouns in your email signature, including them when you write your name on a name tag, or, in some contexts, stating them when you introduce yourself).

Some social conservatives have continued to sound alarm bells over these practices, claiming (as Canadian Gender Report did in 2021) that "employers have started mandating that their employees include pronouns in their signature lines." In fact, however, few (if any) employers have taken such a coercive approach. Employers recognize that some people simply prefer not to foreground gender identity over other aspects of themselves—and that some who are trans or gender-nonconforming but have not come out as such may also prefer not to specify any pronouns. Attempts to coerce may for all sorts of reasons be counterproductive. But *encouraging* the practice of specifying pronouns is another matter. Most institutions and most employers are now quite reasonably of the view that providing one's pronouns in conveniently accessible form may be of practical assistance to others, and may also help to normalize conversations about gender identity. In the 2010s there was for some time fierce resistance in many quarters to the use of non-traditional and non-gendered pronouns. In the 2020s there is much less contention over the issue; it has become broadly accepted that people should have the freedom to choose their own pronouns, that others have an obligation to respect those choices, and that everyone should have the freedom to choose to what degree they publicize their preferred pronouns.

• **non-human and human animals**: No one nowadays thinks it odd to refer to a pet as *he* or *she*, but beyond that there is a great deal of inconsistency. In contexts where non-human animals are portrayed as pets or as friendly and lovable, using *he* or *she* seems to be quite accepted. Wild animals too we seem comfortable referring to as living creatures rather than things. In the case of the non-human animals many humans make a practice of eating, though, *it* is used far more frequently. Does this mean a cow is more like a *thing* while a tail-wagging Labrador is more like a *person*? Is a calf or a piglet any more a thing than is a kitten or a puppy? What about a shrimp? Or a clam? Where does one draw a line? For many people there may be no easy answers to such questions, but they are surely worth asking; as has often been the case in human history, debates over appropriate linguistic usage provide some of the most interesting windows into large ethical, political, and epistemological issues.

Of course, if you cannot tell whether the bird you see flashing by in the sky or the fish you see flashing by in the water is male or female, you are surely not likely to refer to the creature as *he* or *she*. But if you do know whether what you are looking at is male or female, there is no good reason not to refer to that animal as *he* or *she*, and to use the same pronouns we use for people as appropriate: *his*, *her*, *who*, *whose*, etc.

worth checking Our new puppy, which is six months old, chewed on my shoes.

revised Our new puppy, who is six months old, chewed on my shoes.

worth checking The cow on the milk carton looks like it is happier than the real cows in the milking barn.

revised The cow on the milk carton looks like she is happier than the real cows in the milking barn.

• **relative pronouns and word order**: When a relative pronoun is used to begin a subordinate clause, the clause should be placed as close as possible to the noun or noun phrase that is the antecedent to the pronoun.

needs checking He purchased his friend's shop, whom he had known for many years.

(The relative pronoun *whom* refers to *friend*, not *shop*. Change the word order to put *whom* directly after *friend*.)

revised He purchased the shop from his friend, whom he had known for many years.

needs checking On Saturday I went to my brother's wedding, whose new wife is a senior government official.

revised On Saturday I went to the wedding of my brother, whose new wife is a senior government official.

needs checking Brett Kavanaugh was the next Supreme Court choice of Trump, who was confirmed in the Senate by a narrow margin, 52–48.

revised Trump's next Supreme Court choice was Brett Kavanaugh, who was confirmed in the Senate by a narrow margin, 52–48.

needs checking In the 1950s, office designers increasingly chose to install lightbulbs made of argon, which could last up to twice as long as incandescent bulbs.

revised In the 1950s, office designers increasingly chose to install argon lightbulbs, which could last up to twice as long as incandescent bulbs.

needs checking The presentation was made to Max Verstappen's team, who had won almost half of the Formula One races held that year.

revised The presentation was made to the team of Max Verstappen, who had won almost half of the Formula One races held in that year.

(Here the relative pronoun *who* refers to Verstappen.)

or The presentation was made to Max Verstappen's team, which had won almost half of the Formula One races held in that year.

(Here the relative pronoun *which* refers to the team. [Note that in car racing some awards are to the driver and some to the entire team.])

• **than**: Does *than* take a subject or an object pronoun? Purists argue that we should say *She's brighter than I* [*am*], and *He's louder than she* [*is*]—that the verb is always understood in such sentences, even when we do not say it or write it, and that the unspoken verb requires a subject. It's hard to argue, however, that the increasingly widespread use of object pronouns after *than* is either ugly or confusing.

less formal She always sleeps later than him.
more formal She always sleeps later than he [does].

• **unreferenced or wrongly referenced pronoun**: Normally a pronoun must refer to a noun in the previous sentence or clause. In the following sentence, for example, the pronoun *she* clearly refers to the noun *Charity*, which is the subject of the first clause in the sentence:

- Charity told Alfred that she would start work at nine.

Notice how confusing the sentence becomes, however, if there are two possible *shes* in the first part of the sentence:

- Charity told Mavis that she would start work at nine.

Does this mean that Charity will start work at nine, or that Mavis will? From the sentence it is impossible to tell. In cases like this, where it is not absolutely clear whom or what a pronoun refers to, use the noun again instead:

clear Charity told Mavis that she (Charity) would start work at nine.

In the following case the writer has gone astray by mentioning two things—one singular, one plural—and then matching only one of the two with a pronoun. In this instance the best remedy is to substitute a noun for the pronoun:

needs checking Shields's characters are so exquisitely crafted and her plot so artfully conceived that it keeps the reader riveted until the final page.

revised Shields's characters are so exquisitely crafted and her plot so artfully conceived that the book keeps the reader riveted until the final page.

Similar mistakes are often made in writing about a general class of people, such as police officers, or doctors, or football players. When writing in this way one can use either the third person singular (e.g., *A doctor helps patients. She* ....) or the third person plural (*Doctors help patients. They* ....). Mixing the two in such situations often leads people to write unreferenced pronouns:

needs checking A herbalist knows a lot about plants. They can often cure you by giving you medicine.

(Here the pronoun *they* is presumably meant to refer to the plural noun *herbalists*, but the writer has referred only to *a herbalist*.)

revised A herbalist knows a lot about plants. He can often cure you by giving you medicine.

or Herbalists know a lot about plants. They can often cure you by giving you medicine.

It may also not be clear what or whom a pronoun refers to if it is placed too far away from the noun:

needs checking The Board of Trustees increased tuition fees by an average of 43 percent. Other measures taken included a $100 million cut in student assistance and the closing of the office of the ombudsman. They also introduced a variety of measures to help recruitment.

revised The Board of Trustees increased tuition fees by an average of 43 percent. Other measures taken included a $100 million cut in student assistance and the closing of the office of the ombudsman. The Board also introduced a variety of measures to help recruitment.

Be particularly careful when using *this* as a pronoun; if the preceding sentence is a long one, it may not be at all clear what *this* refers to:

needs checking	The deficit was forecast to be $800 million, but turned out to be over $6 billion. This reflected the government's failure to predict the increase in interest rates and the onset of a recession.
	(*This what?*)
revised	The deficit was forecast to be $800 million, but turned out to be over $6 billion. This vast discrepancy reflected the government's failure to predict the increase in interest rates and the onset of a recession.

Sometimes the meaning may be clear, but the omission of a pronoun may create unintended and humorous ambiguity:

needs checking	She visited a doctor with a bad case of the flu.
	(Did the doctor have the flu?)
revised	She visited a doctor when she had a bad case of the flu.
needs checking	The Cougar was a sporty car aimed at the youthful-feeling who wanted luxury in their automobiles. Its buyers were similar to Mustangs, but more affluent.
revised	The Cougar was a sporty car aimed at the youthful-feeling who wanted luxury in their automobiles. Its buyers were similar to those who bought Mustangs, but more affluent.

- **who/whom**: The subject pronoun and the object pronoun, but it's not as simple as that. Nor is the distinction merely a matter of stuffiness or pedantry on the part of grammar purists. Sound has a great deal to do with it. Even purists must sometimes find themselves saying, *I didn't know who I was talking to*, even though the rules say it should be *whom* (subject—*I*; object—*whom*). In similar fashion the enemies of *whom* must surely be tempted to sacrifice principle rather than attempt such an owlish mouthful as *To who was he talking*? They would do so not on the grammatical grounds of *whom*, the object pronoun, being correct since it is acting as the object of the preposition *to*, but on the grounds of *whom*, the word with an *m* on the end, being in that sentence a lot easier to say. In such circumstances convenience of pronunciation occasionally overrides arguments either for or against formality.

less formal	Scott Fitzgerald never cared who he irritated.
more formal	Scott Fitzgerald never cared whom he irritated.

2 Usage

2.3.3 Noun and Pronoun Issues with Authors and Speakers

A tangle of issues surrounding authorship can make it difficult to phrase sentences having to do with what an author says, or what a text says. Views expressed by a character or narrator must not be confused with those of the author, and—for works of drama, poetry, and fiction—it is important to use phrasing that focuses on what the text does rather than making assumptions about what the author might have intended. But we must also be careful of phrases such as "the book says..." that seem to grant authorial status to the text itself. Over time writers have developed a wide variety of strategies to deal with these sorts of awkwardness—to enable us to speak without obvious absurdity about the ways in which texts convey meanings. This is one area in which the passive voice often proves helpful.

needs checking In the book it says that Victor Frankenstein becomes "capable of bestowing animation upon lifeless matter" (Ch. 3).

revised Victor Frankenstein tells Robert Walton the story of how he became "capable of bestowing animation upon lifeless matter" (Ch. 3).

or In Shelley's novel the lead character, Victor Frankenstein, recounts his great scientific discovery: "I succeeded in discovering the cause of generation and life; [and] more, I became myself capable of bestowing animation upon lifeless matter" (Ch. 3).

needs checking In Genesis they give two quite different versions of the creation of Eve.

(The use of *they* when assigning responsibility where the actual people are unknown ["they should fix the potholes on this street," "they never used to do it this way," etc.] is colloquial and should be avoided in formal written work.)

revised Genesis offers us two quite different versions of the creation of Eve.

or Two quite different versions of the creation of Eve are given in Genesis.

(Notice how the passive voice ["are given"] is used here.)

needs checking The poem says that the 1930s were "a low dishonest decade."

needs checking In the poem it says that the 1930s were "a low dishonest decade."

revised In the poem's first stanza the 1930s are described as "a low dishonest decade."

(This construction, using the passive voice, can be used whether or not it is a character speaking, or the author speaking to us directly.)

or The speaker refers to the 1930s as "a low dishonest decade."

When referencing text that is not attributed to a specific character, it is conventional to use phrases such as *the speaker* (in the case of a poem) or *the narrator* (in the case of a novel) instead of saying *the poet* or *the author*. For some poems where the author does not seem to have adopted a persona—such as, arguably, "September 1, 1939"—it can be acceptable to refer to the author directly:

- Auden refers to the 1930s as "a low dishonest decade."

If you are at all in doubt it is safest to use a phrase such as "the speaker."

The next example shows the danger of equating statements in a book with the author's opinions:

needs checking In More's *Utopia* he says that landowners are "no longer content with leading an idle life and doing no harm to the country." In his view, they have now chosen to do real harm: "they leave no ground to be tilled, enclose every bit of land for pasture, pull down houses, and destroy towns."

(There are several problems here. The first is grammatical: *he* is a pronoun, and pronouns need to refer to nouns, whereas *More's* is a possessive adjective.)

needs checking In his *Utopia* More declares that English landowners are "no longer content with leading an idle life and doing no harm to the country." In his view, they have now chosen to do real harm: "they leave no ground to be tilled, enclose every bit of land for pasture, pull down houses, and destroy towns."

(Thomas More's *Utopia* is a work of fiction in which various characters give their views; it cannot be assumed that any of the views put forward by the characters were also those of the author.)

revised In More's *Utopia* Raphael Hythloday declares that landowners are "no longer content with leading an idle life and doing no harm to the country." In Raphael's view, they have now chosen to do real harm: "they leave no ground to be tilled, enclose every bit of land for pasture, pull down houses, and destroy towns."

(Can we take this as More's own view? That question cannot be answered readily.)

needs checking The novel *The Jungle* tells us that the meatpacking industry is cruel to the workers in a wide variety of ways.

(We are not told this in so many words by the novel, as a non-fiction book or magazine article might tell us such things; rather we are shown the cruelties of the industry.)

revised The novel *The Jungle* depicts the cruel treatment of workers in the early twentieth-century meatpacking industry.

(Here the emphasis is on the novel as a work that may still speak to us today—as literature rather than a historical artifact.)

or Upton Sinclair's 1906 novel *The Jungle* depicted the cruel treatment of workers in the meatpacking industry; it had a powerful effect on public opinion.

(Here the emphasis is on the historical impact of the novel.)

Here are some other approaches to wording that may be useful as you write about texts—and try to negotiate the many issues involving what the characters have said, what the text has said, and what the author has said:

In the poem we are led to believe that …
Throughout the story we are led to sympathize with …
These lines in the poem suggest that …
The way this sentence is phrased implies that …
The fact that these deeds go unpunished at the end of the story suggests that …
The imagery in this stanza suggests that …
Characters who make us laugh tend to be easy to relate to, and Falstaff … (*not* Characters who make us laugh tend to be easily relateable, …)

2.4 Word Order

Word order problems are of many sorts. See also, for example, the discussions elsewhere in this book of syntax; of ambiguity; of split infinitives; of indefinite pronouns such as *each*, *every*, and *anyone*; and of *not only ... but also*.

• **ambiguity/confusion**: Inappropriate word order is one of the most common sources of ambiguity and confusion. Often a change in punctuation may also be required to correct the problem.

needs checking The liner tilted dramatically after fire broke out in the engine room, 50 miles south of Cyprus.

revised The liner tilted dramatically after fire broke out in the engine room. At the time the ship was 50 miles south of Cyprus.

needs checking He has not come under any pressure to make way for a new leader, despite the failure of any tangible benefits from his government's economic policies.

revised He has not come under any pressure to make way for a new leader, despite the failure of his government's economic policies to bring any tangible benefits.

needs checking Proportion of overweight people between 18 and 64 years trying to lose weight by sex in Alberta, 1990.

(Heading on chart, Alberta Heart Health Survey, reprinted in *The Calgary Herald*)

revised Proportion in Alberta, Canada, of overweight people between 18 and 64 years, by sex, who were trying to lose weight, 1990.

See page 144 for more on ambiguity.

• **amounts**: For no good reason, adjectives having to do with amounts or quantities (e.g., *much*, *few*, *many*) normally precede the noun or pronoun to which they refer, even when the verb *to be* is used. In this way such adjectives differ from other adjectives. For example, we can talk about a happy man, putting the adjective *happy* before the noun *man*, or we can use the present tense of the verb *to be* and say, *The man is happy*, in which case the adjective *happy* comes after the noun *man*. In contrast, it is considered awkward to say, *We were many at the meeting*, or *The people here are few*. Instead the sentence should be changed around, and the adjectives put before the nouns. The easiest way to do this is by using *there* and the verb *to be*. The revised versions of the above sentences are as follows:

revised	There were many of us at the meeting.
revised	There are few people here.

A further example:

needs checking	The students at the football game were many.
revised	There were many students at the football game.

EAL

For particular problems with word order faced by those whose native language is not English, see Section 4.

• **balance and parallelism**: Paired connectives (*if ... then*, *either ... or* [given a separate entry below], *not only ... but also*, *both ... and*) can help in achieving balance. But difficulties in getting all the words in the right order can easily arise.

needs checking	As a critic she is both fully aware of the tricks used by popular novelists, as well as realizing that "serious" novelists sometimes resort to the same tricks.
revised	As a critic she is fully aware both of the tricks used by popular novelists, and of the fact that "serious" novelists sometimes resort to the same tricks.

needs checking	The argument that Hellman puts forward not only fails to rebut the strongest arguments of Singer and Regan, but he also does not even directly engage with those arguments.
revised	Hellman not only fails to rebut the strongest arguments of Singer and Regan; he does not even directly engage with those arguments.

We tend to think of constructions involving words such as *both ... and* and *not only ... but also* when we think of balance and parallelism in written work. But the principles involved extend far more widely. Finding the right order for the words in a long sentence can be surprisingly challenging, even for experienced writers. Keeping words, phrases, and clauses grammatically balanced is less difficult where a pairing of two is concerned—though even here it is easy enough to go astray if you're not careful:

needs checking This holiday we plan on keeping healthy and we'll get lots of rest.

revised This holiday we plan on keeping healthy and getting lots of rest.

needs checking The new government aims to reduce conflict with its neighbors and increasing the rate of economic growth.

revised The new government aims to reduce conflict with its neighbors and to increase the rate of economic growth.

needs checking The study concludes that Facebook use is associated with declines in subjective measures of well-being, and the more people use Facebook, the worse they tend to feel.

revised The study concludes that Facebook use is associated with declines in subjective measures of well-being, and that the more people use Facebook, the worse they tend to feel.

(Repetition of the function word *that* makes clear to the reader how the second part of the sentence is connected to the first; the sentence's second part reports another of the same study's conclusions.)

When it is a matter of keeping three or more elements parallel or in balance, everything becomes more difficult.

needs checking His accomplishments included a succession of strategic successes during World War II, helping to revive Europe after the war, and he founded an important new international organization.

revised His accomplishments included a succession of strategic successes during World War II, a plan to revive Europe after the war, and the foundation of an important new international organization.

or He is remembered for his strategic successes during World War II, for his plan to revive Europe after the war, and for the foundation of an important new international organization.

(These are only two of many ways in which the sentence might be revised so as to make its three parts grammatically parallel.)

needs checking A plant-based, whole foods diet is associated with improvements in heart condition, greater life expectancy, diabetes is reduced, lowering of cancer rates, less chance of Alzheimer's, and also there are other health benefits.

revised A plant-based, whole foods diet is associated with improvements in heart condition, greater life expectancy, lower rates of diabetes, lower incidence of cancer, lower incidence of Alzheimer's, and many other health benefits.

or A plant-based, whole foods diet typically improves heart condition; increases one's life expectancy; significantly lowers one's chances of being afflicted with diabetes, heart disease, cancer, or Alzheimer's; and is associated with many other health benefits.

(Again, these are only two of many ways in which the problem of the sentence's faulty parallelism may be corrected.)

2 Usage

In the above examples parallelism is a matter of grammatical structure first and foremost. But the importance of balance and parallelism to writing is not only a matter of grammar. Sentences that are balanced and that include parallel structures tend to be both more comprehensible and more pleasing to the reader. In the following examples the initial sentence is not grammatically incorrect; the revisions are a matter of style rather than of correctness. You may judge for yourself as to how they compare in terms of the reader's experience.

worth checking Teams with very low payrolls are unlikely to achieve much success, even in the regular season, and very unlikely to be able to win in the postseason against teams who are able to afford the best-paid stars. The Oakland As are often cited as an exception to the rule that low budget teams are unlikely to succeed in baseball, and it's true that they have enjoyed a surprising degree of success in the regular season. Perhaps inevitably, however, they have not enjoyed much success in the postseason.

revised Teams with very low payrolls are likely to struggle in the regular season, and to struggle even more if they reach the playoffs and face teams who can afford the best-paid stars. If the Oakland As's low payroll makes their regular season success seem surprising, it also makes their postseason failures seem inevitable.

worth checking What Marianne and her mother conjectured one moment as perhaps being possible, the next moment they believed to be probable. Anything they wished might happen they soon found themselves hoping for, and soon after that the hope would become an expectation.

revised What Marianne and her mother conjectured one moment, they believed the next; with them, to wish was to hope, and to hope was to expect.

(Jane Austen, *Sense and Sensibility*)

worth checking Our nation is made up of people of all sorts of religious beliefs. Many Americans are Christians but we also have Jews, Muslims, and Hindus among us, and there are also many American nonbelievers. America has also been shaped by many languages and cultures, from all over the world.

revised We are a nation of Christians and Muslims, Jews and Hindus, and nonbelievers. We are shaped by every language and culture, drawn from every end of this earth.

(Barack Obama, First Inaugural Address)

In most cases, revising to strengthen parallel structures in your writing will have the happy byproduct of making it more concise. But that's not always the case; the second sentence from the Obama passage quoted above is longer than it need be, but a pleasing instance of parallelism nonetheless.

• **direct object position**: The normal position for direct objects is after the verb. When the direct object is put at the beginning of a sentence it usually sounds awkward, and the word order may lead writers to include an extra, unwanted pronoun later in the sentence. It is usually best to keep the direct object after the verb.

needs checking Some of the money I put it in the bank.

(Notice the extra pronoun *it*.)

revised I put some of the money in the bank.

(*I* is the subject; *some of the money* is the direct object of *put*.)

• **either ... or**: These words should directly precede the pair of things to which they refer. The same applies to *neither ... nor*.

needs checking I will either pick an apple or a banana.

revised I will pick either an apple or a banana.

(*Either* and *or* refer to *apple* and *banana*. Therefore they must come immediately before those words.)

needs checking He will go either to New York for the holiday or remain here.

revised He will either go to New York for the holiday or remain here.

(The choice is between *going* and *remaining*.)

needs checking We will either buy a poodle or a spaniel.

revised We will buy either a poodle or a spaniel.

(The choice is between breeds of dogs, not between *buying* and a dog breed.)

- **except**: A phrase beginning with *except* should appear directly after the noun or pronoun to which *except* refers.

needs checking We all had to wait except for those who had bought tickets in advance.

revised All except those who had bought tickets in advance had to wait.

- **first person last**: When speaking about both yourself and another person (or other people), always mention the other person first. The first person pronoun (*I*, *me*) should come last.

needs checking I and my brother decided to go shopping.

revised My brother and I decided to go shopping.

On the Companion Website

Word order mistakes involving words such as *only* are often classed as one variety of misplaced modifier error; a full discussion of the category **misplaced modifier** (including how it relates to the category **dangling modifier**) is provided alongside a range of relevant exercises at **sites.broadviewpress.com/grammar**. Click on **Exercises** and go to **"Verbs and Verb Issues."**

- **only**: The adverb *only* should come directly before the word or words it refers to. *She could only see him* implies that she could not hear, smell, or touch him; *She could see only him* implies that she had eyes for no one else.

needs checking She only asked six people to the party.

revised She asked only six people to the party.

- **questions in indirect speech**: In a question we normally reverse the order of the subject and the verb. For example, to change the statement *She was sad* to a question, we reverse the order of *she* and *was* and ask,

Was she sad? The same rule does not apply, however, to questions in indirect speech. These are considered to be part of a statement and, as in any other statement, the entire verb should come after the subject. For example, to turn the above sentence into indirect speech we would say, *I asked her if she was sad* (not *I asked her was she sad*).

needs checking I asked him how was he.
revised I asked him how he was.
needs checking She asked her brother where was he going.
revised She asked her brother where he was going.

Notice as well that these sentences are statements, not questions. They therefore do not end with a question mark.

On the Companion Website

Exercises on word order and on one-word/two-word problems may be found at **sites.broadviewpress.com/grammar**. Click on **Exercises** and go to **"Word Order"** and **"Spelling: One Word or Two?"**

2.5 Word Meanings

• **accept/except**: These two words are often confused because of their similar sounds. *Accept* is a verb meaning *to receive something favorably* (or at least without complaining). Examples:

- We accepted the invitation to his party.
- We will have to accept the decision of the judge.

Except, on the other hand, is a conjunction (or sometimes a preposition) which means *not including* or *but.*

needs checking All the permanent members of the Security Council accept China voted to authorize the use of force.
revised All the permanent members of the Security Council except China voted to authorize the use of force.

• **adapt/adopt/adept**: *To adapt something* is *to alter or modify it*; *to adopt something* is *to approve it* or *accept responsibility for it*; *adept* is an adjective meaning *skillful.*

needs checking The board adapted the resolution unanimously.
revised The board adopted the resolution unanimously.

• **adverse/averse**: *Adverse* means *unfavorable*; *averse* means *reluctant* or *unwilling.*

needs checking The plane was forced to land because of averse weather conditions.

revised The plane was forced to land because of adverse weather conditions.

or The pilot was averse to the idea of landing in the fog.

• **afflict/inflict**: A person *inflicts* pain or hardship on someone else, who is *afflicted* by the pain and hardship.

needs checking The Mugabe government began as early as 1983 to afflict terrible suffering on large numbers of Zimbabweans living in Matabeleland.

revised The Mugabe government began as early as 1983 to inflict terrible suffering on large numbers of Zimbabweans living in Matabeleland.

• **aggravate/annoy/irritate**: *Aggravate* means *make worse.* Here is an example:

- The injury was aggravated by the bumpy ride in the ambulance.

In formal English *aggravate* should not be used to mean *annoy* or *irritate.*

needs checking She found his constant complaints very aggravating.

revised She found his constant complaints very irritating.

• **alliterate/illiterate**: *Alliterate* is a verb meaning *to use consecutively two or more words that begin with the same sound.*

- The big, burly brute was frighteningly fierce.

Illiterate is an adjective meaning either *unable to read* or *unable to read and write well.* Those who confuse the two are sometimes, if unfairly, accused of being illiterate.

needs checking Over forty percent of the population of Zambia is functionally alliterate.

revised Over forty percent of the population of Zambia is functionally illiterate.

• **alternately/alternatively**: *Alternately* means *happening in turn, first one and then the other*; alternatively means *instead of.* Be careful as well with the adjectives *alternate* and *alternative.*

needs checking An alternate method of arriving at this theoretical value would be to divide the difference between the two prices by the number of warrants.

revised An alternative method of arriving at this theoretical value would be to divide the difference between the two prices by the number of warrants. (or Another method of ...)

needs checking Professor Beit-Hallahmi seems to have trouble alternatively in reading his own book accurately and in reading my review of it correctly.

revised Professor Beit-Hallahmi seems to have trouble alternately in reading his own book accurately and in reading my review of it correctly.

• **ambiguity**: Two broad categories of English language ambiguity are **semantic ambiguity** and **syntactic ambiguity** (also known as structural ambiguity). Semantic ambiguity occurs as a result of a word or words having two or more possible meanings. Since the word *light* has two unrelated meanings, a *light box* can refer either to a box that is not heavy or to a box with a sheet of glass on one side through which light shines. In the newspaper headline "Red tape holds up new bridge," there are two sources of semantic ambiguity; to *hold up* something can mean either to keep it off the ground or to delay it, and the expression *red tape* has both a literal and an idiomatic meaning.

Syntactic ambiguity is a matter of grammar—of the way in which words are arranged in a sentence, and of how they are interpreted grammatically. One circumstance in which syntactical ambiguity can arise is when there is uncertainty as to whether or not a compound noun is being used. Someone who is employed to perform safety inspections of large barges might be described as a "large barge inspector"—but if his job title is *barge inspector* (a compound noun), then the word *large* in "large barge inspector" could reasonably be taken to refer to the size of the inspector rather than of the barges. Is a *plastic fruit bowl* necessarily made of plastic? Or can it be a bowl of any sort that happens to hold pieces of plastic fruit?

Within the broad categories there may be ambiguities of several types. For further discussions of ambiguity in these pages—sorry, that should be "for further discussions in these pages of ambiguity"—see pages 83–88 (on dangling constructions), pages 130–32 (on pronouns), page 136 (on word order problems), and the entries below for words such as *flammable*.

Red Tape Holds Up New Bridge

The following are all examples of ambiguity in newspaper headlines. In some cases it may take several moments to decipher the intended meaning.

Two pedestrians struck by bridge
Man held over giant L.A. brush fire
Undocumented immigrants cut in half by new law
Passerby injured by post office
Red tape holds up new bridge
Village water holds up well

(The above examples come courtesy of columnist Bob Swift of Knight-Ridder Newspapers, and Prof. A. Levey of the University of Calgary.)

Here are two gems provided by editor Beth Humphries:

The fossils were found by scientists embedded in red sandstone.

She walked into the bathroom tiled in sea-green marble.

Here is a weather prediction from a Global News *telecast:*

"Out west tomorrow, they're going to see the sun, as well as Atlantic Canada."

And, from a 19 Jan. 2024 Globe and Mail *article about a pole vault champion:*

"According to the report, Barber ingested the cocaine on July 8, the night before he won the Canadian title in Edmonton, in a sexual encounter with a woman."

• **amiable/amicable**: *Amiable* is used to describe someone's personality; *amicable* describes the state of relations between people.

needs checking Navratilova said that the split with her former tennis partner had been an amiable one.
revised Navratilova said that the split with her former tennis partner had been an amicable one.

• **amoral/immoral**: An *amoral* act is one to which moral standards do not apply; an *immoral* act, on the other hand, is one that goes against a moral standard.

needs checking The reader is unlikely to share Austen's views as to what constitutes amoral behavior.
revised The reader is unlikely to share Austen's views as to what constitutes immoral behavior.

• **amused/bemused**: If you are *bemused*, you are a bit puzzled about something—though not in any troubled fashion, and perhaps even in a somewhat amused one. From that slight point of connection (as well as the similarity in sound) has arisen the erroneous belief that the two words are synonymous.

• **anti/ante**: If you remember that *anti* means *against* and *ante* means *before* you are less likely to misspell the many words that have one or the other as a prefix.

needs checking The UN had many anticedents—most notably the League of Nations formed after World War I.
revised The UN had many antecedents—most notably the League of Nations formed after World War I.

• **antonym/homonym/synonym**: Antonyms are opposites—two words with opposite meanings (e.g., *hot* and *cold*, *good* and *bad*). Homonyms have different meanings but the same spelling or sound. There are thus two types of homonyms; homophones have the same sound but may have different spellings, like *sight* and *site*, while homographs have the same spelling but may be pronounced differently, like *bass* (the instrument, rhymes with "pace") and *bass* (the fish, rhymes with "pass"). *Pole* meaning *long stick* and *pole* meaning *extremity of a planet* are homonyms that are both homophones and homographs. Synonyms (e.g., the verbs *shut* and *close*) are words with the same meaning.

• **anxious/eager**: The adjective *anxious* means *uneasy*, *nervous*, *worried*;

it should not be used in formal writing to mean *eager*.

needs checking	He was anxious to help in any way he could.
revised	He was eager to help in any way he could.

• **appraise/apprise**: *To appraise something* is *to estimate its value*; *to apprise someone of something* is *to inform him or her of it.*

needs checking	The house has been apprised at $660,000.
revised	The house has been appraised at $660,000.
or	He apprised her of the house's jump in value.

• **assure/ensure/insure**: To *assure* someone of something is to tell her with confidence or certainty; to *ensure* that something will happen is to make sure that it does; to *insure* something is to purchase insurance on it so as to protect yourself in case of loss. In American English especially, it is common—and acceptable to some—to use *insure* in the sense of *ensure*, but the difference in meaning is significant enough that the distinction should really be maintained.

needs checking	Our inventory is ensured for $10,000,000.
revised	Our inventory is insured for $10,000,000.
needs checking	He ensured us that it would not happen again.
revised	He assured us that it would not happen again.
less widely accepted	Please insure that it does not happen again.
more widely accepted	Please ensure that it does not happen again.

• **be/become**: The difference between the two is that *to be* simply indicates existence, while *to become* indicates a process of change. Whenever you are talking about a change, use *become* instead of *be*.

needs checking	I had been quite contented, but as time went by I was unhappy.
revised	I had been quite contented, but as time went by I became unhappy.
needs checking	After years of struggle, East Timor finally was independent in 2002.
revised	After years of struggle, East Timor finally became independent in 2002.

• **beg the question**: The original meaning of *beg the question* is *take for granted the very thing to be argued about*—not *invite the question*. In the words of philosopher Thomas Hurka, "'begging the question' is not what the host does on Jeopardy." The extension of the phrase to mean *invite the question* or *prompt the question* has become so widespread in recent years that it may be vain to think of the tide being reversed, but the original concept of question begging is a useful one, and we should be reluctant to allow it to disappear.

needs checking This sort of sexual abuse case begs the question as to how such behavior could be hidden for so many years.
revised This sort of sexual abuse case makes us wonder how such behavior could be hidden for so many years.

• **beside/besides**: *Besides* can mean *in addition to*, *moreover* (as in the sentence *Besides, he deserved to lose*), *other than*, or *except* (as in *no one was there besides me*). *Beside* may mean *at the side of* (as in *no one was there beside me*) or *irrelevant to* (as in the common phrase *beside the point*); in this latter meaning confusion with *besides* sometimes arises.

needs checking Much of Dawkins's argument is besides the point.
revised Much of Dawkins's argument is beside the point.

• **bored/boring**: *Bored* is the opposite of *interested* and *boring* is the opposite of *interesting*. In other words, one is quite likely to be bored when someone reads out what one has already read in the newspaper, or when one is watching a football game when the score is 38–0, or when one is doing an uninteresting job. To be bored, however, is not the same as to be sad, or depressed, or irritated, or angry.

needs checking She was so bored with her husband that she tried to kill him.
revised She was so angry with her husband that she tried to kill him.

• **breach/breech**: *To breach a wall or a contract* is *to break or break through it*, and *the breach* is *the breaking*. *Breech* refers to a part of a cannon or rifle—or to *the buttocks* (hence a *breech birth*, in which the buttocks or feet emerge before the head).

needs checking The lawyers claimed that her actions constituted a breech of contract.
revised The lawyers claimed that her actions constituted a breach of contract.

• **brusque/brisk**: *To be brusque* is *to be abrupt or slightly rude in speech or manner*; *brisk* means *quick* or *lively*.

needs checking He didn't say anything rude to me, but his manner was rather brisk.

revised He didn't say anything rude to me, but his manner was rather brusque.

• **can/may**: In formal writing *can* should be used to refer to *ability*, *may* to refer to *permission*.

needs checking Can I leave the room?

(This makes literal sense only if you are an injured person conversing with your doctor.)

revised May I leave the room?

• **capital/capitol**: As a noun, *capital* can refer to *wealth*, to *the city from which the government operates*, to *an upper case letter*, or to *the top of a pillar*. It can also be used as an adjective to mean *most important* or *principal*. *Capitol* is much more restricted in its meaning—*a specific American legislative building or Roman temple*.

needs checking The prosecution alleged that he had committed a capitol offense.

revised The prosecution alleged that he had committed a capital offense.

• **career/careen**: As a verb, *career* means *to swerve wildly*. *Careen* originally meant *tilt or lean*, but now is often treated as a synonym for *career*. Since *careen* has other specifically nautical meanings, some authorities resist the conflation of the two verbs—but the fact that *career* carries unintended echoes of the noun meaning *profession* leads many, not unreasonably, to prefer *careen*.

• **careless/uncaring**: *Careless* means *negligent* or *thoughtless*; you can be careless about your work, for example, or careless about your appearance. Do not use *careless*, however, when you want to talk about *not caring enough about other people*.

needs checking He acted in a very careless way towards his mother when she was sick.

revised He acted in an uncaring way towards his mother when she was sick.

• **censor/censure**: *To censor something* is *to prevent it, or those parts of it that are considered objectionable, from being available to the public. To censure someone* is *to express strong criticism or condemnation*.

needs checking The Senate censored the attorney general for his part in the scandal.

revised The Senate censured the attorney general for his part in the scandal.

• **childish/childlike**: The first is a term of abuse, the second a term of praise.

needs checking Her writing expresses a childish innocence.
revised Her writing expresses a childlike innocence.

• **classic/classical**: As an adjective *classic* means *of such a high quality that it has lasted or is likely to last for a very long time. Classical* is used to refer to *ancient Greece and Rome*, or, particularly when speaking of music, to refer to *a traditional style.*

needs checking Sophocles was one of the greatest classic authors; his plays are classical.
revised Sophocles was one of the greatest classical authors; his plays are acknowledged classics.

• **climatic/climactic**: Weather is not necessarily the high point of life.

needs checking Difficulties in predicting long-term trends are inherent in any climactic projections.
revised Difficulties in predicting long-term trends are inherent in any climatic projections.

• **collaborate/corroborate**: *To collaborate* is *to work together*, whereas *to corroborate* is *to give supporting evidence.*

needs checking He collaborated her claim that the Americans had corroborated with the Nazi colonel Klaus Barbie.
revised He corroborated her claim that the Americans had collaborated with the Nazi colonel Klaus Barbie.

• **compliment/complement**: *To compliment someone* is *to praise him*, and a *compliment* is the *praise*; *to complement something* is *to add to it to make it better or complete*, and a *complement* is *the number or amount needed to make it complete.*

needs checking None of the divisions had its full compliment of troops.
revised None of the divisions had its full complement of troops.
needs checking Prince Fielder's mission in Detroit was to compliment Miguel Cabrera, who was at that time the best hitter in baseball.

(Literally, this would mean that Fielder's job was to keep saying, "Nice work, Miguel," and so on.)

2 Usage

revised Prince Fielder's mission in Detroit was to complement Miguel Cabrera, who was at that time the best hitter in baseball.

On the Companion Website

Exercises on word meanings may be found at **sites.broadviewpress.com/grammar**. Click on **Exercises** and go to **2.5.**

• **comprise/compose/constitute**: The whole *comprises* or includes the various parts; the parts *compose* the whole. The verb *constitute*, similar in meaning to *compose*, is commonly used to refer to abstract concepts (e.g., *The point you make does not constitute an argument*, *The case you refer to constitutes a legal precedent*).

needs checking The British government is comprised of far fewer ministries than is the French government.

revised The British government comprises far fewer ministries than does the French government.

or The British government is composed of far fewer ministries than is the French government.

• **conscience/conscious/consciousness**: *To be conscious* is *to be awake and aware of what is happening*, whereas *conscience* is *the part of our mind that tells us it is right to do some things and wrong to do other things (such as steal or murder). Conscience* and *consciousness* are both nouns; the adjectives are *conscientious (aware of what is right and wrong)* and *conscious (aware).*

needs checking She was tempted to steal the chocolate bar, but her conscious told her not to.

revised She was tempted to steal the chocolate bar, but her conscience told her not to.

• **contemptuous/contemptible**: We are *contemptuous* of anyone or anything we find *contemptible.*

needs checking The judge called the delinquent's behavior utterly contemptuous.

revised The judge called the delinquent's behavior utterly contemptible.

• **continual/continuous**: If something is *continuous* it *never stops*; something *continual* is *frequently repeated but not unceasing*. The same distinction holds for the adverbs *continually* and *continuously*.

needs checking	He has been phoning me continuously for the past two weeks.
	(Surely he stopped for a bite to eat or a short nap.)

• **decimate**: Most etymologists agree that originally this word meant *kill one of every ten*. It has come to be used more loosely to mean *destroy a considerable number of*, and sometimes *kill nine of every ten*, but many authorities advise against using the word in any way that expressly contradicts the original sense.

needs checking	The regiment was decimated; fewer than 40 percent of the troops survived.
revised	The regiment suffered extreme losses; fewer than 40 percent of the troops survived.

• **deduce/deduct**: *Deduction* is the noun stemming from both these verbs, which is perhaps why they are sometimes confused. *To deduce* is *to draw a conclusion*, whereas *to deduct* is *to subtract*.

needs checking	Sherlock Holmes deducted that Moriarty had committed the crime.
revised	Sherlock Holmes deduced that Moriarty had committed the crime.

• **definite/definitive**: If something is *definite* then there is *no uncertainty about it*; a *definitive* version of something *fixes it in its final or permanent form*—just as a dictionary definition attempts to fix the meaning of a word. Often a sentence is better with neither of these words.

needs checking	Glenn Gould's recording of Bach's Goldberg Variations is often thought of as the definite modern version.
revised	Glenn Gould's recording of Bach's Goldberg Variations is often thought of as the definitive modern version.
needs checking	Once we have completed our caucus discussion I will be making a very definitive statement.
revised	Once we have completed our caucus discussion I will be making a statement.
or	Once we have completed our caucus discussion I will have something definite to say.

• **degradation/decline**: *Degradation* carries the connotation of *shame* *and disgrace. To degrade something* is not *to reduce it*, or *downgrade it*, or *destroy it.*

needs checking	Among those units in which women played a combat role there was no degradation in operational effectiveness.
revised	Among those units in which women played a combat role there was no decline in operational effectiveness.
or	... there was no reduction in operational effectiveness.
needs checking	According to some authorities, the threat of war has now been significantly degraded.
revised	According to some authorities, the threat of war has now been significantly reduced.

• **demur/demure**: To *demur* is to raise an objection; to be *demure* is to be modest and shy in an appealing way.

• **deny/rebut/refute**: *To deny something* is *to assert that it is not true*; *to rebut an argument* is *to oppose it*; *to refute it* is *to prove conclusively that it is not true.*

needs checking	During yesterday's press conference the president angrily refuted the allegations: "There has been no improper relationship," he said.
revised	During yesterday's press conference, the president angrily denied the allegations: "There has been no improper relationship," he said.

• **deprecate/depreciate**: *To deprecate something* is *to suggest that it is not valuable or worthy of praise*; something that *depreciates* loses its value.

needs checking	Leonard Cohen was very self-depreciating throughout the interview.
revised	Leonard Cohen was very self-deprecating throughout the interview.

• **discrete/discreet**: *Discrete* means *separate* or *distinct*, whereas *discreet* means *prudent* and *tactful; unwilling to give away secrets.*

needs checking	Madonna is not renowned for being discrete.
revised	Madonna is not renowned for being discreet.

• **disinterested/uninterested**: A *disinterested* person is *unbiased; uninfluenced by self-interest, especially of a monetary sort.* It is thus quite possible for a person who is entirely disinterested in a particular matter to be completely fascinated by it. If one is *uninterested in* something, on the other hand, one is *bored by* it.

needs checking	He was so disinterested in the game that he left after the fifth inning with the score at 2–2.
revised	He was so uninterested in the game that he left after the fifth inning with the score at 2–2.
needs checking	The controlling shareholders had grown tired of the CEO's futuristic strategies and disinterest in day-to-day operations.
revised	The controlling shareholders had grown tired of the CEO's futuristic strategies and lack of interest in day-to-day operations.

• **disorient/disorientate**: Both are considered correct by many authorities, but the extra syllable of the second grates on the ear.

needs checking	I was entirely disorientated in the darkness.
revised	I was entirely disoriented in the darkness.

• **dissemble/disassemble**: *To dissemble* is *to disguise your feelings*—a mild form of lying. *To disassemble* is *to take apart.*

needs checking	For the test we are required to first assemble and then dissemble a six-cylinder engine.
revised	For the test we are required to first assemble and then disassemble a six-cylinder engine.

• **dissociate/disassociate**: There is no need for the extra syllable.

needs checking	T.S. Eliot speaks of a disassociation of sensibility that began in the seventeenth century.
revised	T.S. Eliot speaks of a dissociation of sensibility that began in the seventeenth century.

• **distinct/distinctive**: *Distinct* means *able to be seen or perceived clearly; easily distinguishable from those around it. Distinctive* means *unusual; not commonly found.* There is a similar contrast between the adverbs *distinctly* and *distinctively*, and the nouns *distinction* and *distinctiveness.*

needs checking	I distinctively heard the sound of a car engine.
revised	I distinctly heard the sound of a car engine.

• **ecology/environment**: *Ecology* is the study of some aspects of the environment; you cannot "harm the ecology."

• **economic/economical**: *Economic* means *pertaining to economics*, or *sufficient to allow a reasonable return for the amount of money or effort put* *in*. *Economical* is a word applied to people, which means *thrifty*. The difference applies as well to *uneconomic* and *uneconomical.*

needs checking Controversy over whether it would be economical to develop the vast Hibernia oilfield continued for many years.

revised Controversy over whether it would be economic to develop the vast Hibernia oilfield continued for many years.

• **effective/efficacious/effectual/efficient**: *Effective*, *efficacious*, and *effectual* all mean *sufficient to produce the desired effect. Efficacious*, however, applies only to *strategies* or *things* (though it strikes many as a rather pompous word in any application). A person, then, cannot be efficacious. *Effectual* was once applied only to actions, but is now sometimes applied to people as well. *Effective* can apply to actions or people. *Efficient* has an added connotation: *producing results with little waste of money or effort*. Thus a promotional campaign to persuade people to buy a product by giving away free samples to every man, woman, and child in the country might be effective, but it would certainly not be efficient; a good deal of waste would be involved. The same difference applies to the nouns *effectiveness* and *efficiency*. (*Efficacy* is a rather pretentious noun that is usually best avoided.)

needs checking The board wants to increase the efficacy of the machinery we use.

revised The board wants to increase the efficiency of the machinery we use.

needs checking He is the most efficacious worker in the office.

revised He is the most effective worker in the office.

• **e.g./i.e.**: The abbreviation *e.g.* is short for *exemplum gratia* ("example given"; or, in the plural *exempli gratia*, "examples given"). It is sometimes confused with the abbreviation *i.e.*, which is short for *id est* ("that is to say").

needs checking Those citizens of India who speak Hindi (e.g., over 500 million people) are being encouraged to learn a second language.

revised Those citizens of India who speak Hindi (i.e., over 500 million people) are being encouraged to learn a second language.

• **elemental/elementary**: A thing is *elemental* if it forms *an important or essential element of the whole*; it is *elementary* if it is *easy to understand*, or *at a relatively simple level.*

needs checking	He lacked even the most elemental understanding of the problem.
revised	He lacked even the most elementary understanding of the problem.

• **elicit/illicit**: *Elicit* is a verb; one elicits information about something. *Illicit* is an adjective meaning *illegal* or *not approved.*

needs checking	She has been dealing in elicit drugs for some time.
revised	She has been dealing in illicit drugs for some time.
or	The police elicited details about her drug use.

• **eligible/illegible**: One is *eligible* for a job or for membership in an organization if one *meets the standard* set for applicants. One of the requirements might be that one's handwriting not be *illegible.*

needs checking	He regretted that I was not illegible to join his club.
revised	He regretted that I was not eligible to join his club.

• **emigrant/immigrant**: *To migrate* is *to move from one place to another.* The prefix *ex*, shortened to *e*, means *out of*, so an *emigrant* from a country is *someone who is moving out of it.* The prefix *in* or *im* means *in* or *into*, so an *immigrant* to a country is *someone moving into it.* Similarly, *emigration* is *the movement of people out of a country*, while *immigration* is *the movement of people into a country*. Notice the spelling in both cases: *e-migrant* (one *m*), *im-migrant* (two *m*s).

needs checking	More than one million emigrants entered America last year.
revised	More than one million immigrants entered America last year.

• **eminent/imminent/immanent**: An *eminent* person is one who is *well-known and well-respected*; an event is *imminent* if it is *about to happen*; a quality (or a god) is *immanent* if it *pervades* everything.

needs checking	Even those working for the party in the campaign did not believe that a majority victory was immanent.
revised	Even those working for the party in the campaign did not believe that a majority victory was imminent.

• **empathy/sympathy**: To *sympathize* with another person is to feel for that person; to *empathize* is to do so in a way that identifies oneself with that person.

• **enervate/invigorate**: Because of the similarity in sound between *enervate* and *energy*, *enervate* is often thought to mean *make more energetic.*

In fact *enervate* means just the opposite—*to lessen the strength of.* If something makes you more *energetic* it *invigorates* you.

needs checking She found the fresh air quite enervating; I haven't seen her so lively in months.

revised She found the fresh air quite invigorating; I haven't seen her so lively in months.

• **enormity/enormousness**: Originally the adjective *enormous* simply meant *deviating from the norm*, but by the early nineteenth century it had also come to mean *abnormal, monstrous,* or *extraordinarily wicked.* Today the only meaning is of course *vast in size or quantity*, but the connotation of wickedness is preserved in the noun *enormity*. We may speak of the enormity of a person's crime, but if we want a noun to express vast size we should use *enormousness* or *vastness*.

needs checking What most impresses visitors to the Grand Canyon is its sheer enormity.

revised What most impresses visitors to the Grand Canyon is its sheer enormousness.

better What most impresses visitors to the Grand Canyon is its vastness.

• **envious/jealous**: One is envious of someone else's good fortune, jealous of one's own possessions. In common parlance *jealous* is often used as a synonym for *envious*, but arguably the distinction between the two words is worth preserving.

needs checking He felt jealous whenever he thought of how much land his brother owned.

revised He felt envious whenever he thought of how much land his brother owned.

• **epithet/epigraph/epitaph/epigram**: four words often confused. Here are their meanings:

- Epithet—an adjective or short phrase describing someone *("The Legion of Boom"—an epithet first used in 2012 to describe the secondary defense of the Seattle Seahawks—involves an allusion to another epithet, "Legion of Doom," which has been used by teams both in ice hockey and in professional wrestling).*
- Epigraph—an inscription, especially one placed upon a building, tomb, or statue to indicate its name or purpose; or a motto or quotation appearing at the beginning of a book (or the beginning of a chapter in a book).

- Epitaph—words describing a dead person, often the words inscribed on the tomb.
- Epigram—a short, witty, or pointed saying.

needs checking His epigram will read, "A good man lies here."
revised His epitaph will read, "A good man lies here."

• **equal/equitable/equable**: Things that are *equal* have the *same value*. Arrangements that are *equitable* are *fair and just*. An *equable* person is one who is *moderate and even-tempered*.

needs checking The distribution of seats in the American Senate is not an equable one; Rhode Island, with its one million people, is allocated two senators, while California, with its forty million people, is also allocated two senators.
revised The distribution of seats in the American Senate is not an equitable one; Rhode Island, with its one million people, is allocated two senators, while California, with its forty-five million people, is also allocated two senators.

• **explicit/implicit**: If something is *explicit* it is *unfolded—stated in precise terms, not merely suggested or implied*. Something that is *implicit* is *folded in—not stated overtly*. By extension *implicit* has also come to mean *complete or absolute* in expressions such as *implicit trust* (i.e., trust so complete that it does not have to be put into words).

needs checking I told you implicitly to have the report on my desk first thing this morning.
revised I told you explicitly to have the report on my desk first thing this morning.

• **financial/fiscal/monetary/economic**: The terms used in personal, business, and government finance are not always the same. Here are four that are often not clearly understood:

- Financial—having to do with finance or the handling of money.
- Fiscal—having to do with public revenue.
- Monetary—having to do with the currency of a country. (Only in very limited circumstances, such as the expression *monetary value*, can *monetary* have the more general meaning of *having to do with money*.)
- Economic—having to do with the economy. Thus a government's economic program embraces both fiscal and monetary policies.

needs checking My brother is a nice person, but he has no monetary ability.
revised My brother is a nice person, but he has no financial ability.

• **finish/be finished/have finished**: In informal usage *to be finished* means *to be at the end of one's life or career (If that player's knee is seriously injured again, he will be finished).* In formal writing, this special use should not be extended to the verb *finish* in its normal meaning.

needs checking When you are finished the experiment, tabulate the results carefully.
revised When you have finished the experiment, tabulate the results carefully.

• **flammable/inflammable**: The two words share the same meaning; *flammable* may have originated because of the possibility for confusion with the word *inflammable*, which looks like a negative but isn't. *Non-flammable* should be used to mean *difficult or impossible to burn.*

needs checking Asbestos is an inflammable material.
revised Asbestos is a non-flammable material.

• **fleshing/flushing**: The expression *flesh out* means add to—just as flesh is added to a growing animal. The similarity in sounds often leads people to write *flush* instead of *flesh*, but if you suggest someone *flush out* their argument, you are surely not suggesting they expand it.

• **flout/flaunt**: *To flout* is *to disobey or show disrespect for*; *to flaunt* is *to display very openly.*

needs checking Aggressive policing seems to have had no effect on the number of people flaunting the law.
revised Aggressive policing seems to have had no effect on the number of people flouting the law.

• **formerly/formally**: The similarity of sound often leads to confusion.

needs checking In August Mr. Laurel formerly broke with Mrs. Aquino.
revised In August Mr. Laurel formally broke with Mrs. Aquino.

• **fortunate/fortuitous**: *Fortunate* means *lucky* and can refer to people as well as occurrences; *fortuitous* means *happening by chance*, and can refer only to occurrences or situations, not people.

needs checking This combination of circumstances is not a fortuitous one for our company; we shall have to expect reduced sales in the coming year.

revised This combination of circumstances is not a fortunate one for our company; we shall have to expect reduced sales in the coming year.

• **forward/foreword**: You find a *foreword* before the other words in a book (and an *afterword* after the other words).

needs checking The author admits in the forward to her book that the research was not comprehensive.

revised The author admits in the foreword to her book that the research was not comprehensive.

• **founder/flounder**: As a verb, *founder* means *to get into difficulty*, *to stumble or fall*, *to sink* (when speaking of a ship), or *to fail* (when speaking of a plan). *To flounder* is *to move clumsily or with difficulty*, or *to become confused in an effort to do something*.

needs checking He foundered about in a hopeless attempt to solve the problem.

revised He floundered about in a hopeless attempt to solve the problem.

• **fulsome/effusive**: *Fulsome* means *insincere* or *excessively flattering*; fulsome praise is not the sort one wants to receive. But we all like to receive *effusive* (or *enthusiastic*) praise.

needs checking He was pleased to be showered with fulsome compliments.

revised He was pleased to be showered with effusive compliments.

• **further/farther**: *Farther* refers only to *physical distance*.

needs checking Eisenhower argued that the plan should receive farther study.

revised Eisenhower argued that the plan should receive further study.

• **gender/sex**: The word *gender* is used to refer to characteristics that are associated with one's sex but that have been formed through social influences. When we refer to the *female sex* or the *male sex*, on the other hand, we are speaking of biological difference.

• **herbs/spices**: The difference lies in the origin; *herbs* come from the stems, leaves, or flowers of plants, while *spices* come from the roots, the bark, the seeds, or the buds.

• **historic/historical**: *Historic* means *of sufficient importance that it is likely to become famous in history*; *historical* means *having to do with history* (*historical research, historical scholarship*, etc.).

needs checking	We are gathered here for a historical occasion—the opening of the city's first sewage treatment plant.
revised	We are gathered here for a historic occasion—the opening of the city's first sewage treatment plant.

• **hopefully**: one of the greatest causes of disagreement among grammarians. Traditionalists argue that the correct meaning of the adverb *hopefully* is *filled with hope*, and that the use of the word to mean *it is to be hoped that* is therefore incorrect. On the other side it is plausibly argued that many adverbs can function as independent comments at the beginning of a sentence. (*Finally, let me point out that ...* ; *Clearly, we have much to do if we are to ...* ; *Obviously, it will not be possible to ...*). Why should *hopefully* be treated differently? Why indeed? Using *hopefully* for this purpose might not make for beautiful English, but it should not be regarded as a grievous error.

needs checking	Hopefully, it will be possible to finish before tomorrow. (As often happens, *hopefully* is here used with the passive, making for a wordy sentence.)
revised	We hope we can finish before tomorrow.
needs checking	Hopefully, we will arrive before dusk. (This sentence should be rewritten in order to ensure that the sentence does not suggest the meaning, *we will arrive filled with hope before dusk.*)
revised	I hope we will arrive before dusk.

• **human/humane**: Until the eighteenth century there was no distinction made between the two in either meaning or pronunciation; they were simply alternative ways of spelling the same word. In recent centuries *humane* has come to be used to refer exclusively to the more attractive human qualities—kindness, compassion, and so forth.

needs checking	Their group is campaigning for the human treatment of whales and dolphins.
revised	Their group is campaigning for the humane treatment of whales and dolphins.

• **idioms**: Similarity in sound and meaning between words often leads to the mixing-up of idioms.

needs checking	Authorities termed it a democratic transition, but for all intensive purposes it was a coup d'état.
revised	Authorities termed it a democratic transition, but for all intents and purposes it was a coup d'état.

needs checking The new recruits were reminded that they would have to tow the line.

revised The new recruits were reminded that they would have to toe the line.

• **illusion/allusion**: An *allusion* is *an indirect reference to something*; an *illusion* is *something falsely supposed to exist.*

needs checking Joyce is making an illusion in this passage to a Shakespearean sonnet.

revised Joyce is making an allusion in this passage to a Shakespearean sonnet.

• **imply/infer**: *To imply something* is *to suggest it without stating it directly*; the other person will have to *infer* your meaning.

needs checking I implied from his tone that he disliked our plan.

revised I inferred from his tone that he disliked our plan.

• **in to/into**: The difference is that *into* is used to indicate movement from outside to inside.

needs checking Many expressed sympathy for Rushdie's decision, although some said he was caving into pressure.

revised Many expressed sympathy for Rushdie's decision, although some said he was caving in to pressure.

For more on these words see pages 275–76.

• **incidents/incidence**: *Incidents* is the plural of *incident* (*happening*), whereas *incidence* is a singular noun meaning *the rate at which something occurs.*

needs checking The incidents of lung cancer is much lower in Zambia than it is in North America.

revised The incidence of lung cancer is much lower in Zambia than it is in North America.

• **ingenious/ingenuous**: *Ingenious* means *clever*; *ingenuous* means *pleasantly open and unsophisticated.*

needs checking Her manner was completely ingenious; I cannot imagine she was trying to deceive us.

revised Her manner was completely ingenuous; I cannot imagine she was trying to deceive us.

• **innumerable**: *so numerous that it is impossible to count*; do not use this word as a synonym for *many*.

needs checking Scholars have advanced innumerable explanations for the dinosaurs' disappearance.

revised Scholars have advanced many explanations for the dinosaurs' disappearance.

• **insist/persist**: To *insist* (that something be done, or on doing something) is to *express yourself very forcefully.* To *persist in doing something* is to *keep on doing it, usually despite some difficulty or opposition.*

needs checking Even after he had been convicted of the crime, he persisted that he was innocent.

revised Even after he had been convicted of the crime, he insisted that he was innocent.

• **instinctive/instinctual**: There is no difference in meaning; arguably, it is thus better to stay with the older (and more pleasant sounding) *instinctive.*

needs checking Biologists disagree as to what constitutes instinctual behavior.

revised Biologists disagree as to what constitutes instinctive behavior.

• **judicial/judicious**: *Judicial* means *having to do with law courts and the administration of justice. Judicious* means *having good judgment.*

needs checking He made one or two judicial comments about the quality of the production.

revised He made one or two judicious comments about the quality of the production.

• **know**: When one *knows* something, that piece of knowledge has been in one's mind for some time. The process of gathering or acquiring knowledge is called *discovering.*

needs checking Although I noticed the new employee on Monday, I did not know her name until today.

revised Although I noticed the new employee on Monday, I did not discover her name until today.

• **later/latter**: *Later* means *afterwards in time*, whereas the *latter* is the *last mentioned (of two things).*

needs checking I looked up the battle of Stalingrad in both the *Encyclopedia Britannica* and Wikipedia. The later provided much more information.

revised I looked up the battle of Stalingrad in both the *Encyclopedia Britannica* and Wikipedia. The latter provided much more information.

• **laudable/laudatory**: *Laudable* means *worthy of praise*; *laudatory* means *expressing praise.*

needs checking His efforts to combat poverty are very laudatory.
revised His efforts to combat poverty are very laudable.

• **liable/likely**: *Liable* means *obliged by law* or *responsible under the law (You will be liable for any damage caused when you are driving the vehicle)*; or *in danger of doing or suffering from something undesirable (That chimney is liable to fall)*. Since in the latter meaning *likely* can often be used in place of *liable*, it is often assumed that there is really no distinction between the two. Careful writers, however, do not use *liable* unless they are referring to possible consequences of an undesirable nature.

needs checking Last Sunday Rahm won the Colonial Open. He's liable to win again before the end of the year.
revised Last Sunday Rahm won the Colonial Open. He's likely to win again before the end of the year.

• **libel/slander**: *Libel* is written (and published); *slander* is oral.

needs checking He was careful in his speech to avoid making any libellous remarks.
revised He was careful in his speech to avoid making any slanderous remarks.

• **lightning/lightening**: One is not likely to see the sky *lightening* until after the thunder and *lightning* are over.

needs checking Three of the men were severely injured by the lightening.
revised Three of the men were severely injured by the lightning.

• **like/such as**: In formal writing, *like* is used to draw comparisons, while *such as* is used when you want to provide examples. *We need someone like LeBron James on this team* means *We need someone who resembles LeBron James*—a superb all-round basketball player. If you say *The Miami Heat teams of 2012 and 2013 featured stars like LeBron James and Dwyane Wade*, the literal meaning of the sentence is that those teams featured stars who *resembled* LeBron James and Dwyane Wade—which presumably is not what you mean to say, since these players didn't resemble the leading stars; they were the leading stars. In a case such as this the words you want are *such as*: *The Miami Heat teams of 2012 and 2013 featured stars such as LeBron James and Dwyane Wade.*

needs checking In the early twentieth century, writers like T.S. Eliot, Ezra Pound, and Virginia Woolf were leading figures in the movement we now call modernism.

revised In the early twentieth century, writers such as T.S. Eliot, Ezra Pound, and Virginia Woolf were leading figures in the movement we now call modernism.

or T.S. Eliot, Ezra Pound, and Virginia Woolf were leading figures in the early twentieth-century movement we now call modernism.

(It was not writers similar to Eliot, Pound, and Woolf who led the literary movement; it was Eliot, Pound and Woolf themselves.)

See also pages 186-87 below—**like/as**.

• **literally**: *Literal* means *by the letter—in exact agreement with what is said or written.* A literal meaning is thus the opposite of a figurative or metaphorical meaning. Do not use the adverb *literally* simply to emphasize something.

needs checking As silviculturalists, we are—literally—babes in the woods. (Ken Drushka, *Stumped: The Forest Industry in Transition*)

(Silviculturalists may be literally in the woods, but they are not literally babes.)

revised As silviculturalists, we are babes in the woods.

• **make/allow/make possible**: *To make someone do something* is *to force them to do it (often against their wishes)*; *to allow someone to do something* is *to permit them or make it possible for them to do something that they want to do.*

needs checking A new hospital wing is being built; this will make many more people come for treatment.

revised A new hospital wing is being built; this will allow many more people to come for treatment.

or A new hospital wing is being built; this will make it possible for many more people to come for treatment.

• **masterful/masterly**: *Masterful* means *domineering*; *masterly* means *exhibiting mastery or great skill.*

needs checking Once again last night, Diana Krall gave the audience a masterful performance.

revised Once again last night, Diana Krall gave the audience a masterly performance.

• **mitigate/militate**: To *mitigate something* is to *make it less harsh or severe*; thus, mitigating circumstances are those that make a criminal offense less serious. *To militate against something* is *to act as a strong influence against it.*

needs checking The natural history orientation of early anthropology mitigated against studies of change. (Bruce G. Trigger in *Natives and Newcomers*)

revised The natural history orientation of early anthropology militated against studies of change.

• **momentarily**: *Momentarily* means *lasting only a moment (He was momentarily confused).* Common usage also allows the word to mean *in a moment* or *soon*; in formal writing it is best to avoid this use.

needs checking Ms. Billings has informed me that she will join us momentarily.

revised Ms. Billings told me that she will join us soon.

• **moot/mute**: A *moot court* discusses a hypothetical case; a *moot point* is one that may be argued from either side. *Mute* means *silent* or *incapable of speech.*

needs checking In her recent article Nussbaum suggests that Williams's point is mute.

revised In her recent article Nussbaum suggests that Williams's point is moot.

• **moral/morale**: The *morale* of a group is their level of confidence, optimism, shared positive feeling—not to be confused with the *moral* of a story, or with *moral* issues.

• **nauseous/nauseated**: Something that is *nauseous* makes you feel *nauseated.* Informally many people speak of feeling *nauseous*; in the context of formal writing they should feel *nauseated* instead.

• **need/want**: The verb *need* conveys the idea that it would be difficult or impossible for you to do without the needed thing. If you are talking about acquiring something that is not necessary or essential, use *want* instead; everyone *needs* water and food, but no one really *needs* a new smartphone. Be careful too not to commit to paper the slang use of *need to* for *should.*

needs checking I need to marry someone who is very beautiful, very intelligent, very kind, and very rich.

revised I want to marry someone who is very beautiful, very intelligent, very kind, and very rich.

needs checking The government needs to improve the roads in this area.

revised The government should improve the roads in this area.

• **non sequitur**: A *non sequitur* is a *statement that has no clear relationship with what has preceded it*. There may be some connection within the mind of the speaker or writer, but it has not been expressed in words.

needs checking It's time our government did more to help southern Africa. Besides, consumers appreciate inexpensive clothes.

revised It's time our government did more to help southern Africa. Lowering the current barriers against importing cheap food and textiles would be an important step in that direction. Such a move would benefit our own citizens too; consumers appreciate inexpensive food and clothing.

• **novel**: A novel is an extended work of prose fiction. Perhaps because students in high school are rarely asked to read extended works of prose *non*-fiction, the mistaken idea often takes root that any extended prose work can be called a novel. It can't. Extended works of non-fiction—of history or philosophy or political theory or science, for example—are not works of fiction, so they cannot be novels.

needs checking Darwin's *The Voyage of the Beagle* appeared twenty years before his greatest novel, *On the Origin of Species*, was published.

revised Darwin's *The Voyage of the Beagle* appeared twenty years before his greatest work, *On the Origin of Species*, was published.

needs checking In Chapter 25 of his novel, Machiavelli writes that it is "better to be adventurous than cautious."

revised In Chapter 25 of *The Prince*, Machiavelli writes that it is "better to be adventurous than cautious."

or In Chapter 25, Machiavelli writes that it is "better to be adventurous than cautious."

(if the context makes clear which text is being referred to)

• **numbers and things**: In any sentence about things and numbers associated with those things, it can be easy enough to become grammatically tangled up between the things and the measure of number. Always have this question in the back of your mind: what is the subject of the verb? Here's an example:

needs checking Delays in new product launches have hammered the company's share price, which started the year at about $60 and now trades at less than $30.

That may seem fine at first glance, but look again. What is the subject of the verb *trades*? It's the noun *price*. But is it in fact the price that trades at under $30? No; it's the shares that trade at less than $30.

revised Delays in new product launches have hammered the company's share price, which started the year at about $60 and is now less than $30.

or Delays in new product launches have hammered the company's shares, which started the year at about $60; now the stock trades at less than $30.

Here are other examples of the same sort of problem:

needs checking Many people said that the price of the Tesla was too expensive.

revised Many people said that the price of the Tesla was too high.

or Many people said that the Tesla was too expensive.

needs checking The height of the Shanghai Tower rises more than 2,000 feet.

revised The Shanghai Tower rises more than 2,000 feet.

or The height of the Shanghai Tower is more than 2,000 feet.

needs checking The speed of the Sopwith Camel flew at just over 100 miles per hour during WWI.

revised The Sopwith Camel flew at just over 100 miles per hour during WWI.

or The maximum speed of the WWI Sopwith Camel was just over 100 miles per hour.

• **obsolescent/obsolete**: Something *obsolescent* is becoming out of date; something *obsolete* is completely outmoded.

• **obtuse/abstruse**: *Obtuse* means *rounded* or *blunt* (as opposed to sharp)—and by extension, when used about humans, *dull* or *dim-witted* (sometimes with the implication that the person is wilfully refusing to see the truth). *Abstruse* refers to ideas, not people, and means *obscure*, *difficult to understand* (sometimes with the implication that the material is of considerable weight or importance).

• **of/have**: The difference in meaning is obvious, but the similarity in sound consistently leads people to write sentences involving such meaningless expressions as *should of, would of, could of, may of, might of,* and *must of.*

needs checking The experiment would of succeeded if the solution had been prepared correctly.

revised The experiment would have succeeded if the solution had been prepared correctly.

needs checking Hitler believed that Rommel should of been able to defeat Montgomery at El Alamein.

revised Hitler believed that Rommel should have been able to defeat Montgomery at El Alamein.

• **other**: If one uses the words *the other* it suggests that the thing or person you are about to mention is the **only** other one you are going to write about. If there are several others to be mentioned, *another* is the word to choose.

On the Companion Website

Exercises on word meanings may be found at **sites.broadviewpress.com/grammar**. Click on **Exercises** and go to **2.5.**

needs checking One reason Germany lost the Second World War was that Hitler underestimated the importance of keeping the United States out of the conflict. The other reason was that the German intelligence network was inferior to that of the Allies. Moreover, Hitler's decision to invade Russia was a disastrous mistake.

(Here the use of *the other* in the second sentence leads the reader to believe this is the only other reason. When a third reason is mentioned in the next sentence, the reader is taken by surprise.)

revised One reason Germany lost the Second World War was that Hitler underestimated the importance of keeping the United States out of the conflict. Another reason was that the German intelligence network was inferior to that of the

Allies. Moreover, Hitler's decision to invade Russia was a disastrous mistake.

• **our/are**: Like the substitution of *of* for *have*, the confusion of *our* and *are* should never survive the rough draft stage.

needs checking Almost all are time is spent together.
revised Almost all our time is spent together.

• **palate/palette/pallet**: Your *palate* is in your mouth. An artist uses a *palette* to mix paint on. (By extension, people often refer to the range of colors typically used by a painter as her *palette*.) Finally, a *pallet* (or skid) is a *wooden frame designed for transporting goods*.

needs checking In his later work Matisse's pallet was more limited; much of his work was in unmodulated, primary colors.
revised In his later work Matisse's palette was more limited; much of his work was in unmodulated, primary colors.

• **partake/participate**: *Partake* refers to *things* (especially food and drink), *participate* to *activities*.

needs checking The mayor made a brief appearance, but did not partake in the festivities.
revised The mayor made a brief appearance, but did not participate in the festivities.

• **penultimate/ultimate**: The *penultimate* one comes just before the last one; the *ultimate* one is the last one. A widespread misconception is that *penultimate* carries the implication of being higher than or better than or beyond the *ultimate*; not so.

• **persecute/prosecute**: To *persecute* someone is to treat them in a harsh and unfair manner, especially because of their political or religious beliefs. To *prosecute* someone is to take legal action against them in the belief that they have committed a crime.

needs checking Catholics began to be prosecuted in England in the sixteenth century.
revised Catholics began to be persecuted in England in the sixteenth century.

• **persuade**: To persuade someone *of* something is to make that person believe that it is true. To persuade someone *to do* something is to lead that person, through what one says, to do the desired thing. If one does not succeed in making people believe or do what one wants, then one has not persuaded or convinced them, but only tried to persuade them. (The confusion of *refute* with *deny* [page 153] is a parallel mistake.)

needs checking After all Portia's persuasion, Shylock still refuses to change his mind.

revised After all Portia's attempts to persuade him, Shylock still refuses to change his mind.

• **pore/pour**: As *The Globe and Mail Style Book* puts it, one should "not write of someone pouring over a book unless the tome in question is getting wet."

needs checking After pouring over the evidence, the committee could find no evidence of wrongdoing.

revised After poring over the evidence, the committee could find no evidence of wrongdoing.

• **practical/practicable**: *Practical* means *suitable for use*, or *involving activity rather than theory. Practicable* means *able to be done*. Changing the railway system back to steam locomotives would be practicable but extremely impractical. In most cases *practical* is the word the writer wants; excessive use of *practicable* will make writing sound pretentious rather than important.

needs checking We do not feel that the construction of a new facility would be practicable at this time.

revised It would not be practical to construct a new facility now.

• **prescribe/proscribe**: To *prescribe* something is to recommend or order its use; to *proscribe* something is to forbid its use.

needs checking One local physician has already proscribed this new drug for a dozen of her patients, and in every case their condition has improved after they take it.

revised One local physician has already prescribed this new drug for a dozen of her patients, and in every case their condition has improved after they take it.

• **presently**: This word is the subject of much disagreement among grammarians; should *presently* be restricted to its original meaning of *soon*, or should common usage of the word to mean *now* be allowed to spread unopposed? Traditionalists argue that the acceptance of both meanings encourages ambiguity, but in fact the verb tense usually makes clear whether the speaker means *soon* or *now* (*I will be there presently, I am presently working on a large project*, etc.). Perhaps the best solution is to avoid the rather pompous *presently* altogether, and stick to those fine simple words *soon* and *now*.

needs checking	I am seeing Mr. Jones presently.
revised	I am seeing Mr. Jones now.
or	I will be seeing Mr. Jones soon.

• **proposition/proposal**: The only formally correct meaning of *proposition* is *a statement that expresses an idea*, as in *This country is dedicated to the proposition that all humans are created equal*. It is better not to use it to mean *proposal*.

needs checking	The department has put forward a proposition for increasing sales.
revised	The department has put forward a proposal for increasing sales.

• **prove**: *To prove something* is *to eliminate any doubt whatsoever as to its truth*. Outside of mathematical or philosophical logic, proof is rarely possible; what one is doing when writing about history or political science or literature is presenting an argument, not a proof. Be cautious in the claims you make in formal writing.

needs checking	The following passage proves that T.S. Eliot was antisemitic.
revised	The following passage strongly suggests that T.S. Eliot was antisemitic.
or	Antisemitic feeling is clearly present in the following passage.

• **raise/rise**: As a verb, *raise* means *to lift*; *rise* means *to come up*.

needs checking	They rose the curtain at 8 o'clock.
revised	They raised the curtain at 8 o'clock.
or	The curtain rose at 8 o'clock.

(Note: Both words are also used as nouns; in North America a *raise* is an *increase in salary*; the UK equivalent is a *rise* in salary.)

• **rational/rationale**: *Rational* is an adjective meaning *logical* or *sensible*. A *rationale* is an *explanation for something*.

needs checking	The underlying rational for the proliferation of soaps and detergents is not to make our skin or clothes any cleaner, but to increase the profits of the manufacturers.
revised	The underlying rationale for the proliferation of soaps and

detergents is not to make our skin or clothes any cleaner, but to increase the profits of the manufacturers.

• **ravish/ravage**: *Ravish* has two quite unrelated meanings—*to rape*, or *to fill with delight*. *To ravage* is *to damage or destroy*.

needs checking The tree had been ravished by insects.
revised The tree had been ravaged by insects.

• **real/genuine**: The basic meaning of *real* is *existing*; the opposite of *fake* or *forged* is *genuine*.

needs checking The buyer had thought the painting was a Cézanne, but he soon discovered it was not real.
revised The buyer had thought the painting was a Cézanne, but he soon discovered it was not genuine.

• **regime/regimen/regiment**: A *regime* is either a *system of government* or a *period in which a particular government is in power* (e.g., *military regime, democratic regime*). A *regimen* is a *precisely fixed course of activity* (e.g., a *program of daily exercise and dieting*, a *schedule according to which medication must be taken*). A *regiment* is an *army unit*. Sometimes medical authorities use *regime* and *regimen* interchangeably; there is some benefit to keeping all three clearly separate.

needs checking A regiment of exercise and heavy medication kept Kennedy performing into his third year as president.
(*The National Post*, 7 June 2003)
revised A regimen of exercise and heavy medication kept Kennedy performing into his third year as president.

• **reign/rein**: A monarch *reigns* over a territory; to control a horse you *rein* it in (using the reins). A new manager takes up the *reins* of an organization.

needs checking The new leader has so far shown no signs of reigning in the armed forces.
revised The new leader has so far shown no signs of reining in the armed forces.

• **relatable**: Until relatively recently, most people were in the habit of using phrases such as *easy to relate to* where many now use *relatable*. Some traditionalists see *relatable* as an awkward or inappropriate coinage, arguing that the word does not follow the usual pattern of adjectives formed from transitive verbs (*catchable*, *hittable*, etc.). But, as Ben Zimmer and others have pointed out, many useful adjectives (*reliable*, *laughable*, etc.) have been formed from intransitive verbs, and are regarded as entirely acceptable. There is thus no good reason not to accept *relatable* as perfectly correct English; indeed, the argument may fairly be made that using *relatable* in some contexts reduces wordiness; compare *Most people will find the premise of Greta Gerwig's new film easy to relate to* (15 words) with *Most people will find the premise of Greta Gerwig's new film relatable* (12 words).

The problem with *relatable* is not that it shouldn't ever be used; it's that many people use it too often to mean too many different things. If you're going to write that something is *relatable*, it may be useful to ask yourself before you do so *who* is likely to find that thing easy to relate to, and *why* they may be likely to find it easy to relate to. It will sharpen what you write if you can be more specific:

> That's something that anyone under 30 can probably relate to.
>
> That's a feeling that any young woman in twenty-first-century North America is likely to be able to relate to.
>
> This is a book that young people of color are particularly likely to find relatable—but it's also a book that may help whites to better understand the challenges that people of color face.
>
> It's difficult for most modern readers to directly relate to the situation that Shylock finds himself in when Portia turns the tables on him in *The Merchant of Venice*, but the way in which Shakespeare structures the scene—and, in particular, the inclusion of Shylock's "Hath not a Jew eyes?" speech at this point in the play—makes it easy for us to feel some sympathy for his predicament.

The unfortunate habit that many students fall into when using *relatable* to describe a book or a film or an idea is using the word as a vague catch-all term that in the end means little more than *I can relate to this*; or *I like this*. The more you can train yourself to think in terms of specifics, the less likely you will be to use *relatable* to convey meanings that are vague and unhelpful—and it may be that you'll find yourself using *relatable* a good deal less frequently.

• **respectively/respectfully**: *Respectively* means *in the order mentioned*; *respectfully* means *done with respect*.

needs checking Seattle, Denver, and New England were, respectfully, the three best teams in the NFL last season.

revised Seattle, Denver, and New England were, respectively, the three best teams in the NFL last season.

• **reticent/reluctant**: *Reticent* means *reluctant to speak*; *reserved about speaking*. A country may be *reluctant* to go to war; it cannot be *reticent* to go to war. And to say *reticent to speak* is to repeat oneself.

needs checking She was reticent to speak up, even when her family's reputation had been attacked.

revised She was reluctant to speak up, even when her family's reputation had been attacked.

or She remained reticent, even when her family's reputation had been attacked.

• **rite/right**: A *rite* is a *ceremonial or ritualistic act*; the word is most frequently used to denote formal acts, such as those of religious ceremonies (e.g., *marriage rites*). Many cultures have formal ceremonies to mark a new stage in a person's life—ceremonies referred to by social scientists as *rites of passage*. That phrase has come to be used informally to refer to any event marking a significant life change. Perhaps because rights and privileges are sometimes conferred during a ceremonial *rite*, the two words are sometimes confused and two *right*s end up making a wrong.

needs checking For some students, political protests are a right of passage.

revised For some students, political protests are a rite of passage.

• **sensory/sensuous/sensual**: Advertising and pornography have dulled the distinction among these three adjectives. The meanings of *sensory* and *sensuous* are similar—*sensual* is the sexy one:

- Sensory—having to do with the senses.
- Sensuous—having to do with the senses, or appealing to the senses.
- Sensual—offering physical pleasure, especially of a sexual sort.

needs checking Boswell suggested they go to a house of ill repute, but Johnson had no desire for sensuous pleasures.

revised Boswell suggested they go to a house of ill repute, but Johnson had no desire for sensual pleasures.

• **set/sit**: *To set* means *to place something somewhere*.

needs checking I could remember everything, but I had difficulty sitting it down on paper.

2 Usage

revised I could remember everything, but I had difficulty setting it down on paper.

needs checking He asked me to set down on the couch.

revised He asked me to sit down on the couch.

• **shall/will**: Historically *shall* was used primarily for simple statements or questions in the first person—both singular (*I*) and plural (*we*)—and *will* primarily for simple statements or questions in the second person and third person. When *shall* was used in the second or third person it implied control or authority, expressing promises, commands, or a sense of determination. The old distinctions are still maintained in questions (*shall I eat a peach?, will you have some tea?*) but in other respects the distinctions long ago weakened. A sense of control is expressed with just as much force in the second person using *will* (*you'll do as I say*) and expressions of determination in the first person often use *shall* (*we shall overcome*). At most, then, a slight difference in tone lingers. In legal documents, for example, *shall* is often used rather than *will*, but either wording carries with it the same meaning—and confers the same legal obligation.

correct The undersigned shall fulfill the said requirements on or before December 31, 2027.

also correct The undersigned will fulfill the said requirements on or before December 31, 2027.

• **simple/simplistic**: *Simplistic* is a derogatory word meaning *too simple* or *excessively simplified.*

needs checking The questions were so simplistic that I was able to answer all but one correctly.

revised The questions were so simple that I was able to answer all but one correctly.

• **somehow**: *Somehow* means *by some method (Somehow I must repair my car so that I can arrive in time for my appointment)*. It does not mean *in some ways, to some extent,* or *somewhat.*

needs checking His brother is somehow mentally disturbed.

revised His brother is mentally disturbed in some way.

or His brother is somewhat disturbed mentally.

• **specially/especially**: *Specially* means *for a particular purpose (These utensils are specially designed for left-handed people)*. *Especially* means *particularly* or *more than in other cases.*

needs checking The entire system pleased her, but she was specially happy to see that the computer program had been especially created for small business users.

revised The entire system pleased her, but she was especially happy to see that the computer program had been specially created for small business users.

• **stationary/stationery**: *Stationary* means *not moving*; *stationery* is *what you write on.*

needs checking As Mr. Blakeney remembered it, Lord Taylor "would always park his car in the no-parking zone outside the Bessborough Hotel, leaving House of Lords stationary on the windshield."

revised As Mr. Blakeney remembered it, Lord Taylor "would always park his car in the no-parking zone outside the Bessborough Hotel, leaving House of Lords stationery on the windshield."

• **stimulant/stimulus**: *Stimulus* (plural *stimuli*) is the more general word for *anything that produces a reaction*; *stimulant* normally refers to *a drink or drug that has a stimulating effect.*

needs checking The shocks were intended to act as stimulants to the rats that we used as subjects for the experiment.

revised The shocks were intended to act as stimuli to the rats that we used as subjects for the experiment.

• **tack/tact**: *Tack* is a sailing term; *a different tack* means *a different direction relative to the wind. Tact* is *skill in saying or doing the right or polite thing.*

needs checking We will have to exercise all our tack in the coming negotiations.

revised We will have to exercise all our tact in the coming negotiations.

• **then/than/that**: The difference in meaning is obvious, but slips of the pen or keyboard too often allow the error to make it to the final draft.

needs checking It turns out that the company needs more money that we had expected.

revised It turns out that the company needs more money than we had expected.

needs checking There were fewer people in attendance then had been predicted.

revised	There were fewer people in attendance than had been predicted.

• **they/their/there/they're**: These four words are confused perhaps more frequently than any others. *They* is a pronoun used to replace any plural noun (e.g., books, people, numbers). *There* can be used to mean *in* (or *at*) *that place*, or can be used as an introductory word before various forms of the verb *to be* (*there is*, *there had been*, etc.). *Their* is a possessive adjective meaning *belonging to them*. *They're* is a contraction of *They are*. Beware in particular of substituting *they* for *there*:

needs checking	They were many people in the crowd.
revised	There were many people in the crowd.

The easiest way to check whether one is making this mistake is to ask if it would make sense to replace *they* with a noun. In the above sentence, for example, it would obviously be absurd to say, *The people were many people in the crowd.*

The confusion of *they*, *there*, and *their* is the sort of mistake that all writers are able to catch if they proofread carefully—particularly if they do so out loud.

needs checking	Defenseman Zdeno Chára was considered to be there toughest player.
revised	Defenseman Zdeno Chára was considered to be their toughest player.
needs checking	There all going to the dance this Saturday.
revised	They're all going to the dance this Saturday.
or	They are all going to the dance this Saturday.

• **tiring/tiresome**: Something that is *tiring makes you feel tired*, though you may have enjoyed it very much. Something that is *tiresome* is *tedious and unpleasant*.

needs checking	Although it is tiresome for him, my father likes to play tennis at least twice a week.
revised	Although it is tiring for him, my father likes to play tennis at least twice a week.

• **to/too/two**: Too can mean *also* or be used to indicate *excess* (*too many*, *too heavy*); *two* is of course the number.

needs checking	She seemed to feel that there was to much to do.
revised	She seemed to feel that there was too much to do.

• **to/towards**: *To* indicates *direction*; *towards* indicates *motion*.

(Note that *toward* and *towards* may be used interchangeably.)

needs checking The deer moved slowly to me through the tall grass.
revised The deer moved slowly towards me through the tall grass.

• **tortuous/torturous**: *Tortuous* means *full of twists and turns*; *torturous* means *having to do with torture*.

• **unexceptional/unexceptionable**: *Unexceptional* means *ordinary, not an exception*; *unexceptionable* is used when you do not object (or take exception) to the thing or person in question.

needs checking A great deal of confusion and controversy surrounded the unexceptional White House plan to reflag 11 Kuwaiti tankers with the Stars and Stripes. It was a modest proposal that in itself should not have caused the handwringing it did on Capitol Hill.

(The plan to reflag Kuwaiti tankers as American ships clearly was an exception; the US had not done anything similar for years. What the writer means to say is that the plan was unexceptionable—that no one should have any objection to it.)

revised A great deal of confusion and controversy surrounded the unexceptionable White House plan to reflag 11 Kuwaiti tankers with the Stars and Stripes. It was a modest proposal that in itself should not have caused the handwringing it did on Capitol Hill.

• **unique/universal/perfect/complete/correct**: Many authorities insist that none of these terms can be a matter of degree. According to this line of thought, something must be either *unique* or *not unique*, *perfect* or *imperfect*, and so on; it is thought to be wrong to speak of something as being *very unique* or *largely correct*, or as being *more complete* than something else. Instead, we are instructed to use phrases such as *almost unique* and *more nearly complete*. It's worth noting that not all authorities agree as to the importance of drawing a clear line in this way between adjectives and adverbs which admit of comparison and adjectives and adverbs which do not. Not a few have pointed out that the phrase "more perfect union" has been lent authority through its inclusion in the preamble to the American constitution. Nevertheless, students are well advised to pay attention to this issue in formal writing.

needs checking Frida Kahlo made a rather unique contribution to twentieth-century art.

revised Frida Kahlo made a unique contribution to twentieth-century art.

or It is arguable that Frida Kahlo made a unique contribution to twentieth-century art.

• **valid/true/accurate**: An *accurate* statement is one that is *factually correct*. (A combination of accurate facts may not always give a true picture, however.) *Valid* is often used carelessly and as a consequence might seem fuzzy in its meaning. Properly used it can mean *legally acceptable*, or *sound in reasoning*; do not use it to mean *accurate*, *reasonable*, *true*, or *well-founded*.

needs checking Churchill's fear that the Nazis would become a threat to all of Europe turned out to be valid.

revised Churchill's fear that the Nazis would become a threat to all of Europe turned out to be well-founded.

• **vein/vain**: *Veins* run through your body; *to be vain* is *to be conceited*; an effort that fails to bring any of the desired results has been *in vain*.

needs checking Shakespeare portrays Sir John Oldcastle—or Falstaff, as he is usually known—as vein and irresponsible but immensely amusing and likeable.

revised Shakespeare portrays Sir John Oldcastle—or Falstaff, as he is usually known—as vain and irresponsible but immensely amusing and likeable.

• **verbal/oral**: *Oral* means *spoken* rather than written, whereas *verbal* means *having to do with words*. A person who is unable to speak may have a high level of verbal skill.

needs checking I can write well enough, but I have difficulty in expressing ideas verbally.

revised I can write well enough, but I have difficulty in expressing ideas orally.

• **were/where**: *Were* is of course a past tense form of the verb *to be*, while *where* refers to a place.

needs checking This is the place were Dante met Beatrice.

revised This is the place where Dante met Beatrice.

2.6 Part-of-Speech Conversions

A well-known Calvin and Hobbes cartoon strip nicely conveys the amusement that part-of-speech conversions may engender:

Calvin:	"I like to verb words."
Hobbes:	"What?"
Calvin:	"I take nouns and adjectives and use them as verbs. Remember when *access* was a thing? Now it's something you do. It got verbed....Verbing weirds language."
Hobbes:	"Maybe we can eventually make language a complete impediment to understanding."

In fact, however, there is no good reason why a word that has become established as one part of speech should not be used as another; the language has always been changing and growing in this way. As Tom Shippey asks:

> What can be the matter with using nouns as adjectives? Everyone does it; how about *stonewall*? It has been built into the language since before English settlers found Ireland, let alone America.... As for converting nouns to verbs, what about *water*? *Watering the horses* is recorded from before the Conquest. (*Times Literary Supplement*, 19–25 October 1990)

For that matter, what about *chair*, *table*, *paper*, *shelf*, *bottle*, *cup*, *knife*, *fork*, *eye*, *mouth*, *finger*? The list of nouns that have also become verbs or other parts of speech is a very long one, and it includes many of the most basic words in the language. (Ironically enough, the adjective *weird*, used humorously in the cartoon as a verb, began life as a noun; in Old English a weird was the personification of a powerful but unpredictable natural force.) The point in being aware of the conversion of one part of speech to another, then, is not that the practice is always a bad one. Rather it is to keep oneself aware of whether or not one is saying something in the best possible way. If the new creation fills a need, saying something more clearly and concisely than it is possible to do otherwise, then it deserves to survive. But if it fulfills no useful purpose—if clearer and more concise ways of saying the same thing already exist—then it's better to avoid it.

• **access**: For many years authorities felt, except in the vocabulary of computers, *access* should be used as a noun, not a verb. The use of *access* as a verb is now much more widely accepted, but some purists still argue that alternatives such as *enter* and *reach* are usually more precise:

less widely accepted	The cafeteria may be accessed from the warehouse or the accounts department.
more widely accepted	The cafeteria may be reached through the warehouse or the accounts department.

• **adjective for adverb**: If a word is modifying a verb, it should as a general rule be an adverb rather than an adjective. This is normally the case when the descriptive word comes directly after the verb. We say *The boy laughed quietly*, for example (rather than *The boy laughed quiet*), because the descriptive word *quietly* refers to the verb *laughed*, not the noun *boy*. Similarly, in the sentence *The quiet boy laughed* we use the adjective *quiet* to refer to the noun *boy*.

In most cases a descriptive word following a verb will apply to that verb, and should take the form of an adverb:

needs checking	She asked us not to talk so loud.
revised	She asked us not to talk so loudly.
needs checking	According to Mr. Adams, "most books will go heavier into evolution, which is a good thing."
revised	According to Mr. Adams, "most books will go more heavily into evolution, which is a good thing."
needs checking	He performs bad whenever he is under pressure.
revised	He performs badly whenever he is under pressure.

In some cases, however, a descriptive word following a verb may refer not to the verb, but to the subject. This happens most frequently with the verb *to be*, which of course does not name an action in the way that other verbs do. Thus we say *The boy is quiet*, not *The boy is quietly*; we use the adjective rather than the adverb because we are describing the boy, not the action of being. Verbs such as *taste*, *smell*, and *feel* resemble *be* in this respect; it is correct to say *I feel good* rather than *I feel well*, since the descriptive word is clearly intended to describe your condition, and not the act of feeling. Similarly, we say *it tastes good*, not *it tastes well*, and *it smells sweet*, not *it smells sweetly*. In some other cases, too, an adjective rather than an adverb will be appropriate after a verb. It makes perfect sense, for example, to write that *someone sliced the bread thin* (rather than *sliced the bread thinly*), since the descriptive word is intended to refer to the resulting slices, and not to the action of slicing.

The principles outlined above also apply to the comparative and superlative forms of adjectives and adverbs:

needs checking	They both ran quicker in the final than they had in the semi-final.
revised	They both ran more quickly in the final than they had in the semi-final.
needs checking	He performs worse under pressure than he does when he is relaxed.
revised	He performs less well under pressure than he does when he is relaxed.
needs checking	Of all the contestants, Hawkins ran the quickest.
revised	Of all the contestants, Hawkins ran the most quickly.

Given that comparative and superlative adverbs are often more long-winded compound formations, it is not surprising that in everyday speech the shorter adjectival equivalents are often used in their stead. And such usages are becoming more and more common as well in written English. Should the *Financial Post* editor have corrected the headline that read "Northern Miners Breathe Easier"? Certainly it's easier to use the adjective here in place of the two-part adverb *more easily*. Whether or not it's better is less clear; certainly many purists are not pleased by the practice.

less widely accepted	The purpose of desktop publishing is to do the same old thing cheaper, easier, and quicker.
more widely accepted	The purpose of desktop publishing is to do the same old thing more cheaply, more easily, and more quickly.

• **advice/advise**: *Advice* is the noun; *advise* is the verb.

needs checking	They refused to take our advise.
revised	They refused to take our advice.

• **affect/effect**: *Effect* is normally used as a noun meaning *result*. (It can also be used as a verb meaning *put into effect*, as in *The changes were effected by the committee.*) *Affect* is a verb meaning *cause a result*. (It can also be used as a noun meaning *emotion* or *mental state*, as in *affect theory*.)

needs checking When the acid is added to the solution, there is no visible affect.

revised When the acid is added to the solution, there is no visible effect.

needs checking "The issues that effect us here on the reserve are the same issues that effect the whole constituency," Mr. Littlechild said. (*The Globe and Mail*)

revised "The issues that affect us here on the reserve are the same issues that affect the whole constituency," Mr. Littlechild said.

• **author**: The noun *author* seems to have been first used as a verb in the seventeenth century. That usage died out, but it reappeared in the twentieth century, and has become quite common in the twenty-first. Some authorities still regard the use of *author* as a verb to be an outright error, however, and others feel that it has a pretentious feel to it, and in most situations see no need to find substitutes for *write*. As Merrill Perlman has pointed out, however, acceptance of *author* as a verb is much higher in situations where it may not be entirely clear who did the actual writing. In a sentence such as *The Liberal government has authored new legislation on greenhouse gas emissions*, *authored* seems to be regarded as an acceptable alternative to verbs such as *introduced* or *unveiled*.

needs checking Smith is a member of the Appeals Court, and has authored two books on the judicial system.

revised Smith is a member of the Appeals Court, and has written two books on the judicial system.

• **bear/birth/give birth to**: For centuries standard English had no single word to describe the process of giving birth; one spoke of a woman *bearing children* or *giving birth to children*. In the late twentieth century, however, a usage that Walt Whitman had used in an 1855 poem entitled "There was a child went forth every day" (*She that conceived him in her womb and birthed him…*) started to become more and more common, and nowadays it is considered entirely acceptable to use *birth* as a transitive verb. The expression *birth a child* is certainly more concise than *give birth to a child*, and is widely felt as well to better reflect the active nature of the process.

• **breath/breathe**: *Breath* is the noun, *breathe* the verb.

needs checking When you breath, your lungs take in oxygen.

revised When you breathe, your lungs take in oxygen.

• **dependent/dependant**: *Dependent* is an adjective that describes someone or something that depends on someone or something else. In American usage *dependent* can also be a noun; in Canada the noun is spelled *dependant.*

needs checking Emily is still dependant on her parents for financial support.
revised Emily is still dependent on her parents for financial support.

• **dialogue**: As a verb, *talk* serves perfectly well, even after all these years.

awkward The two department heads should dialogue with each other more frequently.
better The two department heads should talk to each other more frequently.

• **enthuse/enthusiastic**: The verb *enthuse* is a relatively recent back formation from the adjective *enthusiastic*; *enthused* is its simple past tense form. Confusion between the two forms is now common.

needs checking In 2022 millions were enthused about Norway's Olympic performance.
revised In 2022 millions were enthusiastic about Norway's Olympic performance.
or In 2022 millions enthused over Norway's Olympic performance.

• **first/firstly**: *Firstly* is now generally thought of as archaic, though it is not incorrect. Be sure to be consistent, though, in the use of *first*, *second*, etc., in lists.

needs checking There were several reasons for France's reluctance to commit more resources to North America. First, she was consumed with the battle for supremacy in Europe. Secondly, the returns on previous investments had been minimal.
revised There were several reasons for France's reluctance to commit more resources to North America. First, she was consumed with the battle for supremacy in Europe. Second, the returns on previous investments had been minimal.

• **give/gift**: Until relatively recently it was universally understood that *give* is a verb and *gift* is a noun. The use of *gift* as a verb seems to have arisen in the context of institutional fundraising; in most cases, it is difficult to see any reason to say "thank you" for this *gift*.

needs checking	Mr. Dench has generously gifted the university with funding for a new library.
revised	Mr. Dench has generously given the university funding for a new library.

• **good/well**: The most common of the adjective-for-adverb mistakes.

needs checking	As the manager put it, "He pitched good, but not real good."
fair	He pitched well, but not really well.
better	He did not pitch very well.

• **impact**: The use of *impact* as a verb has become widespread even in formal English, but *affect* remains an attractive option.

awkward	The government's decision will impact upon wholesalers in all areas of the country.
better	The government's decision will affect wholesalers in all areas of the country.

• **its/it's**: *Its* is an adjective meaning *belonging to it*. *It's* is a contraction of *it is*—a pronoun plus a verb. (Similarly, *whose* is an adjective meaning *belonging to whom*, whereas *who's* is a contraction of *who is*. See pages 190–91.)

needs checking	Its important to remember that the population of North America in this period was less than 10 million.
revised (less formal)	It's important to remember that the population of North America in this period was less than 10 million.
revised (more formal)	It is important to remember that the population of North America in this period was less than 10 million.

needs checking	A coniferous tree continually sheds it's leaves.
revised	A coniferous tree continually sheds its leaves.

• **lend/loan**: In Canadian English *loan* is used only as a noun; *lend* is the verb. In American English, *loan* has long been used as a verb as well.

He was unwilling to loan his sister any money.
He was unwilling to lend his sister any money.

• **like/as**: *Like* is a preposition, not a conjunction; it introduces a noun or pronoun in a phrase. If introducing a clause, which always includes a verb, use *as* in formal writing.

- He looks like his father.

(*Like* introduces the noun *father*.)

- He looks as his father did at his age.
  (*As* introduces the clause *as his father did at his age*.)
- He is acting like a drunkard.
  (*Like* introduces the noun *drunkard*.)
- He is acting as if he were drunk.
  (*As* introduces the clause *as if he were drunk*.)

needs checking Like I said before, smoking is forbidden.
revised As I said before, smoking is forbidden.

needs checking He runs like I do—with short, choppy strides.
revised He runs as I do—with short, choppy strides.
or He runs like me. We both take short, choppy strides.

needs checking Duvalier ran Haiti like his father had done.
revised Duvalier ran Haiti the way his father had.

The attempt is also sometimes made to use *like what* in place of *as*.

needs checking Bush Sr. wanted to appear tough, like what Reagan had when he ordered the invasion of Grenada.
revised Bush Sr. wanted to appear tough, as Reagan had when he ordered the invasion of Grenada.

On the Companion Website

Exercises on part-of-speech conversions may be found at **sites.broadviewpress.com/grammar**. Click on **Exercises** and go to **"Parts of Speech."**

- **loath/loathe**: *Loath* is the adjective; *loathe* is the verb.

needs checking He told me he is beginning to loath his job.
revised He told me he is beginning to loathe his job.
or He is loath to return to his old job.

- **loose/lose**: *Loose* is normally used as an adjective meaning *not tight*; as a verb it means to *make loose* (e.g., *He loosed the reins*). *Lose* is, of course, always a verb.

needs checking As soon as it became dark she began to loose control of herself.

2
Usage

revised As soon as it became dark she began to lose control of herself.

needs checking If this movie doesn't bring the song back to the hit parade, then you know it's flopped—and that Spielberg is loosing his touch.

revised If this movie doesn't bring the song back to the hit parade, then you know it's flopped—and that Spielberg is losing his touch.

• **maybe/may be**: *Maybe* is an adverb that should be replaced by *perhaps* in formal writing. *May be* is a compound verb.

needs checking May be he will come, but I doubt it.
revised Maybe he will come, but I doubt it.
or Perhaps he will come, but I doubt it.

needs checking A prototype maybe ready by 2032.
revised A prototype may be ready by 2032.

• **meantime/meanwhile**: *Meantime* is a noun, used most frequently in the phrase *in the meantime*. *Meanwhile* is an adverb.

needs checking The Germans were preparing for an attack near Calais. Meantime, the Allies were readying themselves for the invasion of Normandy.

revised The Germans were preparing for an attack near Calais. Meanwhile, the Allies were readying themselves for the invasion of Normandy.

• **medal/win a medal**: Until quite recently English lacked a one-word verb meaning *win a medal*. The verb *to medal* now fills that function, but many feel the new coinage has the feel of a counterfeit. In formal writing it is probably still best to use the more widely accepted currency.

less widely accepted She medalled twice at the 2008 Olympics.

more widely accepted She twice won medals at the 2008 Olympics.

or She won two medals at the 2008 Olympics.

• **orgasm/have an orgasm**: For a long time the only one-word synonyms for *have an orgasm* or *achieve orgasm* were colloquial terms that clearly had no place in formal writing. In the late twentieth century people began to use *orgasm* as a verb as well as a noun. That usage is now becoming quite widely accepted.

less widely accepted Twenty percent of the respondents reported that on average they had orgasmed fewer than three times per month.

more widely accepted Twenty percent of the respondents reported that on average they had experienced orgasm fewer than three times per month.

or Twenty percent of the respondents reported that on average they had had fewer than three orgasms per month.

• **practice/practise**: In the US *practice* serves as both noun and verb. In Canada and Britain *practise* (verb) and *practice* (noun) should be distinguished.

US The team will practice on Thursday.
UK/CDA The team will practise on Thursday.

• **predominate/predominant**: *Predominate* is the verb, *predominant* the adjective. (Either *predominately* or *predominantly* may be used as adverbs.)

needs checking The use of the word "hero" for a sandwich was predominate only in New York.
revised The use of the word "hero" for a sandwich was predominant only in New York.
or The use of the word "hero" for a sandwich predominated only in New York.

• **principal/principle**: *Principal* can be either a noun or an adjective. As a noun it means *the person in the highest position of authority in an organization* (e.g., *a school principal*) or *an amount of money*, as distinguished from the interest on it. As an adjective it means *first in rank or importance* (*The principal city of northern Nigeria is Kano*). *Principle* is always a noun, and is never used to describe a person; *a principle* is *a basic truth or doctrine*, *a code of conduct*, or *a law describing how something works*.

needs checking We feel this is a matter of principal.
revised We feel this is a matter of principle.

needs checking Up went the shares of the two principle companies in this emerging field.
revised Up went the shares of the two principal companies in this emerging field.

• **prophecy/prophesy**: *Prophecy* is the noun, *prophesy* the verb.

needs checking His comment should be regarded as a prediction, not a prophesy.
revised His comment should be regarded as a prediction, not a prophecy.

• **quality**: Although in colloquial English *quality* is frequently used as a replacement for *good* or *worthwhile*, in formal writing it should be used as a noun, not an adjective. It is useful to remember that something may as easily be of poor quality as of good quality.

needs checking The salesperson claims that this is a quality product.
revised The salesperson claims that this is a product of high quality.
or The salesperson claims that this is a good product.

• **quote/quotation**: In formal English *quote* is the verb, *quotation* the noun.

needs checking The following quote shows just how determined she is to change the constitution.
revised The following quotation shows just how determined she is to change the constitution.

• **real/really**: One of the most commonly made adjective-for-adverb mistakes.

needs checking Some of the fish we caught were real big.
fair Some of the fish we caught were really big.
better Some of the fish we caught were very big.

• **verb–noun confusion**: Where verbs and nouns have similar forms, be careful not to confuse them. Some of the most common examples are: *advice* (noun) and *advise* (verb); *extent* (noun) and *extend* (verb); *device* (noun) and *devise* (verb); *revenge* (noun) and *avenge* (verb).

needs checking Gerald Ford, president from 1974 to 1976, has now to a large extend been forgotten.
revised Gerald Ford, president from 1974 to 1976, has now to a large extent been forgotten.

needs checking She wanted to revenge the harm he had caused her.
revised She wanted to avenge the harm he had caused her.

• **whose/who's**: *Whose* means *belonging to whom*; *who's* is a contraction of *who is*.

needs checking Kennedy is not normally remembered as the president who's policies embroiled the US in the Vietnam conflict, but several scholars have suggested that he was as much responsible as was Johnson.

revised Kennedy is not normally remembered as the president whose policies embroiled the US in the Vietnam conflict, but several scholars have suggested that he was as much responsible as was Johnson.

2.7 Slang

• **slang/informal English**: The column to the left below lists words and expressions often used in conversation, but not in formal English. The corresponding formal words are listed to the right. The most frequently troublesome words are also given separate entries in this section.

anyways	anyway
anywheres, anyplace	anywhere
awful	poor, miserable, sick
awfully	very, extremely

Some authorities continue to hold that *awful* should retain its original meaning of *filled with or inspiring awe*. In any case, a better replacement can always be found. The same is even more true of the use of the adverb *awfully* as an intensifier to mean *very* (*awfully good*, *awfully small*, etc.).

boss	manager, supervisor
bunch	group
(except for grapes, bananas, etc.)	
buy	bargain
(as a noun—*a good buy*, etc.)	
go (to mean "say")	say
have got	have, own
kid	child, girl, boy
kind of, sort of	rather, in some respects
let's us	let us
lots of	a great deal of
mad	angry
(unless the meaning is *insane*)	

2 Usage

All contractions (*it's*, *he's*, *there's*, *we're*, etc.) should be avoided in formal academic writing, as should conversational markers such as *Well*, ….

• **attitude**: In colloquial English in recent years *attitude* has undergone a considerable transformation, becoming first a synonym for *bad attitude* and then a word that (depending on context) may denote an air of superiority or suggest the audacity and forceful irreverence of an "in-your-face" personality. In formal written English such colloquial usages as *she's got attitude* should be avoided.

• **could care less/couldn't care less**: In the early 1990s people started to say sarcastically *I could care less* to mean the opposite—that they couldn't care less. For some time *I could care less* seemed to be taking over, regardless of the tone of voice used, and the meaning of the words themselves seemed in danger of being lost. In recent years *couldn't care less* has made something of a comeback.

needs checking	Most of the time most people could care less about what their elected representatives are doing.
revised	Most of the time most people couldn't care less about what their elected representatives are doing.

• **get**: should not be used to mean *come*, *go*, *be*, or *become*. Such expressions as *get a hold of* are also inappropriate in formal writing.

needs checking	Henry and Jane Seymour got married in 1536, only ten days after the death of Anne Boleyn.
revised	Henry and Jane Seymour were married in 1536, only ten days after the death of Anne Boleyn.

• **go** (to mean *say*)

needs checking	He goes, "What do you mean?"
revised	He says, "What do you mean?"

• **have got** (to mean *have*)

needs checking	He has got two houses and three cars.
revised	He has two houses and three cars.

In conversational English *got* has become widely used as an auxiliary verb, probably because of the awkwardness of pronouncing certain combinations involving common contractions. Thus we would never shorten *I have you covered* to *I've you covered*; instead we would say, *I've got you covered*. *Have got* is also an informal synonym for *have* in the sense of *possess*. Both these uses of *got* are usually to be avoided in formal writing.

• **let's say**: This expression should be omitted entirely from writing.

needs checking Let's say for example a relative dies, a poor family will have to deal with financial worries as well as with grief.

revised If, for example, a relative dies, a poor family will have to deal with financial worries as well as with grief.

• **like** (to mean *say* or *indicate through gesture*): An expressive idiom, but one to be avoided in formal writing.

conversational She's like, "Why do we have to be here?" and I'm like, "Duh!"

formal She wondered why we had to be there; to me it was obvious.

• **look to**: In formal writing one may speak of *looking to the future*, but the informal use of *look to* to mean *attempt* or *intend* should be avoided.

needs checking From the moment he took power in France, Napoleon was looking to conquer Europe.

revised From the moment he took power in France, Napoleon intended to conquer Europe.

• **off** (to mean *from*)

needs checking I got it off him for two dollars.

revised I bought it from him for two dollars.

• **put across, get across** (one's point): *Express*, *convince*.

needs checking He could not get his point across.

revised He could not persuade us he was right.

• **so** (as discourse marker): It is not incorrect to start various sorts of sentences using *so* as a conjunction—though if you do, the word should always be followed by a comma. Both of the following are correct:

- Sophie greatly enjoyed staying with her grandmother, so when the time came to leave, she was reluctant to say goodbye.
- Sophie greatly enjoyed staying with her grandmother. So, when the time came to leave, she was reluctant to say goodbye.

In both of these sentences the word *so* is used as a conjunction to indicate a connection between the two ideas; Sophie's reluctance to leave is explained by the degree to which she enjoyed staying with her grandmother.

In the following example, on the other hand, the word *so* does not indicate any connection between ideas. It is used simply as what linguists call a "discourse marker"—conversational filler, in other words:

> Nice to see you again. So, did you watch the playoff game last night?

There can be no objection to using *so* in this way in conversation. Be careful not to do so in formal written work, however:

needs checking	This essay has looked at the issue from both sides. So, what conclusions can be drawn?
revised	This essay has looked at the issue from both sides. What conclusions can be drawn?

- **till/until**: In conversation or in literature *till* is a perfectly acceptable informal substitute for *until*. In formal written English, however, *until* should be used.

needs checking	They waited till dawn to launch the attack.
revised	They waited until dawn to launch the attack.

- **well**: In conversation *well* is often added to sentences while you are thinking of what to say. Do not do this in writing.

needs checking	Well, at the end of the meeting there was some doubt within the cabinet as to which course to take.
revised	At the end of the meeting there was some doubt within the cabinet as to which course to take.

- **when you get right down to it**: usually best omitted; use *otherwise*, *indeed*, or *in fact*.

On the Companion Website

An exercise on slang and informal English may be found at **sites.broadviewpress.com/grammar**.
Click on **Exercises** and go to **2.7 "Slang."**

2.8 Word Conventions

• **according to**: This expression normally is used only when one is referring to a person or to a group of people (e.g., *According to his lawyer, the accused was nowhere near the scene when the crime was committed*; *According to Shakespeare, Richard III was a murderer*).

needs checking According to geography, Congo is larger than all of Western Europe.

revised As we learn in geography, Congo is larger than all of Western Europe.

needs checking According to the story of *Cry, the Beloved Country*, Stephen Kumalo has a quick temper.

revised The events of the story show that Stephen Kumalo has a quick temper.

• **age/aged**: Do not use the noun *age* as a participle.

needs checking A woman age 35 was struck and killed by the car.

revised A woman aged 35 was struck and killed by the car.

• **all of**: Many authorities advise that the expression *all of* should be avoided in the interests of economy. Perhaps so, but there is certainly no error involved, and in many cases the addition of the word *of* improves the rhythm of the sentence; Lincoln's famous maxim "You can not fool all the people all of the time" would not be improved by dropping the *of*.

• **amount**: This word should be used only with things that are uncountable (sugar, goodwill, etc.).

needs checking A large amount of books were stolen from the library last night.

revised A large number of books were stolen from the library last night.

• **and**: In most cases *or* rather than *and* should be used as a connective if the statement is negative.

needs checking Moose are not found in South America, Africa, and Australia.

revised Moose are not found in South America, Africa, or Australia.

• **anyways/anywheres**: There is never a need for the *s*.

needs checking We were unable to find him anywheres.

revised We were unable to find him anywhere.

• **as**: When this word is used to relate the times at which two actions happened, the actions must have happened at the same time (e.g., *As I got out of bed, I heard the sound of gunfire*, where the hearing happens during the action of getting out; *As he was walking to work, he remembered that he had left the stove on*, where the remembering happens during the walking). *As* should not be used in this way if the two actions happened at different times. If one action is completed before the other begins, always use *when*.

needs checking	As I had finished my geography assignment, I started my history essay.
revised	When I had finished my geography assignment, I started my history essay. (The finishing happens before the starting.)
needs checking	As she discovered that the engine was overheating, she stopped the car immediately.
revised	When she discovered that the engine was overheating, she stopped the car immediately. (The discovering happens before the stopping.)

Note: Since *when* can be used both when actions happen simultaneously and when they happen at different times, anyone who is at all uncertain about this point is wise to avoid using *as* to refer to time, and always stick to *when*. This has the added advantage of avoiding the possible ambiguity as to whether *as* is being used to mean *because* or to mean *when*.

• **as/that/whether**: Do not use *as* to mean *that* or *whether*.

needs checking	I don't know as how I can do the job in time.
revised	I don't know whether I can do the job in time.

• **back formations**: A back formation is the formation of a word from what one would expect to be its derivative. The verb *laze*, for example, is a back formation from the adjective *lazy*; a more recent (and similar-sounding) back formation is the verb *liaise* from the noun *liaison*. Many back formations may be created from negatives that lack a positive form (*kempt*, *gruntled*, *ruthful*, *solent*, etc.). These may constitute amusing colloquialisms, but should be avoided in formal written English except where the writer is striving for a humorous effect.

informal	Toronto is a pretty ruly place to watch a game. (Baseball manager Lou Piniella, as quoted by Robertson Cochrane in *The Globe and Mail*, 29 Oct. 1994)
more formal	Toronto is a pretty civilized place to watch a game.

• **because of the following reasons/some reasons/many reasons**: The word *because* makes it clear that a cause or reason is being introduced. The addition of a phrase such as *of the following reasons* is redundant. Either use *because* on its own, or use *for the following reasons/many reasons*, etc.

needs checking During her first few years in Chicago, Susanna was unhappy because of several reasons.
revised During her first few years in Chicago, Susanna was unhappy for several reasons.

• **both**: The expressions *both alike*, *both equal*, and *both together* all tend to involve repetition.

needs checking Macdonald and Cartier both arrived together at about eight o'clock.
revised Macdonald and Cartier arrived together at about eight o'clock.

• **can be able**: *I can do it* and *I am able to do it* mean the same thing. Using the verbs together is redundant.

needs checking He thinks Minnesota can be able to win the Cup.
revised He thinks Minnesota can win the Cup.
or He thinks Minnesota will be able to win the Cup.

• **cannot help but**: One too many negatives; use *can but* or *cannot help*.

needs checking He couldn't help but think he had made a mistake.
revised He couldn't help thinking he had made a mistake.
or He could but think he had made a mistake.

• **change**: You *make a change* (not *do a change*).

needs checking The manager did several changes to the roster before the match with Russia.
revised The manager made several changes to the roster before the match with Russia.

• **comment**: We *make comments* (not *say* or *do them*).

needs checking Anyone who wishes to say any comments will have a chance to speak after the lecture.
revised Anyone who wishes to make any comments will have a chance to speak after the lecture.

• **compared to/than**: The use of *compared to* as a participial phrase often leads to ambiguity and error. Unless one is speaking of one person comparing something to something else, it is usually better to use *than*.

needs checking	There were far fewer frogs in the area in 2023 compared to previous years.
revised	There were far fewer frogs in the area in 2023 than there had been in previous years.

• **convince**: You *convince* people that they should do something, or *persuade* them to do it.

needs checking	Reagan's advisers convinced him to approve the arms-for-hostages deal with Iran.
revised	Reagan's advisers persuaded him to approve the arms-for-hostages deal with Iran.

• **elder/older**: *Elder* can act as an adjective (*my elder son*) or a noun (*the elder of the two*). *Older* can act only as an adjective. If using *than*, use *older*.

needs checking	She is four years elder than her sister.
revised	She is four years older than her sister.

• **for**: One use of this preposition is to show purpose. Normally, however, *for* can be used in this way only when the purpose can be expressed in one word (e.g., *for safety*, *for security*). It is not usually correct to try to express purpose by combining *for* with a pronoun and an infinitive: expressions such as *for him to be happy*, *for us to arrive safely* are awkward and should be avoided. Instead, one can express purpose either by beginning with *in order to* (e.g., *in order to make life easier, in order to increase yield per hectare*), or by using *so that* (e.g., *so that life will be made easier, so that yield per hectare will be increased*).

needs checking	Please speak slowly for me to understand what you say.
revised	Please speak slowly so that I can understand what you say.
needs checking	The team must work hard for it to have a chance at the World Series.
revised	The team must work hard if it is to have a chance at the World Series.

On the Companion Website

Exercises on the conventions of English usage may be found at **sites.broadviewpress.com/grammar**. Click on **Exercises** and go to **"Usage."**

• **forget**: *To forget something* is *to fail to remember it*, not *to leave it somewhere*.

needs checking I forgot my textbook at home.
revised I left my textbook at home.
or I forgot to bring my textbook from home.

• **had ought/hadn't ought**: Use *ought* or *ought not* instead.

needs checking He hadn't ought to have risked everything at once.
revised He ought not to have risked everything at once.
or He should not have risked everything at once.

• **hardly**: *Hardly* acts as a negative; there is thus no need to add a second negative.

needs checking The advertisers claim that you can't hardly tell the difference.
revised The advertisers claim that you can hardly tell the difference.

• **how/what**: One may talk about *how something* (*or someone*) is, or *what something* (*or someone*) is like, but not *how they are like*.

needs checking Tell me how it looks like from where you are.
revised Tell me how it looks from where you are.
or Tell me what it looks like from where you are.
needs checking I do not know how the roads are like between Carmel and Santa Barbara.
revised I do not know what the roads are like between Carmel and Santa Barbara.
or I do not know how the roads are between Carmel and Santa Barbara.

• **increase**: Numbers can be *increased* or *decreased*, as can such things as production and population (nouns which refer to certain types of numbers or quantities). Things such as houses, however, or books (nouns which do not refer to numbers or quantities) cannot be increased; only the number of houses, books, etc. can be increased or decreased, raised or lowered. (See also pages 167–68.)

needs checking Tulsa has greatly increased low-rent apartments in the city's core.
revised Tulsa has greatly increased the number of low-rent apartments in the city's core.

2 Usage

• **information**: One *gives information* (not *tells it*).

needs checking He told me all the information I wanted about how to apply.

revised He gave me all the information I wanted about how to apply.

• **investigation**: We *make*, *carry out*, or *hold an investigation* (not *do one*).

needs checking The manager did a thorough investigation into the disappearance of funds from his department.

revised The manager made a thorough investigation into the disappearance of funds from his department.

• **irregardless**: The result of confusion between *regardless* and *irrespective*. Use *regardless*.

needs checking She told us to come for a picnic, irregardless of whether it is rainy or sunny.

revised She told us to come for a picnic, regardless of whether it is rainy or sunny.

• **is when/is where**: Many people use these phrases when attempting to define something. There is always a better way.

needs checking Osmosis is when a fluid moves through a porous partition into another fluid.

revised Osmosis occurs when a fluid moves through a porous partition into another fluid.

or Osmosis is the movement of a fluid through a porous partition into another fluid.

• **journey**: You *make a journey* (not *do one*).

needs checking If we do not stop along the way, we can do the journey in an hour.

revised If we do not stop along the way, we can make the journey in an hour.

• **law**: A law is *passed*, *made*, or *put into effect* by the government, and *enforced* by the police. Laws are not *put* or *done*.

needs checking I think the government should put a law increasing the penalty for drunk driving.

revised I think the government should pass a law increasing the penalty for drunk driving.

• **less/fewer**: When something can be counted (e.g., people, books, trees), use *fewer*. Use *less* only with uncountable nouns (e.g., *sugar, meat, equipment*).

needs checking	As the modern economy spreads through the countryside, less people will die of tropical diseases or infected wounds. (*The New York Times*, 12 May 1997)
revised	As the modern economy spreads through the countryside, fewer people will die of tropical diseases or infected wounds.
needs checking	There are less steps, and that means there is more room for error.
revised	There are fewer steps, and that means there is more room for error.

• **lie** (meaning *speak falsely*): You *lie about something*, not *that something*.

needs checking	He lied that he was eighteen years old.
revised	He lied about his age, stating that he was eighteen.
or	He lied when he said he was eighteen years old.

• **mistake**: Mistakes are *made* (not *done*).

needs checking	He did seven mistakes in that short spelling exercise.
revised	He made seven mistakes in that short spelling exercise.

• **more/most**: Most adjectives and adverbs have comparative and superlative forms; the comparative is used when comparing two things, the superlative when comparing three or more.

needs checking	Smith was the most accomplished of the two.
revised	Smith was the more accomplished of the two.

To use *more* with a comparative adjective, or *most* with a superlative adjective is to repeat oneself.

needs checking	The bride looked like the most happiest person in the world.
revised	The bride looked like the happiest person in the world.
or	The bride looked like the most happy person in the world.
needs checking	Gandalf is much more wiser than Frodo.
revised	Gandalf is much wiser than Frodo.

• **nor**: This word is usually used with *neither*. Do not use it with *not*; when using *not*, use *or* instead of *nor*.

needs checking	She does not drink nor smoke.
revised	She does not drink or smoke.
or	She neither drinks nor smokes.

2 Usage

needs checking Graham does not have the money nor the organizational skills to succeed in business.
revised Graham does not have the money or the organizational skills to succeed in business.
or Graham has neither the money nor the organizational skills to succeed in business.

• **nothing/nobody/nowhere**: These words should not be used with another negative word such as *not*. If one uses *not*, then one should use *anything* instead of *nothing*, *anybody* instead of *nobody*, *anywhere* instead of *nowhere*.

needs checking He could not do nothing while he was in prison.
revised He could not do anything while he was in prison.

• **old-fashioned**: Be sure not to leave off the *-ed* in this adjectival expression.

needs checking Let's do it the old-fashion way.
revised Let's do it the old-fashioned way.

• **opposed**: You are opposed *to* something or someone (not *with* or *against*).

needs checking Charles Darwin was opposed against the literal interpretation of the story of Creation, as found in Genesis.
revised Charles Darwin was opposed to the literal interpretation of the story of Creation, as found in Genesis.

• **percent/percentage**: If you use *per cent*, you must give the number. Otherwise, use *percentage*.

needs checking The percent of people surveyed who reported any change of opinion was very small.
revised The percentage of people surveyed who reported any change of opinion was very small.
or Only six percent of the people surveyed reported any change of opinion.

Note: *Percentage* is always one word; in American usage *percent* is also normally now written as one word; whereas it is often still written as two words in Britain, Australia, and Canada.

• **position/theory**: Positions and theories *are held* or *are argued*; they do not hold or argue themselves.

needs checking Devlin's position holds that a shared public morality is essential to the existence of society.
revised Devlin's position is that a shared public morality is essential to the existence of society.
or Devlin holds that a shared public morality is essential to the existence of society.

• **preclude**: *To preclude something* is *to exclude any possibility of it happening*; people cannot be precluded.

needs checking Our cash flow problems preclude us from entering into any major new commitments before 2030.
revised Our cash flow problems preclude any major new commitments before 2030.
or We do not have enough money to make a commitment to you now.

• **reason**: The phrase *the reason is because* involves repetition; use *that* instead of *because*, or eliminate the phrase completely.

needs checking The reason ice floats is because it is lighter than water.
revised The reason ice floats is that it is lighter than water.
or Ice floats because it is lighter than water.
needs checking The reason I have come is because I want to apply for a job.
revised I have come to apply for a job.

• **short/scarce**: If a person is *short of something*, that thing is *scarce*.

needs checking Food is now desperately short throughout the country.
revised Food is now extremely scarce throughout the country.
or The country is now desperately short of food.

• **since/for**: Both these words can be used to indicate length (or duration) of time, but they are used in slightly different ways. *Since* is used to mention the point at which a period of time began (*since 6 o'clock*, *since the beginning of 2022*, *since last Christmas*, etc.). *For* is used to mention the amount of time that has passed (*for two years*, *for six months*, *for centuries*, etc.).

needs checking She has been staying with us since three weeks.
revised She has been staying with us for three weeks.
or She has been staying with us since three weeks ago.

• **so**: When used to show degree or extent, *so* is normally used with *that*: *so big that ...* , *so hungry that ...* , etc. In formal writing, *so* should not be used as an intensifier in the way that *very* is used.

needs checking	Once the chemical reaction started, the container became so hot.
revised	Once the chemical reaction started, the container became very hot.

• **some/any/someone/anyone**: With negatives (*not*, *never*, etc.) *any* is used in place of *some*.

needs checking	He never gives me some help with my work.
revised	He never gives me any help with my work.

• **speech**: You *make a speech* or *give a speech* (not *do a speech*).

needs checking	The dean was asked to do a speech at the convocation.
revised	The dean was asked to give a speech at the convocation.

• **start**: If both the time at which an event begins and the time that it finishes are mentioned, it is not enough to use only the verb *start*.

needs checking	The dance started from 9 p.m. till midnight.
revised	The dance started at 9 p.m. and finished at midnight.
or	The dance continued from 9 p.m. until midnight.
or	The dance lasted from 9 p.m. until midnight.

• **suppose/supposed**: Be sure to add the *d* in the expression *supposed to*.

needs checking	We are suppose to be there by eight.
revised	We are supposed to be there by eight.

• **supposed to/should**: These two are very similar in meaning, and may often be used interchangeably; if a person is *supposed to* do something, then that is what she *should* do. In the past tense, however, the question of when and when not to use *supposed to* is quite tricky. You may use it when you are clearly talking about a fixed plan that has not been carried out (e.g., *He was supposed to arrive before two o'clock, but he is still not here*). You should not use it to apply to any action that you think was wrong, or you feel should not have been carried out. The safe solution to this problem is always to use *should* instead of *supposed to*.

needs checking	What she said was impolite, but he was not supposed to hit her for saying it.
revised	What she said was impolite, but he should not have hit her for saying it.

needs checking The National Party government was not supposed to keep Nelson Mandela in jail for so many years.

revised The National Party government should not have kept Nelson Mandela in jail for so many years.

• **thankful/grateful**: We are *thankful* that something has happened, and *grateful* for something we have received.

needs checking I am very thankful for the kind thoughts expressed in your letter.

revised I am very grateful for the kind thoughts expressed in your letter.

• **too**: The word *too* suggests that something is *more than necessary*, or *more than desired*. Do not use it indiscriminately to lend emphasis.

needs checking He looked too handsome in his new suit.

revised He looked very handsome in his new suit.

• **try/sure**: Perhaps the most common error of all, in published books and articles as well as in less formal writing, is the use of *and* rather than *to* after *try* and *sure*.

needs checking No one stepped in to try and save the poor animal.

revised No one stepped in to try to save the poor animal.

needs checking Burton had agreed with the Sultan not to try and convert the Africans to Christianity. (Alan Moorehead, *The White Nile*)

revised Burton had agreed with the Sultan not to try to convert the Africans to Christianity.

needs checking Be sure and take out the garbage before you go to bed.

revised Be sure to take out the garbage before you go to bed.

• **use/used**: Be sure to add the *d* in the expression *used to*.

needs checking He use to be much more reckless than he is now.

revised He used to be much more reckless than he is now.

• **where**: Do not use *where* for *that*.

needs checking I read in the paper where the parties are now tied in popularity.

revised I read in the paper that the parties are now tied in popularity.

2.9 Joining Words

The art of combining correct clauses and sentences logically and coherently is as much dependent on taking the time to think through what we are writing—and how the reader will respond to what we write—as it is on knowledge of correct usage. It is all too easy for most of us to assume that the flow of our thoughts will be as clear to the reader as it is to us. In practical terms this leads to the omission of links in the argument or of joining words that help the reader to see those links. Almost as common is the tendency to give too many or contradictory cues to the reader—a tendency that is often an indication that ideas have not yet been thoroughly thought out. That in itself is nothing to be ashamed of; the key is to be willing to take the time to re-read and revise the work. Every good writer makes at least two and sometimes as many as five or six drafts of any piece of writing before considering it finished.

• **too few or too many cues** (see also “Non Sequitur”): Here’s an example of a passage that gives the reader too few cues:

- At the end of World War II there was substantial optimism that the application of Keynesian analysis would lead to economic stability and security. Over the post-war period optimistic rationalism weakened in the face of reality.

What is the connection between the idea of the first sentence and that of the second? One can figure it out without too much difficulty, but the flow of the argument is briefly interrupted while one does so. The problem is easily solved by the addition of one word to the second sentence:

> ***revised*** At the end of World War II there was substantial optimism that the application of Keynesian analysis would lead to economic stability and security. Over the post-war period, however, optimistic rationalism weakened in the face of reality.

Below is an example of a passage that suffers from the opposite problem: too many cues.

- A short report in which you request an increase in your department’s budget should be written in the persuasive mode. Most reports, however, do not have persuasion as their main objective. Persuasion, though, will often be one of their secondary objectives.

The use of *however* and *though* in consecutive sentences gives readers the sense of twisting back on themselves without any clear sense of direction. This sort of difficulty can be removed by rewording or re-arranging the ideas:

> *revised* A short report in which you request an increase in your department's budget should be written in the persuasive mode. Most reports, however, do not have persuasion as their main objective. Persuasion will thus be at most a secondary objective.

The following pages list the chief words and expressions used in English to join ideas together, and discuss problems that are often experienced with them.

Words to Connect Ideas Opposed to Each Other

All these words are used to indicate that the writer is saying two things which seem to go against each other, or are different from each other. For example, in the sentence, *He is very rich, but he is not very happy*, the fact that he is not happy is the reverse of what we might expect of a rich man. The word *but* indicates this opposition of ideas to the reader.

although	nevertheless
but	though
despite	whereas
even if	while
however	yet
in spite of	

Although, though

These words are used to indicate that, within the same sentence, two things that seem to go against each other are being said. *Although* is usually used to introduce subordinate clauses, not phrases.

- Although he has short legs, he can run very quickly.
- Hume and Dr. Johnson, indeed, have a good deal in common, although Hume's attitude towards religion earned him Johnson's scorn.

• **although/but**: Be careful not to use both *although* and *but* in the same sentence; one is enough.

needs checking Although in many African countries the government is not elected by the people, but in Botswana the government is democratically elected.

revised Although in many African countries the government is not elected by the people, in Botswana the government is democratically elected.

or In many African countries the government is not elected by the people, but in Botswana the government is democratically elected.

But

This word is usually used in the middle of a sentence to show that the two ideas in the sentence oppose or seem to oppose each other. It is also quite correct, however, to use *but* at the beginning of a sentence, if what one is saying in the sentence forms a complete clause and if the idea of the sentence seems to oppose the idea of the previous sentence. Examples:

- The civilization of ancient Greece produced some of the world's greatest works of art and gave birth to the idea of democracy, but the Greeks also believed in slavery.
- The civilization of ancient Greece produced some of the world's greatest works of art and gave birth to the idea of democracy. But the Greeks also believed in slavery.

• **opposing or supporting ideas**: When one is dealing with complex combinations of ideas it is sometimes easy to forget which ideas are in fact in opposition and which in support.

needs checking Brandy and bourbon, with the most "congenors," have the highest hangover ratings. Red wine is a close second, followed by dark rum, sherry, scotch, rye, beer, white wine, gin, and vodka. Vintage red wines have 15 times as much histamine (it triggers allergic reactions) as white wine, but vintage whites have fewer congenors.

(The use of *but* is inappropriate here; that whites have both less histamine and fewer congenors is as one would expect; the two facts are both instances of white wines having fewer side effects than reds.)

revised Brandy and bourbon, with the most "congenors," have the highest hangover ratings. Red wine is a close second, followed by dark rum, sherry, scotch, rye, beer, white wine, gin, and vodka. Vintage red wines also have 15 times as much histamine (it triggers allergic reactions) as white wine does.

• **but**: Experienced writers are careful not to use *but* more than once in a single sentence, or in consecutive sentences; they realize that doing so tends to confuse the reader. (It is also unwise to use any combination of *but* and *however* in this way.)

needs checking Detective Smith said that Ryan had been legally in possession of three handguns and two rifles, but he thought it "incredible" that someone should be allowed to keep ammunition at his home. But he said any change in the firearms law was something which would not be discussed by him.

revised Detective Smith said that Ryan had been legally in possession of three handguns and two rifles. Smith said he thought it "incredible" that someone should be allowed to keep ammunition at his home, but he would not comment directly on whether there should be a change in the firearms law.

Despite

This word means the same as *although*, but it is used to introduce phrases, not clauses.

- Despite his old age, his mind is active and alert.
  (*Despite his old age* is a phrase; it has no verb.)
- Although he is very old, his mind is active and alert.
  (*Although he is very old* is a clause, with *he* as a subject and *is* as a verb.)
- Despite the rain, she wanted to go out to the park.
- Although it was raining, she wanted to go to the park.

• **despite**: Remember not to introduce clauses with *despite*.

needs checking Despite that the drink tasted very strong, there was very little alcohol in it.

revised Despite its strong taste, there was very little alcohol in the drink.

or Although the drink tasted very strong, there was very little alcohol in it.

Even if

This expression is used when one is introducing a clause giving a condition. The word *even* emphasizes that the condition is surprising or unusual. Examples:

- Even if I have to stay up all night, I am determined to finish the job.

  (Staying up all night would be very unusual.)

- Even if Bangladesh doubled its food production, some of its people would still be hungry.

  (Doubling its food production would be very surprising.)

However

When used as a joining word,[1] *however* usually indicates that what one is saying seems to go against what one has said in the previous sentence. It should normally be set off by commas when used in this way:

- The country suffered greatly during the three-year drought. This year, however, the rains have been heavy.

• **however**: *However* should not be used to combine ideas within one sentence, unless a semicolon is used.

needs checking Hitler attempted to conquer the Soviet Union however he was defeated.

revised Hitler attempted to conquer the Soviet Union; however, he was defeated.

or Hitler attempted to conquer the Soviet Union. However, he was defeated.

or Hitler attempted to conquer the Soviet Union but he was defeated.

needs checking There will not be regular mail pick-up from boxes this Friday, however regular mail pick-up will resume Monday.

revised There will not be regular mail pick-up from boxes this Friday, but regular mail pick-up will resume Monday.

or There will not be regular mail pick-up from boxes this Friday. However, regular mail pick-up will resume Monday.

(Note that *however* in the sense of *to whatever*

---

1 Note that *however* may also be used as an adverb modifying an adjective or another adverb (e.g., "However rich she may become, she will never be happy," "However quickly he runs, he will never threaten Usain Bolt's record").

extent is an adverb, and does not need to be set off by commas. *However tired we are, we must finish the job tonight.*)

Nevertheless

• Like *however*, *nevertheless* is normally used to show that the idea of one sentence seems to go against the idea of the previous sentence. It should not be used to join two clauses into one sentence. Example:

- According to the known laws of physics it is not possible to walk on water. Nevertheless, this is what the Bible claims Jesus did.

> **On the Companion Website**
>
> Exercises on joining words may be found at **sites.broadviewpress.com/grammar**. Click on **Exercises** and go to **"Putting Ideas Together."**

Whereas

This word is commonly used when one is comparing two things and showing how they differ. Like *although*, it must begin a subordinate clause, and may be used either at the beginning or in the middle of a sentence. Examples:

- Whereas the stereotypical New Yorker is usually thought of as being rude and unwelcoming, Californians are typically characterized as being friendly and relaxed.
- The stereotypical New Yorker is usually thought of as being rude and unwelcoming, whereas Californians are typically characterized as being friendly and relaxed.

• **whereas**: Any sentence that uses *whereas* must have at least two clauses—a subordinate clause beginning with *whereas* and a main clause.

needs checking In "The Rain Horse" a young person feels unhappy when he returns to his old home. Whereas in "The Ice Palace" a young person feels unhappy when she leaves home for the first time.

revised In "The Rain Horse" a young person feels unhappy when he returns to his old home, whereas in "The Ice Palace" a young person feels unhappy when she leaves home for the first time.

While

• **while**: *While* can be used in the same way as *although*. If there is any chance of confusion with the other meanings of *while*, however, it is better to use *although* in such circumstances.

needs checking While I support free trade in principle, I think it hurts this industry.

revised Although I support free trade in principle, I think it hurts this industry.

Yet

This word can be used either to refer to time (e.g., *He is not yet here*), or to connect ideas in opposition to each other. When used in this second way, it may introduce another word or a phrase, or a completely new sentence.

- His spear was firm, yet flexible.
- Jones positions himself as a critic of naturalism in art. Yet the aesthetic criteria he relies on are often founded on naturalistic principles.

• **yet**: *Yet*, like the other words in this group, should not be paired with another conjunction in such a way as to create too many twists and turns in the argument.

needs checking Varying the pace, altering the tone, director Joseph Rubens keeps us off balance. Ultimately, though, the pedestrian script catches up with him, yet not before *Sleeping with the Enemy* has made its point.

(The combination of *yet* and *though* is confusing for the reader.)

revised Varying the pace, altering the tone, director Joseph Rubens keeps us off balance. Ultimately, the pedestrian script catches up with him, yet not before *Sleeping with the Enemy* has made its point.

Words to Join Linked or Supporting Ideas

also	and
as well	besides
further	furthermore
in addition	indeed
in fact	moreover

not only ... but also	plus
similarly	so too
: [colon]	; [semicolon]

Also, and, as well

Also and *as well* are very similar both in meaning and in the way that they are used. Examples:

- He put forward his simplistic credo with enormous conviction. "To do well at school," he assured us, "you must be willing to study. It is also important to eat the right foods, exercise regularly, and get plenty of sleep." All the while, the one thing we all wanted, and none of us had managed to get, was plenty of sex.
- He put forward his simplistic credo with enormous conviction. "To do well at school," he assured us, "you must be willing to study. It is important as well to eat the right foods, exercise regularly, and get plenty of sleep." All the while, the one thing we all wanted, and none of us had managed to get, was plenty of sex.

• **also**: It is best not to use *also* to start sentences or paragraphs. Moreover, *also* should not be used in the way that we often use *and*—to join two clauses together into one sentence.

needs checking We performed the experiment with the beaker half full also we repeated it with the beaker empty.

revised We performed the experiment with the beaker half full, and we repeated it with the beaker empty.

or We performed the experiment with the beaker half full. We also repeated it with the beaker empty.

And

• **and**: If this word appears more than once in the same sentence, it's worth stopping to ask if it would not be better to start a new sentence. Usually the answer will be yes.

needs checking All my family attended the celebration and most of my friends were there and we enjoyed ourselves thoroughly.

revised All my family attended the celebration, and most of my friends were there, too. We enjoyed ourselves thoroughly.

• **as ... as**: When making comparisons one may use the *as ... as* combination or use a comparative adjective with *than*. But the two should not be combined.

needs checking Recent studies indicate that the average smoker is three times as likely to develop cancer than his non-smoking counterpart.

revised Recent studies indicate that the average smoker is three times more likely to develop cancer than is his non-smoking counterpart.

• **as well**: To avoid repetition, do not use *as well* in combination with *both*.

needs checking This method should be rejected, both because it is very expensive as well as because it is inefficient.

revised This method should be rejected, both because it is very expensive and because it is inefficient.

In addition, further, furthermore, moreover

All of these are commonly used to show that what the writer is saying gives additional support to an earlier statement she has made. An example:

- It was easy to see why many countries, despite their intense dislike of apartheid, still traded with South Africa. For one thing, it was the richest country in Africa. Many of its resources, moreover, were of strategic importance.

Notice that all four expressions are often used after sentences that begin with words such as *for one thing* or *first*.

Indeed, in fact

Both of these are used to indicate that what the writer is saying is a restatement or elaboration of the idea he has expressed in the previous sentence. Notice that a colon or semicolon may also be used to show this. Examples:

- Asia is the world's most populous continent. In fact, more people live there than on all the other continents combined.
- Asia is the world's most populous continent: more people live there than on all the other continents combined.

Not only ... but also

• **not only ... but also**: This combination is used to join two pieces of supporting evidence in an argument. The combination can help to create balanced, rhythmic writing, but if it is to do so it must be used carefully. Notice that it is not necessary to use *but also* in all cases, but that if the phrase is omitted a semicolon is normally required in order to avoid a run-on sentence.

needs checking Not only was Nirvana a commercial success, it was also among the first grunge bands to achieve musical respectability.

revised Not only was Nirvana a commercial success; it was also among the first grunge bands to achieve musical respectability.

or Nirvana was not only a commercial success, but also a critical one; it was among the first grunge bands to achieve musical respectability.

Plus

- **plus**: Do not use this word in the same way as *and* or *as well.*

needs checking For one thing, the council did not much like the design for the proposed new City Hall. Plus, there was not enough money available to build it that year.

revised For one thing, the council did not much like the design for the proposed new City Hall. As well, there was not enough money available to build it that year.

Words Used to Introduce Causes or Reasons

Relationships of cause and effect are at the heart of many arguments. It is common to experience some difficulty at first in understanding such relationships clearly. The discussion below of the word *because* may be helpful in this respect. To begin with, though, here is a list of words that are used to introduce causes or reasons:

as	for
as a result of	on account of
because	since
due to	

As

This word can be used either to show the relationship between two events in time, or to indicate that one event is the cause of another. This sometimes leaves room for confusion about meaning (ambiguity). The following sentence is a good example:

- As he was riding on the wrong side of the road, he was hit by a car.

This can mean either *When he was riding on the wrong side of the road* ... or *Because he was riding on the wrong side of the road....* Unless the writer is absolutely certain that the meaning is clear, it may be better to use *while* or *when* instead of *as* to indicate relationships in time, and *because* or *since* instead of *as* to indicate relationships of cause and effect.

Because

This word creates many problems for writers. The first thing to remember is that any group of words introduced with *because* must state a cause or reason. It must not state a result or an example.

- **because**: In the following sentences, *because* has been wrongly used:

needs checking	The wind was blowing because the leaves were moving to and fro.
needs checking	He had been struck by a car because he lay bleeding in the road.

A moment's reflection leads to the realization that both of these sentences are the wrong way round. The movement of the leaves is the result of the blowing of the wind, and the man's bleeding is the result of his having been hit. When the sentences are turned around, they become correct:

revised	The leaves were moving to and fro because the wind was blowing.
revised	He lay bleeding on the road because he had been struck by a car.

What leads many people to make mistakes like these is the sort of question that begins, *How do you know that...* or *Prove that...* or *Show that....* The person who is asked, "How do you know that the wind is blowing?" is likely to answer wrongly, "The wind is blowing because the leaves are moving to and fro." What he really means is, "I know the wind is blowing because I see the leaves moving to and fro." That answer is quite correct, since here the seeing is the cause of the knowing. It is of course awkward to use a lot of phrases such as *I know that* and *I see that*. Here are some easier and better ways of answering such questions:

- The movement of the trees shows that the wind is blowing.
- The fact that the leaves are moving proves that the wind is blowing.

- Since the man lay bleeding in the road, it seems likely that he had been hit by a car.

This problem is quite easily identified in the above sentences. In many formal writing contexts, the same problem can be much more difficult to spot. Look carefully at the following sentences:

needs checking	In the story "The Hero," Dora feels sorry for Julius because she sheds tears when he is expelled from school.
needs checking	A great many politicians are not so concerned about the deficit as they claim to be, because they always call for increases in military spending.

In these sentences the source of the confusion may not be immediately clear. But if we ask whether or not Dora's tears are the *cause* of her feeling sorry for Julius, we realize the answer must be no. The tears, which presumably are the *result* of her feelings, are presented in this context as *evidence* that Dora feels sorry for Julius.

Is the fact that these politicians always call for increases in military spending the *cause* of their being less concerned with the deficit than they claim? Again, the answer must be no. That fact is presumably being presented as an *example* of that lack of concern on the part of these politicians, or as *evidence* in support of the claim that is being made regarding these politicians.

In sentences such as this, in which the writer is trying to present evidence in support of an assertion, reversing the order of the ideas (as we did with the previous set of examples) is not the best solution to the problem. Can we in such circumstances use a word other than *because*? Unfortunately, English lacks any one word that conveys this idea concisely. The word *example* or the word *evidence* might serve this function well, if only the rules of English allowed nouns to be used as conjunctions. In informal conversation, this solution might be worth trying:

- In the story "The Hero," Dora feels sorry for Julius, *evidence*, she sheds tears when he is expelled from school.
- A great many politicians are not so concerned about the deficit as they claim to be, *example*, they always call for increases in military spending.

In formal writing, of course, one cannot use the nouns *evidence* and *example* in this way. What you *can* do in formal writing, though, is use a semi-colon to indicate this sort of link between ideas:

revised In the story "The Hero," Dora feels sorry for Julius; she sheds tears when he is expelled from school.

revised A great many politicians are not so concerned about the deficit as they claim to be; they always call for increases in military spending.

This is one of many situations in which the semi-colon can be extremely useful.

• **because**: It is best not to use *because* when listing several reasons for something; otherwise, the writer gives the reader the impression that the first reason given is to be the only reason. The reader will then be surprised when others are mentioned.

needs checking He was happy because it was Friday. He was also happy because his team had won the game that morning and he had scored the winning goal. Finally, he was happy because he had done well on his exams.

revised He was happy for several reasons: it was Friday, he had scored the winning goal for his team that morning, and he had done well on his exams.

needs checking Frederick was able to enjoy such success because he was adroit at waiting for the right opportunity, and seizing it when it was handed him. He was also successful because he created a military machine that had no equal.

revised One reason Frederick was able to enjoy such success was that he was adroit at waiting for the right opportunity, and seizing it when it was handed him. But none of this would have been possible had he not also created a military machine that had no equal.

• **because**: Some people like to answer *How...?* questions by using *because*. Instead, the word *by* should be used.

needs checking How did she help him? She helped him because she lent him some money.

revised How did she help him? She helped him by lending him some money.

Due to

• **due to**: *Due* is an adjective and therefore should always modify a noun (as in the common phrase *with all due respect*). When followed by *to* it can suggest a causal relationship, but the word *due* must in that case refer to the previous noun:

- The team's success is due to hard work.

(*Due* refers to the noun *success*.)

It is not a good idea to begin a sentence with a phrase such as *Due to unexpected circumstances* ... or *Due to the fact that*.... To avoid such difficulties it is best to use *because*.

needs checking Due to the sudden resignation of our sales manager, the marketing director will take on additional responsibility for a short time.

revised Because our sales manager has resigned suddenly, the marketing director will take on additional responsibility for a short time.

Since

When used to introduce causes or reasons (rather than as a time word) *since* is used in essentially the same way as *because*.

Words Used to Introduce Results or Conclusions

accordingly	it follows that ...
as a result	so
consequently	therefore
hence	thus
in conclusion	to sum up
in consequence	to summarize
in sum	

As a result, hence

Both of these are used to show that the idea being talked about in one sentence follows from, or is the result of, what was spoken of in the previous sentence.

- His car ran out of gas. As a result, he was late for his appointment.
- His car ran out of gas. Hence, he was late for his appointment.

Notice the difference between these two and words such as *because* and *since*; we would say *Because* (or *since*) *his car ran out of gas, he was late for the appointment.*

• **hence**: Hence should not be used to join two clauses into one sentence, or to join words or phrases.

needs checking	Her phone is out of order hence it will be impossible to contact her.
revised	Her phone is out of order. Hence, it will be impossible to contact her.
needs checking	It is not the film but the advertising that is exploitative, hence pornographic.
revised	It is not the film but the advertising that is exploitative, and hence pornographic.

So

This word may be used to introduce results when one wants to mention both cause and result in the same sentence (e.g., *Her phone is out of order, so it will be impossible to contact her*). See pages 29–30 regarding beginning sentences with any of the seven coordinating conjunctions (*and, but, for, nor, or, so, yet*).

• **so**: If *so* is used, *because* is not needed, and vice versa. One of the two is enough.

needs checking	Because he was tired, so he went to bed early.
revised	Because he was tired, he went to bed early.
or	He was tired, so he went to bed early.

Therefore

• **therefore**: *Therefore* should not be used to join two clauses into one sentence.

needs checking	Training is perceived as good, therefore the payment of a $30 million subsidy to McDonald's can be made to look like a benign act.
revised	Training is perceived as good; therefore, the payment of a $30 million subsidy to McDonald's can be made to look like a benign act.

Words Used to Express Purpose

in order to	so that
in such a way as to	so as to

So that

• **so that**: When used beside each other (see also *so ... that* below) these two words show purpose; they indicate that we will be told why an action was taken. Examples:

- He sent the parcel early so that it would arrive before Christmas.
- She wants to see you so that she can ask you a question.

The words *such that* should never be used in this way to indicate purpose.

needs checking	The doctor will give you some medicine such that you will be cured.
revised	The doctor will give you some medicine so that you will be cured.
needs checking	Fold the paper such that it forms a triangle.
revised	Fold the paper so that it forms a triangle.
or	Fold the paper in such a way that it forms a triangle.

Words Used to Introduce Examples

for example	such as
for instance	: [colon]
in that	

For example, for instance, such as

The three expressions are used differently, even though they all introduce examples. *Such as* is used to introduce a single word or short phrase. It always relates to a plural noun that has appeared just before it.

- Crops such as tea and rice require a great deal of water.
  (Here *such as* relates to the noun *crops*.)
- Several African peoples, such as the Yoruba of Nigeria and the Makonde of Tanzania, attach a special ceremonial importance to masks.
  (*Such as* relates to *peoples*.)

For example and *for instance*, on the other hand, are complete phrases in themselves, and are normally set off by commas. Each is used to show that the entire sentence in which it appears gives an example of a statement made in the previous sentence. Examples:

- Some crops require a great deal of water. Tea, for example, requires an annual rainfall of at least 60 inches.
- Several African peoples attach a special ceremonial importance to masks. The Yoruba and the Makonde, for example, both believe that spirits enter the bodies of those who wear certain masks.

- Tornadoes are not only a Midwestern United States phenomenon. In 2023, for instance, a tornado touched down in Los Angeles, California.

• **for example, for instance**: *For example* and *for instance* should not be used to introduce phrases that give examples. In such situations use *such as* instead.

needs checking	In certain months of the year, for example July and August, El Paso, Texas, receives most of its rainfall.
revised	In certain months of the year, such as July and August, El Paso, Texas, receives most of its rainfall.
or	In certain months of the year El Paso, Texas, receives most of its rainfall.

In that

• **in that**: Do not confuse with *in the way that.*

needs checking	He is cruel in the way that he treats his wife harshly.
revised	He is cruel in that he treats his wife harshly.
or	He is cruel in the way that he treats his wife.

Such as

• **such as**: The addition of *and others* at the end of a phrase beginning with *such as* is redundant.

needs checking	In contrast to this perspective, sociological studies of ethnicity written from the "class" perspective (such as Benarez and Lee's 2014 paper, Chang's 2012 monograph, and others) have argued that ethnic inequality is only a special class of inequality in general.
revised	In contrast to this perspective, sociological studies of ethnicity written from the "class" perspective (such as Benarez and Lee's 2014 paper, and Chang's 2012 monograph) have argued that ethnic inequality is only a special class of inequality in general.

Words Used to Indicate Alternatives

either ... or	if only
in that case	instead, instead of
neither ... nor	otherwise
rather than	unless
whether ... or	

If only

This expression is normally used when we wish that something would happen, or were true, but it clearly will not happen, or is not true.

- If only he were here, he would know what to do.
  (This indicates that he is not here.)
- "If only there were thirty hours in a day ...," she kept saying.

In that case

This expression is used when we wish to explain what will happen if the thing spoken of in the previous sentence happens, or turns out to be true. Examples:

- He may arrive before six o'clock. In that case we can all go out to dinner.
- It is quite possible that many people will dislike the new law. In that case the government may decide to change it.

Do not confuse *in that case* with *otherwise*, which is used in the reverse situation (i.e., when one wishes to explain what will happen if the thing spoken of in the previous sentence does not happen, or turns out to be false).

Otherwise

This word has two meanings. The first is *in other ways* (e.g., *I have a slight toothache. Otherwise I am healthy*). The second meaning can sometimes cause confusion: *otherwise* used to mean *if not*. Here the word is used when we want to talk about what will or might happen if the thing spoken of in the previous sentence does not happen. Examples:

- I will have to start immediately. Otherwise, I will not finish in time.
  (This is the same as saying, *If I do not start now, I will not finish in time.*)
- The general decided to retreat. Otherwise, he believed, all his troops would be killed.
  (This is the same as saying, *The general believed that if he decided not to retreat, all his troops would be killed.*)
- You must pay me for the car before Friday. Otherwise, I will offer it to someone else.
  (i.e., *If you do not pay me for the car before Friday, I will offer it to someone else.*)

• **otherwise**: When used to mean *if not*, *otherwise* should normally be used to start a new sentence. It should not be used in the middle of a sentence to join two clauses.

needs checking	I may meet you at the party tonight, otherwise I will see you tomorrow.
revised	I may meet you at the party tonight. Otherwise, I will see you tomorrow.

Words Used to Show Degree or Extent

for the most part	so ... that
such ... that	to a certain extent
to some degree	to some extent
too ... for ... to	

So ... that

• **so ... that**: When separated from each other by an adjective or adverb, these two words express degree or extent, answering questions such as *How far...?*, *How big...?*, *How much...?* (Grammatically, *so* in these contexts introduces adjectives.) Examples:

- How sick is he? He is so sick that he may not last the night.
- How large is Texas? It is so large that you need several days to drive across it.

So ... that is the only combination of words that can be used in this way; it is wrong to say *very sick that* ... or *too large that*, just as it is wrong to leave out the word *so* and simply use *that* in such sentences.

needs checking	She was very late for dinner that there was no food left for her.
revised	She was so late for dinner that there was no food left for her.
needs checking	Dominic speaks quickly that it is often difficult to understand him.
revised	Dominic speaks so quickly that it is often difficult to understand him.

Such ... that

• **such ... that**: Like *so ... that*, the expression *such ... that* is used to express degree or extent, answering questions such as, *How big...?*, *How long...?*, *How fast...?* Grammatically, *such* in these contexts introduces noun phrases. Notice the difference in the way *so … that* and *such … that* are used.

- How far is it? It is such a long way that you would never be able to get there walking.
- It is so far that you would never be able to reach there walking.
- How large is he? He is such a large man that his trousers need to be made specially for him.
- He is so large that his trousers need to be made specially for him.

The difference between the two is of course that only one word is normally used between *so* and *that*, whereas two or three words (usually an article, an adjective, and a noun) are used between *such* and *that*. Be careful not to confuse the two, or to leave out *such*.

needs checking It was a hot day that nobody could stay outside for long.
revised It was such a hot day that nobody could stay outside for long.

That and Which

To understand when to use *that* and when to use *which* (according to traditional grammatical principles), one must first understand the difference between a restrictive clause and a non-restrictive clause (see also pages 240–41). A restrictive clause restricts the application of the noun it modifies. Here is an example:

- The horse that was injured yesterday should recover.

Here the clause *that was injured yesterday* restricts the meaning of the subject of the sentence—*horse*—to a particular horse. The clause helps to define the subject more narrowly. A non-restrictive clause does not restrict the application of the noun it modifies; instead it tells us more about the subject. Again, here is an example:

- The injured horse, which was the favorite to win today's race, should recover in time for the Derby.

Here the clause *which was the favorite to win today's race* tells us more about the horse but is not necessary to its definition. Notice that the non-restrictive clause is set off by commas, while the restrictive clause follows on directly after the noun it describes, with no intervening comma. As these examples illustrate, *that* is typically used with restrictive clauses, *which* with non-restrictive clauses.

• **that/which**: Students have long been taught that it is correct to use *that* in restrictive clauses and *which* in non-restrictive clauses.[1]

needs checking	The only store which sells this brand is now closed.
revised	The only store that sells this brand is now closed.
needs checking	The position which Marx adopted owed much to the philosophy of Hegel.
revised	The position that Marx adopted owed much to the philosophy of Hegel.

Although the use of the word *which* in any restrictive clause provokes a strong reaction among some English instructors, there are clearly instances in which one is quite justified in using *which* in this way. Such is the case when the writer is already using at least one *that* in the sentence:

needs checking	He told me that the radio that he had bought was defective.
revised	He told me that the radio which he had bought was defective.

Better yet, in many cases, is to avoid the use of a second relative pronoun by rephrasing:

revised	He told me that the radio he had bought was defective.

Indeed, instructors who object to *which* point out that rephrasing can often make the sentence shorter and crisper:

needs checking	The ending, which comes as a surprise to most readers, is profoundly unsettling.
revised	The ending is both surprising and unsettling.
needs checking	The 2020 campaign, which had been carefully planned, was an enormous success.
revised	The carefully planned 2020 campaign was an enormous success.

But *which* is not a special case in this regard. *That*, *who*, and *whose* can often be fruitfully removed in the same way:

needs checking	The surplus that we now project for 2026 will probably be exceeded in 2027.
revised	The projected 2026 surplus will probably be exceeded in 2027.

1 See above.

2 Usage

needs checking Eisenhower hired as his personal driver a woman who turned into a long-term friend.
revised Eisenhower and his driver became close friends.

The vice, then, is not *which* per se, but wordiness in general. Those who focus their attention on the one word might do better to treat the excessive use of *which* as a symptom of a much broader disease.

Interestingly, the rule about *that* and *which* seems to be a relatively recent invention, dreamt up by Henry and Francis Fowler and first propounded in their book *The King's English* in 1906. In the words of Joseph M. Williams, they felt

> the random variation between *that* and *which* in restrictive clauses [to be] messy, so they simply asserted that henceforth writers should (with some exceptions) limit *which* to non-restrictive clauses. (*Style: Ten Lessons in Clarity and Grace*, New York, Longman, 2000, 24–25)

Many instructors today are as anxious as were the Fowlers to limit the messiness in English. But, as Robert M. Martin fairly observes, it is "hard to imagine real contexts in which observation of the *that/which* distinction would result in better communication" (*Dalhousie Review*, Spring 2003, 19). Again, the better reason for observing the distinction is that doing so may help to reduce wordiness—not that the distinction itself rests on a particularly strong foundation.

Words Used to Make Comparisons

along the same lines
by comparison
in contrast
in the same way
likewise
on the one hand ...
... on the other hand
similarly

Other Joining Words and Expressions

above/below
as illustrated above/below
as mentioned above/below
as shown in the diagram
as we can see/we can see that
assuming that
firstly/in the first place
for one thing
in light of
in other words
in that
in the event of
in this respect/in some respects
secondly/in the second place
these findings indicate that
to begin with
whereby

2.10 Wordiness

Wordiness is perhaps the most persistent disease afflicting modern writing; references to it permeate this book. Its opposite—the mistake of including too few words in a sentence—is also discussed in this section.

- **actual/actually**: Usually redundant.

needs checking Many people assume that Switzerland is made up entirely of bankers and watchmakers. In actual fact, the Swiss economy is very diversified.

revised Many people assume that Switzerland is made up entirely of bankers and watchmakers. In fact, the Swiss economy is very diversified.

- **as regards**: Use *about*, or rephrase.

needs checking As regards your request for additional funding, we have taken the matter under advisement.

revised We are considering your request for more money.

- **as stated earlier**: If so, why state it again?

needs checking The Venus flytrap, which as stated earlier is an insectivorous plant, grows only in a restricted area of New Jersey.

revised The Venus flytrap grows only in a restricted area of New Jersey.

- **as you know, as we all know**: Usually better omitted.

needs checking As we all know, Barack Obama won in convincing fashion over Mitt Romney in 2012.

revised Barack Obama won in convincing fashion over Mitt Romney in 2012.

- **aspect**: Often a pointer to an entire phrase or clause that can be cut.

needs checking The logging industry is a troubled one at the present time. One of the aspects of this industry that is a cause for concern is the increased production of cheaper timber in South America.

revised The logging industry is now a troubled one. Increased production of cheaper timber in South America has reduced the market for North American wood.

- **at a later date**: *Later.*

needs checking We can decide this at a later date.

revised We can decide this later.

• **at the present time**: *Now*, or nothing.

needs checking At the present time the company has ten employees.
revised The company has ten employees.

• **attention**: *It has come to my attention* that this expression is almost always unnecessarily wordy.

needs checking It has come to my attention that shipments last month were 15 percent below targeted levels.
revised Shipments last month were 15 percent below targeted levels.

• **basis/basically**: Both are often pointers to wordiness.

needs checking On the basis of the information we now possess it is possible to see that William Bligh was not the ogre he was once thought to be. Basically, he was no harsher than most captains of the time.
revised Recent research suggests that William Bligh was not the ogre he was once thought to be. He was no harsher than most captains of the time.

• **cause**: Sentences using *cause* as a verb can often be rephrased more concisely; try to think of other verbs.

needs checking The increased sales tax caused the people to react with fury.
revised The increase in sales tax infuriated the people.

needs checking The change in temperature caused the liquid to freeze within seventeen minutes.
revised The liquid froze within seventeen minutes of the temperature change.

• **close proximity to**: *Near*.

needs checking The office is situated in close proximity to shops and transportation facilities.
revised The office is near a shopping center and a bus stop.

• **e.g. ... etc.**: If you begin by saying *for example*, it is redundant to add *and others* at the end of your list. See *also* and *such as* in "Joining Words."

needs checking In several African nations (e.g., Rwanda, Malawi, Democratic Republic of the Congo, etc.) tyrannical or murderous regimes were overthrown in the 1990s.
revised In several African nations (e.g., Rwanda, Malawi, Democratic Republic of the Congo) tyrannical or murderous regimes were overthrown in the 1990s.

- **etc.**: The Latin *et cetera*, or *etc.* for short, means *and the rest* or *and others*. To say *and etc.* is really to say *and and others*. Beware as well of combining *etc.* with expressions such as *such as.*

needs checking During recent years several countries (Greece, Argentina, and etc.) have amassed huge debts, which they are now unable to pay.

revised During recent years several countries (Greece, Argentina, etc.) have amassed huge debts, which they are now unable to pay.

needs checking Plants such as Venus flytraps, pitcher plants, etc. feed on insects.

revised Plants such as Venus flytraps and pitcher plants feed on insects.

or Some plants (Venus flytraps, pitcher plants, etc.) feed on insects.

- **exists**: Often a pointer to wordiness.

needs checking A situation now exists in which voters suspect the government's motives, regardless of whether or not they approve of its actions.

revised Voters now suspect the government's motives even if they approve of its actions.

- **fact**: Be wary of *the fact that* (as well as *in point of fact* and *actual fact*).

needs checking Due to the fact that we have discontinued this product, we are unable to provide spare parts.

revised Because we have discontinued this product, we are unable to provide spare parts.

needs checking The fact that every member nation has one vote in the General Assembly does not give each one equal influence.

revised Each member nation has one vote in the General Assembly, but some have more influence than others.

needs checking Despite the fact that virtually no one in those days could foresee the end of American surpluses, Jones could.

revised Jones was one of the few to foresee the end of American surpluses.

- **factor**: Heavily overused, and a frequent cause of wordiness.

needs checking An important factor contributing to the French Revolution was the poverty of the peasantry.

revised The poverty of the peasantry was a major cause of the French Revolution.

• **from my point of view, according to my point of view, in my opinion**: All three expressions are usually redundant.

needs checking From my point of view, basic health care is more important than esoteric and expensive machines or procedures that benefit few.
fair I think that basic health care is more important than esoteric and expensive machines or procedures that benefit few.
better Basic health care is more important than esoteric and expensive machines or procedures that benefit few.

• **I myself**: In almost all cases the addition of *myself* is needlessly repetitive.

needs checking I myself believe in freedom of speech.
revised I believe in freedom of speech.
(Note: For more on *myself* see page 127.)

• **in all probability**: *Probably*.

needs checking In all probability we will be finished tomorrow.
revised We will probably be finished tomorrow.

• **include**: Often a needed word or two is omitted after this verb. The best solution may be to rephrase or find another verb.

needs checking The report includes both secondary and post-secondary education.
revised The report includes material on both secondary and post-secondary education.
or The report deals with both secondary and post-secondary education.
needs checking The Thirty Years' War included most countries in Europe.
revised The list of countries that fought in the Thirty Years' War includes almost every European nation.
revised Almost every European country fought in the Thirty Years' War.

• **interesting**: In most cases the writer should not have to tell the reader that what he is saying is interesting.

needs checking It is interesting to observe that illiteracy affects almost as high a proportion of native-born Americans as it does immigrants.
revised Illiteracy affects almost as high a proportion of native-born Americans as it does immigrants.

• **mean for**: The preposition is unnecessary.

needs checking I did not mean for him to do it all himself.
revised I did not want him to do it all himself.

• **nature**: Often contributes to wordiness.

needs checking The nature of the brain is to process information incredibly swiftly.
revised The brain processes information extremely swiftly.

• **personally**: As a way of distinguishing views expressed by the same person acting in different capacities, *personally* serves a very useful function (e.g., *As a member of the cabinet he is obliged to support the measure, but personally he has doubts as to its appropriateness*). If you are not making this sort of distinction, though, it is safe to let your reader take it for granted that you are speaking for yourself rather than on behalf of others.

needs checking Personally, I feel that the Supreme Court has usually exercised its constitutional authority wisely in recent years.
revised I feel the Supreme Court has usually exercised its constitutional authority wisely in recent years.

• **point in time**: *Now* or *then*.

needs checking At that point in time central Africa was very sparsely populated.
revised Central Africa was then very sparsely populated.

• **really**: The adverb *really* has a place in formal writing when used to mean *in reality, truly* (*Vervoerd said he would change the regulations, but really he had no intention of doing so*). If you want to use an intensifier, however, *very* is preferable.

needs checking It is really important that this be done today.
revised It is very important that this be done today.
or This must be done today.

Often in such cases your point may be made more effectively without using intensifiers—and even without using adjectives:

needs checking Like any other animal raised in a modern factory farm, a factory-farmed pig leads a very appalling life. It spends its entire life in really hideous pens that do not permit it to turn around, let alone to walk or run. Such incredibly barbaric cruelty is rationalized on the grounds that without it, humans would be forced to pay somewhat more for bacon and ham.

revised Like any other animal raised in a modern factory farm, a factory-farmed pig leads an appalling life. It spends its entire life in pens that do not permit it to turn around, let alone to walk or run. Such cruelty is rationalized on the grounds that without it, humans would be forced to pay somewhat more for bacon and ham.

• **redundancy**: *Redundancies* are words or expressions that repeat in different words a meaning already expressed. Commonly used expressions that involve redundancy include *ATM machine, end result, plans for the future, general public, nod your head, optimistic about the future, a personal friend of mine,* and *mutual cooperation*. Sometimes a case may be made for using a phrase of this sort in order to emphasize a point. What is to be avoided is thoughtless and purposeless wordiness.

needs checking This property will appreciate greatly in value.
revised This property will appreciate greatly.
needs checking The house is very large in size.
revised The house is very large.
needs checking It was decided it would be mutually beneficial to both of us if he left.
revised It was decided it would be mutually beneficial if he left.
or We agreed it would be better for both of us if he left.

• **regard, with regard to, as regards**: Try *about* or *over*, or rephrase.

needs checking I am writing with regard to your proposal to centralize production.
revised I am writing about your proposal to centralize production.
needs checking As regards the trend in interest rates, it is likely to continue to be upward.
revised Interest rates are likely to continue to increase.
needs checking This Act gave the government powers with regard to the readjustment of industry.
revised This Act gave the government powers over the readjustment of industry.

• **situation**: By avoiding this word you will usually make your sentence shorter and better.

needs checking This treaty created a situation in which European countries gave up a degree of autonomy in return for greater security.
revised Through this treaty European countries gave up a degree of autonomy in return for greater security.

• **there is/are/was/were**: These constructions often produce sentences that are needlessly long.

needs checking There were many factors which undermined the government's popularity in this period.
revised Many things undermined the government's popularity in this period.
needs checking There are many historians who accept this thesis.
revised Many historians accept this thesis.

• **too few words**: This mistake can happen anywhere in a sentence. One of the best tests of whether or not a writer has checked their work is whether or not there are missing words. In almost all cases, such omissions will be noticed through careful proofreading.

needs checking She rushed home to tell my family and about the accident.
revised She rushed home to tell my family and me about the accident.
needs checking Gandhi reminded the Conference that just one intercontinental ballistic missile could plant 200 million trees, irrigate one million hectares of land, or build 6,500 health care centers.
revised Gandhi reminded the Conference that the money spent on just one intercontinental ballistic missile could be used to plant 200 million trees, irrigate one million hectares of land, or build 6,500 health care centers.

• **too many words**: Many of the causes of this problem have been given separate entries.

needs checking So far as the purpose of this essay is concerned, it will concentrate on the expansion of Chinese influence.
revised This essay will concentrate on the expansion of Chinese influence.
needs checking Although the author does not claim to be writing a social study, the question arises whether the social implications of his analysis can be ignored.
revised Although the author does not claim to be writing a social study, his analysis does have social implications.

• **tragic/tragically**: Unnecessary use of either the adjective or the adverb constitutes overkill.

needs checking Her husband, her child, and more than one hundred others died in a tragic plane crash in March, 2023.

revised Her husband, her child, and more than one hundred others died in a plane crash in March, 2023.

• **would like to take this opportunity to**: *Would like*.

needs checking I would like to take this opportunity to thank my cousin in Peoria.

revised I am very grateful to my cousin in Peoria.

or I would like to thank my cousin in Peoria.

On the Companion Website

Exercises on wordiness may be found at **sites.broadviewpress.com/grammar**. Click on **Exercises** and go to **2.10 "Wordiness."**

3 PUNCTUATION AND OTHER CONVENTIONS

3.1 Punctuation Marks

The Period •

The most important mark of punctuation is the period, which is used to end sentences. The most common punctuation mistakes involve using (or failing to use) a period; for a full discussion of complete and incomplete sentences, comma splices, run-on sentences, and sentence fragments, see 1.3.

See below under "The Question Mark" for a discussion of statements concerning questions; like other statements, these should end with a period (not a question mark).

abbreviations: The period is also used to form abbreviations. Here are some examples:

Mr. Ms. Prof. e.g. etc. i.e. St. Ave. Feb.

With many abbreviations, whether periods are included or not has become a matter of convention. For abbreviations such as the following, most style guides now recommend omitting the periods:

academic degrees:	BA	MA	PhD	
directions	NW	SE	NNE	
eras	BCE	CE	(Before the Common Era; Common Era)	
institutions	UBC	CIBC	EU	UN
states and provinces	AB	ON	CA	NY

Some common abbreviations (*et al.*, for example) require a period in one position only. If you are in any doubt about whether or not to use a period in an abbreviation, or where to put it, look up the full form of what is being abbreviated.

needs checking Jones, Smithers et. al. will be there in person.
revised Jones, Smithers et al. will be there in person.
(*Et al.* is short for the Latin *et alia*, meaning *and others*.)

The Ellipsis • • •

Three dots are used to indicate the omission of one or more words needed to complete a sentence or other grammatical construction.

• **ellipsis**: When used in quotation, an ellipsis comes inside the quotation marks. Note as well that when an ellipsis precedes a period the sentence should end with four dots (essentially the three-dot ellipsis followed by the period).

needs checking Harris shows more than a trace of paranoia in her book; she speaks, for example, of "the elements trying to subvert the essence of liberal society, of tolerance, of goodwill ... They are all around us."

revised Harris shows more than a trace of paranoia in her book; she speaks, for example, of "the elements trying to subvert the essence of liberal society, of tolerance, of goodwill.... They are all around us."

Ellipses may also be used to indicate the trailing off of speech: *Violet struggled for breath. "All my money," she gasped, "goes to...." Those were her last words.*

The Comma ,

(See 1.3 for a discussion of comma splices and run-on sentences.)

You may be familiar with this famous example of how important a comma can be:

It's time to eat, children.   It's time to eat children.

If you're reading aloud, the comma indicates a good point to pause. But even more importantly, the comma shows the grammatical structure of the sentence; the comma indicates clearly that the noun "children" is not meant to be taken as the direct object of the verb "eat." This is the central function of the comma in modern English—to help the reader recognize the grammatical structure of the sentences being read. As a side benefit, commas also help those reading aloud to pause at places in a sentence where there are natural breaks in the grammatical structure. But commas should not be used simply to create pauses at any point in a long sentence where the writer thinks the reader might run out of breath.

It was not always thus. When commas began to appear in English prose (in the late sixteenth century), they were used simply as a way of suggesting pauses in speech. Given the extent to which people's natural speech patterns differ, it is no wonder that the placing of commas in seventeenth- and eighteenth-century usage seems to us haphazard. (In this respect eighteenth-century habits of punctuation resemble eighteenth-century habits of capitalization—see page 262.) A striking example is the Second Amendment to the American Constitution:

> A well regulated Militia, being necessary to the security of a free State, the right of the people to keep and bear Arms, shall not be infringed.

This is a sentence comprising two clauses, with a subordinate clause at the beginning providing context for the declaration made in the main clause. Though it is a long sentence, there is according to grammatical principles no good reason to include a comma anywhere except at the break between the two clauses:

> A well regulated Militia being necessary to the security of a free State, the right of the people to keep and bear Arms shall not be infringed.

In saying this sentence aloud some readers will undoubtedly pause slightly at points other than at the one marked by the comma. But it is at that point alone that there should be a comma (at least according to the conventions of modern English). The additional commas in early texts are in this case far more than a historical curiosity; they have fueled endless debate and more than one court case over the constitutionality of twentieth- and twenty-first-century gun control measures in America.

The above should not be taken to imply that there is no room for individuality when it comes to the inclusion of "structural" commas; far from it. Many writers, for example, like to use a comma to set off an opening phrase from the sentence that follows. And that is perfectly acceptable; both versions below of a sentence that appeared in the previous paragraph are correct, as are both versions of the other sample sentence below:

> In saying this sentence aloud some readers will undoubtedly pause slightly at points other than at the one marked by the comma.

> In saying this sentence aloud, some readers will undoubtedly pause slightly at points other than at the one marked by the comma.

> In the spring of 2023 she left her family and moved to Rome.

> In the spring of 2023, she left her family and moved to Rome.

Again, the key point is that if structural commas are to be included, they must come at points in the sentence where there are natural breaks in the grammatical structure.

Although the omission or wrong use of a comma sounds like a small mistake, it can be very important. The following group of words, for example, forms a sentence only if a comma is included:

The Comma Worth a Million Dollars

In a 2006 case, a disagreement between two telecommunications companies over a comma was the subject of a million-dollar lawsuit. One company (Rogers Communications Inc.) argued that the contract between the two parties was valid for a minimum of five years, while the other (Bell Aliant Inc.) argued that it could be terminated at any time by either party, provided one year's notice was given.

Have a look at the relevant clause in the agreement and see what you think:

> This agreement shall be effective from the date it is made and shall continue in force for a period of five (5) years from the date it is made, and thereafter for successive five (5) year terms, unless and until terminated by one year prior notice in writing by either party.

How (if at all) would the meaning change if the last comma were removed?

> This agreement shall be effective from the date it is made and shall continue in force for a period of five (5) years from the date it is made, and thereafter for successive five (5) year terms unless and until terminated by one year prior notice in writing by either party.

The telecommunications regulator who decided the case ruled that that comma made all the difference. If the comma had been omitted, he ruled, the "unless and until terminated..." phrase would have applied only to the "thereafter" part of the agreement. With the inclusion of the comma, however, the "unless and until terminated..." phrase could reasonably be taken to apply to the initial five-year period as well as to the subsequent five-year terms that were contemplated. Bell Aliant was thus free to terminate the contract with one year's notice, even within the initial five-year period.

If the parties had used different punctuation, of course, they could have easily made the meaning plain:

> This agreement shall be effective from the date it is made and shall continue in force for a period of five (5) years from the date it is made. Thereafter it shall continue for successive five (5) year terms, unless and until terminated by one year prior notice in writing by either party.

What do you think? Was the regulator's ruling fair?

needs checking Because of the work that we had done before we were ready to hand in the assignment.

revised Because of the work that we had done before, we were ready to hand in the assignment.

Restrictive and non-restrictive modifiers: The omission or addition of commas can also completely alter the meaning of a sentence—as it did in the Queen's University Alumni letter that spoke of the warm emotions still felt by alumni for *our friends, who are dead* (rather than *our friends who are dead*). The second would have been merely a polite remembrance of those alumni who have died; the first suggests that all the friends are dead.

Such differences in meaning are not usually matters of life and death. In the following two sentences, the difference is a matter of how many stroganoffs are on the menu.

> The stroganoff, made with mushrooms and cashew cream, is the most popular item on our menu.
>
> The stroganoff made with mushrooms and cashew cream is the most popular item on our menu.

In the first sentence the implication is that there is only one stroganoff available; the one and only stroganoff is the most popular item on the menu, and in mentioning the mushrooms and cashew cream the server is simply providing some additional, incidental information. In the second sentence the omission of commas leaves open the possibility that there may be several stroganoffs on the menu; it's the one with the mushrooms and cashew cream that's the most popular. (Hint from the server: *don't order the beef stroganoff.*)

The grammatical distinction involved here is between restrictive and non-restrictive modifiers. Restrictive modifiers are essential to the full meaning of the word being modified; they restrict or limit the meaning of that word within the sentence. To indicate that they are essential to the meaning of the noun, they are not separated from it by commas. (The meaning of the second sentence is restricted to *the stroganoff made with mushrooms and cashew cream.*)

Non-restrictive modifiers, on the other hand, provide additional information that is not essential to the core meaning of the word being modified. As a way of indicating that the information provided by non-restrictive modifiers is incidental rather than essential to the word being modified, non-restrictive modifiers should be set off with commas.

(In the first stroganoff sentence, in which the information about the mushrooms and the cashew cream is not essential to the meaning of *stroganoff* within the sentence, *made with mushrooms and cashew cream* is set off by commas.)

needs checking Shoppers, who spend $100 or more, are eligible for the prize.

(The modifying clause *who spend $100 or more* is in this case essential to the meaning of *shoppers* in the context of this sentence; the group of people eligible is restricted to those who spend $100 or more.)

revised Shoppers who spend $100 or more are eligible for the prize.

The distinction between restrictive and non-restrictive modifiers may apply to adjective clauses (such as those above), adjective phrases, and also to appositives—nouns or noun phrases in apposition to another noun. Mistakes with appositives are common.

needs checking In Shakespeare's play, *The Tempest*, Gonzalo uses the same words that appear in Florio's translation of Montaigne's "Of Cannibals."

(This could be taken to imply that Shakespeare wrote only one play.)

revised In Shakespeare's play *The Tempest* Gonzalo echoes the language of John Florio's translation of Montaigne's "Of Cannibals."

(For more on restrictive and non-restrictive modifiers, see the discussion of *that* and *which* on pages 225–27.)

• **omission of commas**: Commas very commonly come in pairs, and it is wrong to omit the second comma in a pair. Be particularly careful when putting commas around a name, or around an adjectival subordinate clause.

needs checking My sister Caroline, has done very well this year in her studies.

revised My sister, Caroline, has done very well this year in her studies.

needs checking The snake which had been killed the day before, was already half-eaten by ants.

revised The snake, which had been killed the day before, was already half-eaten by ants.

• **extra comma:** Writers often add a comma when they feel a sentence is getting long, regardless of whether one is needed or is appropriate.

needs checking The ever-increasing gravitational pull of the global economy, is drawing almost every area of the world into its orbit.

revised The ever-increasing gravitational pull of the global economy is drawing almost every area of the world into its orbit.

• **serial comma (also known as the Oxford comma):** An important use of commas is to separate the entries in lists. Many authorities feel that a comma need not appear between the last and second-last entries in a list, since these are usually separated already by the word *and*. Omitting the last comma in a series will occasionally lead to ambiguity, though; when in doubt, we recommend that you include the serial comma. And when the list includes items that have commas within them, use a semicolon to separate the items in the list.

needs checking This book is dedicated to my parents, Jane Goodall and God.

revised This book is dedicated to my parents, Jane Goodall, and God.

(The serial comma makes clear that Goodall and God are not the writer's parents.)

needs checking The three firms involved were McCarthy and Walters, Harris, Jones, and Engleby, and Cassells and Wirtz.

revised The three firms involved were McCarthy and Walters; Harris, Jones, and Engleby; and Cassells and Wirtz.

On the Companion Website

Exercises on comma splices (and, more generally, on complete and incomplete sentences) may be found at **sites.broadviewpress.com/grammar**. Click on **Exercises** and go to **1.3 "Parts of Sentences."**

The Question Mark ?

• **question mark:** Everyone knows that a question should be followed by a question mark, but it is easy to forget, particularly if one is writing quickly or if the question mark should appear within other punctuation.

needs checking Would Britain benefit from closer ties with Europe. The question continues to bedevil British political life.

revised Would Britain benefit from closer ties with Europe? The question continues to bedevil British political life.

It is easy to forget that sentences beginning with combinations such as *He asked if...* or *She wondered whether...* are statements, not questions. They may report a question in indirect speech, but they are not themselves questions, and should thus not end with a question mark.

needs checking Many scholars have asked whether Truman was justified in dropping the atomic bomb on Japan, or whether he should have relied on conventional weapons?

revised Many scholars have asked whether Truman was justified in dropping the atomic bomb on Japan, or whether he should have relied on conventional weapons.

or Many scholars have asked the following question: was Truman justified in dropping the atomic bomb on Japan, or should he have relied on conventional weapons?

The Exclamation Mark !

This mark is used to give extremely strong emphasis to a statement. It should be used very sparingly, if at all, in formal written work.

The Semicolon ;

This mark is used to separate independent clauses where the ideas are closely related to each other. In most cases a period could be used instead; the semicolon simply signals to the reader the close relationship between the two ideas. In the following example the second sentence reinforces the statement of the first; a semicolon is thus appropriate, although a period is also correct:

- This book is both exciting and profound. It is one of the best books I have read.
- This book is both exciting and profound; it is one of the best books I have read.

Similarly in the following example the second sentence gives evidence supporting the statement made in the first sentence. Again, a semicolon is appropriate:

- The team is not as good as it used to be. It has lost four of its past five games.
- The team is not as good as it used to be; it has lost four of its last five games.

The semicolon is also used occasionally to divide items in a series that includes other punctuation:

- The following were told to report to the coach after practice: Jackson, a sophomore; Marshall, a junior; Nicola, a senior.

The semicolon, then, has a set of precise grammatical functions;

A common notion is that the central distinction among punctuation marks such as the comma, semicolon, colon, and period is rooted simply in the length of the pause they ask the reader to make. Such indeed was the norm several centuries ago, when punctuation was designed less to indicate grammatical relationships than to mark pauses as an aid to the listener's understanding when the text was read aloud. Under that system, a period counted as four beats, a colon as three, a semicolon as two, and a comma as one. Ian Coutts, in an interesting article in *Quill and Quire* ("All about the Pause"), uses a passage from the 1549 *Book of Common Prayer* as an example of how strangely such a system strikes the modern sensibility:

> Easter Day. The Collect.
>
> Almighty God, who through thine only begotten Son Jesus Christ hast overcome death, and opened unto us the gate of everlasting life; We humbly beseech thee, that, as by thy special grace preventing us thou dost put into our minds good desires, so by thy continual help we may bring the same to good effect; through Jesus Christ our Lord, who liveth and reigneth with thee and the Holy Ghost, ever one God, world without end.

Perhaps even stranger to modern eyes is the fashion in which the reading that follows is punctuated in sixteenth-century style:

> Mortify therefore your members which are upon the earth; fornication, uncleanness, inordinate affection, evil concupiscence, and covetousness, which is idolatry: For which things, sake the wrath of God cometh on the children of disobedience. In the which ye also walked some time, when ye lived in them.

it is not to be used simply to indicate a longer-than-usual pause, any more than the comma is to be used to join independent clauses.

needs checking The threat to the planet is constant and growing, it is to be found in the factories of Ohio; in the shrinking rain forests of Brazil; in the massive growth and massive pollution of China's cities; and in the coal-fired generation stations that still produce much of the world's electricity.

revised The threat to the planet is constant and growing. It is to be found in the factories of Ohio, in the shrinking rain forests of Brazil, in the massive growth and massive pollution of

It is not only the practice of punctuation here that is at odds with today's practice; so too are the principles of capitalization and of grammar considerably different. Here are the two passages again, set down according to modern practice:

> Almighty God, who through thine only begotten Son Jesus Christ hast overcome death, and opened unto us the gate of everlasting life, we humbly beseech thee that, as by thy special grace preventing us thou dost put into our minds good desires, so by thy continual help we may bring the same to good effect; through Jesus Christ our Lord, who liveth and reigneth with thee and the Holy Ghost, ever one God, world without end.

> Mortify therefore your members which are upon the earth: fornication; uncleanness; inordinate affection; evil concupiscence; and covetousness, which is idolatry. For these things' sake the wrath of God cometh on the children of disobedience, in the which ye also walked some time, when ye lived in them.

Echoes of the ancient principles of punctuation are still to be found in surprising places. The section on punctuation in the fifteenth edition of *The Chicago Manual of Style* advises at one point that "the semicolon, stronger than a comma but weaker than a period, can assume either role." As Louis Menand fairly commented in discussing this passage in his review of the fifteenth edition, "What could the authors possibly have been thinking?" To retain elements of the old system of "pause punctuation" in the context of modern academic practice is simply to sow the seeds of confusion.

China's cities, and in the coal-fired generation stations that still produce much of the world's electricity.

or The threat to the planet is constant and growing; it is to be found in the factories of Ohio, in the shrinking rain forests of Brazil, in the massive growth and massive pollution of China's cities, and in the coal-fired generation stations that still produce much of the world's electricity.

(For more on the uses of the semi-colon, see Section 1.3.1.)

The Colon :

• **colon**: This mark is often believed to be virtually the same as the semicolon in the way it is used. In fact, there are some important differences. The most common uses of the colon are as follows:

- in headings, to announce that more is to follow, or that the writer is about to list a series of things.
- to introduce a quotation.
- between two clauses, to indicate that the second one illustrates or provides an explanation of what was stated in the first.

Here are a few examples of how the colon may be used:

- Unquiet Union: A Study of the Federation of Rhodesia and Nyasaland.
- In the last four weeks he has visited five countries: Mexico, Venezuela, Panama, Haiti, and Belize.
- The theory of the Communists may be summed up in a single phrase: abolition of private property.
- There was one point she kept emphasizing: a vote for any of the smaller parties would be unproductive.

Be sure to use a colon (rather than a comma or a semicolon) to introduce a list.

needs checking The operation has supplied Mr. Bomersbach with four luxury cars, two Cadillacs, a Mercedes, and a Jaguar.

revised The operation has supplied Mr. Bomersbach with four luxury cars: two Cadillacs, a Mercedes, and a Jaguar.

The Hyphen -

• **hyphen**: This mark may be used to separate two parts of a compound word (e.g., *tax-free*, *hand-operated*). Notice that many such word combinations are hyphenated only if the combination acts as an adjective:

- No change is planned for the short term.
  (*Term* acts here as a noun, with the adjective *short* modifying it.)
- This is only a short-term plan.
  (Here the compound *short-term* acts as a single adjective, modifying the noun *plan*.)
- George Eliot is one of the major figures in the literature of the nineteenth century.
  (*Century* acts here as a noun, with the adjective *nineteenth* modifying it.)
- George Eliot is one of the major figures of nineteenth-century literature.
  (Here the compound *nineteenth-century* acts as a single adjective, modifying the noun *literature*.)

Hyphens are also used to break a word at the end of a line if there is not enough space. A hyphen should never be used to break up proper nouns, and should be used to break up other words only when it is placed between syllables. Any noun beginning with a capital letter (e.g., *Halifax*, *Blair*, *January*, *Harriet*) is a proper noun.

Whenever one is uncertain about whether or not to use a hyphen to break up a word, the easy solution is to put the entire word on the next line.

The Dash —

• **dash**: Dashes are often used in much the same way as parentheses, to set off an idea within a sentence. Dashes, however, call attention to the set-off idea in a way that parentheses do not:

- Peterborough (home of Broadview Press's distribution facility) is a pleasant city with a population of just over 100,000.
- Peterborough—home of Broadview Press's distribution facility—is a pleasant city with a population of just over 100,000.

A dash may also be used in place of a colon to set off a word or phrase at the end of a sentence:

- He fainted when he heard how much he had won: one million dollars.
- He fainted when he heard how much he had won—one million dollars.

• **em dashes and en dashes:** The above applies to what is known as the em dash—so-called because in most typefaces it is about the same length as the letter *m*. There is also a slightly shortened form of dash—known as the en dash—which fulfills a different function. Whereas an em dash is used to separate groups of words, an en dash is used to separate numbers, as in these examples:

- Paul Newman (1925–2008) was both a philanthropist and a noted actor.
- The street numbers are as follows: in the first block west of Main Street, 1–100; in the second block, 101–200; and so on.

Although it is standard to use the en dash in such circumstances in published work, the en dash does not appear on most keyboards, and the hyphen is usually used in its stead in everyday work. In most word processing programs an em dash may be formed by typing two hyphens (--). Note that no spaces should be left either before or after the dash. In some word processing programs a dash may be chosen from the menu symbols.

needs checking Taipei 101-at the time the tallest building in the world-was completed in 2004. Towers in Dubai and elsewhere have since surpassed it.

revised Taipei 101—at the time the tallest building in the world—was completed in 2004. Towers in Dubai and elsewhere have since surpassed it.

Parentheses

• **parentheses:** Parentheses are used to set off an interruption in the middle of a sentence, or to make a point which is not part of the main flow of the sentence. They are frequently used to give examples, or to express something in other words using the abbreviation i.e. Example:

- Several world leaders of the 1980s (Deng in China, Reagan in the US, etc.) were very old men.

Square Brackets [ ]

• **square brackets:** Square brackets are used for parentheses within parentheses, or to show that the words within the parentheses are added by another person.

- Lentricchia claims that "in reading James's Preface [to *What Maisie Knew*] one is struck as much by what is omitted as by what is revealed."
- Smith writes that as the end of the trial approached, "Sacco and Vanzetti had a good idea of what there [sic] fate would be."
  (Here the Latin *sic*, meaning *thus*, is used to indicate that the error is reproduced just as it appears in the original quotation.)

The Apostrophe ’

• **apostrophe**: The two main uses of the apostrophe are to show possession (e.g., *Peter's book*) and to shorten certain common word combinations. The shortened forms (e.g., *can't*, *shouldn't*, *he's*) are known as contractions.

contractions: Contractions are used frequently in this book, which is relatively informal in its style. Contractions, however, should not be used in more formal written work. Use *cannot*, not *can't*; *do not*, not *don't*; and so on.

informal	The experiment wasn't a success because we'd heated the solution to too high a temperature.
more formal	The experiment was not a success because we had heated the solution to too high a temperature.

• **possession**: The correct placing of the apostrophe to show possession can be a tricky matter. When the noun is singular and does not already end with an *s*, an *s* at the end of the word, preceded by an apostrophe, shows possession (e.g., *Peter's*, *George's*, *Canada's*). When the noun is plural and ends in an *s* already, the apostrophe should be added after the *s*.

needs checking	We have been asked to dinner by Harriets mother.
revised	We have been asked to dinner by Harriet's mother.
needs checking	His parent's house is filled with antiques.
revised	His parents' house is filled with antiques.
needs checking	All three groups of parents attended their infant's one-month pediatric checkup, and observations were made of father's interactions with their infants.

revised All three groups of parents attended their infants' one-month pediatric checkup, and observations were made of fathers' interactions with their infants.

Authorities differ on how one should show possession with singular nouns that already end in *s*. The MLA recommends that an *s* always be added at the end of such nouns, even where they are multi-syllabic and pronunciation with an additional *s* is ungainly:

- Dickens's next novel was *Bleak House*.
- Ulysses's voyage was a long one.
- Socrates's method of communicating his ideas has been as influential as the ideas themselves.

The Chicago Manual of Style, on the other hand, recommends adding just the apostrophe (with no additional *s*) where a singular noun ending in *s* is already more than one syllable. This approach has the great advantage of avoiding amusing but distracting tongue twisters:

- Dickens' next novel was *Bleak House*.
- Ulysses' voyage was a long one.
- Socrates' method of communicating his ideas has been as influential as the ideas themselves.

Whichever convention a writer chooses, they should be consistent. And be sure in such cases not to put an apostrophe before the first *s* in a noun ending with *s*.

needs checking Shield's novel is finely, yet delicately constructed. (concerning novelist Carol Shields)

revised Shields's novel is finely, yet delicately constructed.

Where possession is joint, an *s* should be added to the last mentioned noun:

- Bob and Carol's view is that this can be settled amicably.
- Woodward and Bernstein's persistence eventually paid off.

One important exception to the convention of using an apostrophe to show possession is the possessive *its*. In that case the form *it's* is used as a contraction of *it is*, and no apostrophe is included in the possessive *its*. If you are ever uncertain as to whether or not you are making the correct choice between *it's* and *its*, ask yourself if the sentence would make sense if you substituted *it is*. If it would, *it's* is the one you want; if not, you should be using *its*.

Apostrophes are used by some writers to form the plurals of letters and numbers:

- That sort of music was popular in the 1990's.
- She received straight A's in high school.

Since apostrophes are not otherwise used to show plurality, most authorities now prefer to omit the apostrophe:

- That sort of music was popular in the 1990s.
- She received straight As in high school.

Quotation Marks “ ”

The main use of quotation marks is to show that the words are repeated exactly as they were originally spoken or written. For a discussion of difficulties associated with this use see the discussion of direct and indirect speech in 3.2 below.

According to different conventions, words that are being mentioned in a grammatical sense, rather than used to convey meaning, may be set off by quotation marks, single quotation marks, or italics:

- The words “except” and “accept” are sometimes confused.
- The words ‘except’ and ‘accept’ are sometimes confused.
- The words *except* and *accept* are sometimes confused.

The use-mention distinction originated in analytic philosophy, but it has come to be recognized as a useful one in many contexts.

- It was not until the Renaissance that ‘meat’ began to refer specifically to animal flesh; before that time the term could be used to refer to food of any sort.

  (In the above sentence, the word ‘meat’ is being mentioned, not used.)
- Though links between meat consumption and cancer have been observed since the 1960s, humans in many parts of the world continue to consume meat in large quantities.

  (In the above sentence the word ‘meat’ is being used, not mentioned.)

Quotation marks (or single quotation marks) are sometimes used to indicate that the writer does not endorse the quoted statement, claim, or description. Quotation marks are usually used in this way only with a word or a brief phrase. When they are so used they have the connotation of *supposed* or *so-called*; they suggest that the quoted word or phrase is either euphemistic or downright false:

- After a violent workout the weightlifters would each consume a "snack" of a steak sandwich, a half-dozen eggs, several pieces of bread and butter, and a quart of tomato juice.

In the following two versions of the same report, the more sparing use of quotation marks in the second version signals clearly to the reader the writer's skepticism as to the honesty of the quoted claim, and may be taken to imply that the former Russian president indulged his legendary fondness for alcohol during the flight.

- President Yeltsin appeared to stagger as he left the plane. "The president is feeling tired and emotional," his press secretary later reported.
- A "tired and emotional" President Yeltsin appeared to stagger as he left the plane.

• **misuse of quotation marks to indicate emphasis:** Quotation marks (unlike italics, bold letters, capital letters, or underlining) should never be used to try to lend emphasis to a particular word or phrase. Because quotation marks may be used to convey the sense *supposed* or *so-called* (see above), the common misuse of quotation marks to try to lend emphasis often creates ludicrous effects.

needs checking	All our bagels are served "fresh" daily.
	(The unintended suggestion here is that the claim of freshness is a dubious one.)
revised	All our bagels are served fresh daily.
or	All our bagels are served *fresh* daily.
	(if emphasis is required in an advertisement)
needs checking	Dogs must be "leashed." (BC Ferries sign)
revised	Dogs must be leashed.

Single Quotation Marks ‘ ’

In North America the main use of single quotation marks is to mark quotations within quotations:

- According to Obama's press secretary, "When the president said, 'I will bring change to Washington,' he meant it."

Depending on convention, single quotation marks may also be used to show that a word or phrase is being mentioned rather than used (see above).

In the United Kingdom and some other countries, quotation marks and single quotation marks are used for direct speech in precisely the opposite way that North Americans use them; single quotation marks (or inverted commas, as they are sometimes called) are used for direct speech, and double quotation marks are used for quotations within quotations. Here is the correct British version of the above sentence:

- According to Obama's press secretary, 'When the president said, "I will bring change to Washington", he meant it.'

Note here that UK usage also places the comma outside the quotation mark.

3.2 Quotations

Direct Speech

Direct speech is a written record of the exact words used by the person speaking. The main rules for writing direct speech in English are as follows:

- The exact words spoken—and no other words—must be surrounded by quotation marks.
- A comma should precede a quotation, but according to American convention other punctuation should be placed inside the quotation marks. Examples:

    He said, "I think I can help you."
    (The period after *you* comes before the quotation marks.)
    "Drive slowly," she said, "and be very careful."
    (The comma after *slowly* and period after *careful* both come inside the quotation marks.)

On the Companion Website

An exercise on direct and indirect speech may be found at **sites.broadviewpress.com/grammar**. Click on **Exercises** and go to **3 "Punctuation and Other Conventions."**

With each change in speaker a new paragraph should begin. Example:

> "Let's go fishing this weekend," Mary suggested. "It should be nice and cool by the water."
>
> "Good idea," agreed Faith. "I'll meet you by the store early Saturday morning."

American convention places the punctuation inside the quotation marks:

- "An iron curtain is descending across Europe," declared Winston Churchill in 1946.

Canadian usage demands that all punctuation go inside the quotation marks in quotations that are stand-alone sentences. At the same time, it allows writers either to follow the American convention or to make an exception when the punctuation clearly pertains only to the structure of the surrounding sentence and not to the quoted word or phrase:

- "An iron curtain is descending across Europe," declared Winston Churchill in 1946.
- Was it Churchill who described the post-war divide between newly Communist Eastern Europe and the West as "an iron curtain"?

The most common difficulties experienced when recording direct speech are as follows:

• **omission of quotation marks:** This happens particularly frequently at the end of a quotation.

needs checking She said, "I will try to come to see you tomorrow. Then she left.

revised She said, "I will try to come to see you tomorrow." Then she left.

• **placing punctuation outside the quotation marks:**

needs checking He shouted, "The house is on fire"!

revised He shouted, "The house is on fire!"

• **including the word *that* before direct speech:** *That* is used before passages of indirect speech, not before passages of direct speech.

needs checking My brother said that, "I think I have acted stupidly."

revised My brother said, "I think I have acted stupidly."

or My brother said that he thought he had acted stupidly.

needs checking The official indicated that, "we are not prepared to allow galloping inflation."

revised The official said, "We are not prepared to allow galloping inflation."

or The official indicated that his government was not prepared to allow galloping inflation.

• **when to indent**: In a formal essay, any quotation longer than four lines[1] should normally be indented to set it off from the body of the text. Any quotation of more than three lines from a poem should also be single-spaced and indented. Quotations set off from the body of the text in this way should not be preceded or followed by quotation marks.

needs checking Larkin's "Days" opens with childlike simplicity: "What are days for? / Days are where we live. / They come, they wake us / Time and time over." But with Larkin, the shadow of mortality is never far distant.

revised Larkin's "Days" opens with childlike simplicity:

What are days for?
Days are where we live.
They come, they wake us
Time and time over.

But with Larkin, the shadow of mortality is never far distant.

Indirect Speech

Indirect speech reports what was said without using the same words that were used by the speaker. The rules for writing indirect speech are as follows:

- Do not use quotation marks.
- Introduce statements with the word *that,* and do not put a comma after *that.* Questions should be introduced with the appropriate question word (*what, why, whether, if, how, when,* etc.).
- First-person pronouns and adjectives (e.g., *I, me, we, us, my, our*) must often be changed to third person (*he, she, they, him, her, them,* etc.) if the subject of the main clause is in third person.

correct "I am not happy with our team's performance," said Paul.

also correct Paul said that he was not happy with his team's performance.

correct I said, "I want my money back."

1 This is what the MLA recommends; the APA specifies forty words.

also correct I said that I wanted my money back.
(Here the subject, *I*, is first person.)

- Second-person pronouns must also sometimes be changed.
- Change the tenses of the verbs to agree with the main verb of the sentence. Usually this involves moving the verbs one step back into the past from the tenses used by the speaker in direct speech. Notice in the first example above, for instance, that the present tense *am* has been changed to the past tense *was* in indirect speech. Here are other examples:

correct "We will do everything we can," he assured me.
correct He assured me that they would do everything they could.
(*Will* and *can* change to *would* and *could*.)
correct "You went to school near Brandon, didn't you?" he asked me.
correct He asked me if I had gone to school near Brandon.
(*Went* changes to *had gone*.)

- Change expressions having to do with time. This is made necessary by the changes in verbs discussed above. For example, *today* in direct speech normally becomes *on that day* in indirect speech, *yesterday* becomes *on the day before*, *tomorrow* becomes *the next day*, and so on.

The most common problems experienced when indirect speech is being used are as follows:

• **confusion of pronouns:** Many writers do not remember to change all the necessary pronouns when shifting from direct to indirect speech.

- When I met him he said, "You have cheated me." (direct)

needs checking When I met him he said that you had cheated me.
revised When I met him he said that I had cheated him.

- He will probably say to you, "I am poor. I need money."

needs checking He will probably tell you that he is poor and that I need money.
revised He will probably tell you that he is poor and that he needs money.

• **verb tenses:** Remember to shift the tenses of the verbs one step back into the past when changing something into indirect speech.

- She said, "I will check my tires tomorrow."

needs checking She said that she will check her tires the next day.
revised She said that she would check her tires the next day.

- "Can I go with you later this afternoon?" he asked.

needs checking He asked if he can go with us later that afternoon.
revised He asked if he could go with us later that afternoon.

Formatting Quotations

There are two ways to signal an exact borrowing: by enclosing it in double quotation marks and by indenting it as a block of text. Which you should choose depends on the length and genre of the quotation and the style guide you are following.

Short Prose Quotations

What counts as a short prose quotation differs among the various reference guides. In MLA style, "short" means up to four lines; in APA style, up to forty words; and in Chicago Style, up to one hundred words. All the guides agree, however, that short quotations must be enclosed in double quotation marks, as in the examples below.

Short quotation, full sentence:
According to Terrence W. Deacon, linguists agree that a human child's capacity to acquire language is inborn: "Without question, children enter the world predisposed to learn human languages" (102).

Short quotation, partial sentence:
According to Terrence W. Deacon, linguists agree that human "children enter the world predisposed to learn human languages" (102).

Long Prose Quotations

Longer prose quotations should be double-spaced and indented, as a block, one tab space from the left margin. Do not include quotation marks; the indentation indicates that the words come exactly from the source. Note that indented quotations are often introduced with a full sentence followed by a colon.

Terrence W. Deacon, like most other linguists, believes that human beings are born with a unique cognitive capacity:

> Without question, children enter the world predisposed to learn human languages. All normal children, raised in normal social environments, inevitably learn their local language, whereas other species, even when raised and taught in this same environment, do not. This demonstrates that human brains come into the world specially equipped for this function. (102)

Verse Quotations

Quoting from verse is a special case. Poetry quotations of three or fewer lines (MLA) may be integrated into your paragraph and enclosed in double quotation marks, with lines separated by a forward slash with a space on either side of it, as in the example below.

> Pope's "Epistle II. To a Lady," in its vivid portrayal of wasted lives, sharply criticizes the social values that render older women superfluous objects of contempt: "Still round and round the Ghosts of Beauty glide, / And haunt the places where their Honor dy'd" (lines 241–42).

If your quotation of three or fewer lines includes a stanza break, MLA style requires you to mark the break by inserting two forward slashes (//), with spaces on either side of them.

> The speaker in "Ode to a Nightingale" seeks, in various ways, to free himself from human consciousness, leaving suffering behind. Keats uses alliteration and repetition to mimic the gradual dissolution of self, the process of intoxication or death: "That I might drink, and leave the world unseen, / And with thee fade away into the forest dim: // Fade far away, dissolve, and quite forget" (lines 19–21).

Poetry quotations of more than three lines in MLA, or two or more lines in Chicago Style, should be, like long prose quotations, indented and set off in a block from your main text. Arrange the lines just as they appear in the original.

> The ending of Margaret Avison's "September Street" moves from the decaying, discordant city toward a glimpse of an outer/inner infinitude:
>
> On the yellow porch
> one sits, not reading headlines; the old eyes
> read far out into the mild
> air, runes.
> See. There: a stray sea-gull. (lines 20–24)

3 Punctuation

Quotations within Quotations

You may sometimes find, within the original passage you wish to quote, words already enclosed in double quotation marks. If your quotation is short, enclose it all in double quotation marks, and use single quotation marks for the embedded quotation.

> Terrence W. Deacon is firm in maintaining that human language differs from other communication systems in kind rather than degree: "Of no other natural form of communication is it legitimate to say that 'language is a more complicated version of that'" (44).

If your quotation is long, keep the double quotation marks of the original.

> Terrence W. Deacon is firm in maintaining that human language differs from other communication systems in kind rather than degree:
>
>> Of no other natural form of communication is it legitimate to say that "language is a more complicated version of that." It is just as misleading to call other species' communication systems *simple* languages as it is to call them languages. In addition to asserting that a Procrustean mapping of one to the other is possible, the analogy ignores the sophistication and power of animals' non-linguistic communication, whose capabilities may also be without language parallels. (44)

Adding to or Deleting from a Quotation

While it is important to use the original's exact wording in a quotation, it is allowable to modify a quotation somewhat, as long as the changes are clearly indicated and do not distort the meaning of the original.

USING SQUARE BRACKETS TO ADD TO A QUOTATION

You may want to add to a quotation in order to clarify what would otherwise be puzzling or ambiguous to someone who does not know its context; in that case, put whatever you add in square brackets.

> Terrence W. Deacon writes that children are born "specially equipped for this [language] function" (102).

USING AN ELLIPSIS TO DELETE FROM A QUOTATION

If you would like to streamline a quotation by omitting anything unnecessary to your point, insert an ellipsis (three spaced dots) to show that you've left material out.

When the quotation looks like a complete sentence but is actually part of a longer sentence, you should provide an ellipsis to show that there is more to the original than you are using.

> As Terrence W. Deacon says, "… children enter the world predisposed to learn human languages" (102).

Note that if the quotation is clearly a partial sentence, ellipses aren't necessary.

> Terrence W. Deacon writes that children are born "specially equipped" to learn human language (102).

When the omitted material runs over a sentence boundary or constitutes a whole sentence or more, insert a period plus an ellipsis.

> Terrence W. Deacon, like most other linguists, believes that human children are born with a unique ability to acquire their native language: "Without question, children enter the world predisposed to learn human languages. . . . [H]uman brains come into the world specially equipped for this function" (102).

Be sparing in modifying quotations; it is all right to have one or two altered quotations in a paper, but if you find yourself changing quotations often, or adding to and omitting from one quotation more than once, reconsider quoting at all. A paraphrase or summary is very often a more effective choice.

Integrating Quotations

Quotations must be worked smoothly and grammatically into your sentences and paragraphs. Always, of course, mark quotations as such, but for the purpose of integrating them into your writing, treat them as if they were your own words. The boundary between what you say and what your source says should be grammatically seamless.

needs checking Terrence W. Deacon points out, "whereas other species, even when raised and taught in this same environment, do not" (102).

revised According to Terrence W. Deacon, while human children brought up under normal conditions acquire the language they are exposed to, "other species, even when raised and taught in this same environment, do not" (102).

AVOIDING "DUMPED" QUOTATIONS

Integrating quotations well also means providing a context for them.

Don't merely drop them into your paper or string them together like beads on a necklace; make sure to introduce them by noting where the material comes from and how it connects to whatever point you are making.

needs checking For many years, linguists have studied how human children acquire language. "Without question, children enter the world predisposed to learn human language" (Deacon 102).

revised Most linguists studying how human children acquire language have come to share the conclusion articulated here by Terrence W. Deacon: "Without question, children enter the world predisposed to learn human language" (102).

needs checking "Without question, children enter the world predisposed to learn human language" (Deacon 102). "There is . . . something special about human brains that enables us to do with ease what no other species can do even minimally without intense effort and remarkably insightful training" (Deacon 103).

revised Terrence W. Deacon bases his claim that we "enter the world predisposed to learn human language" on the fact that very young humans can "do with ease what no other species can do even minimally without intense effort and remarkably insightful training" (102–03).

Signal Phrases

To leave no doubt in your readers' minds about which parts of your essay are yours and which come from elsewhere, identify the sources of your summaries, paraphrases, and quotations with signal phrases, as in the following examples.

- As Carter and Rosenthal have demonstrated, . . .
- In the words of one researcher, . . .
- In his most recent book McGann advances the view that, as he puts it, . . .
- As Nussbaum observes, . . .
- Kendal suggests that . . .
- Freschi and other scholars have rejected these claims, arguing that . . .
- Morgan has emphasized this point in her recent research: . . .
- As Sacks puts it, . . .
- To be sure, Mtele allows that . . .

- In his later novels Hardy takes a bleaker view, frequently suggesting that . . .

In order to help establish your paper's credibility, you may also find it useful at times to include in a signal phrase information that shows why readers should take the source seriously, as in the following example:

> In her landmark work, biologist and conservationist Rachel Carson warns that . . .

Here, the signal phrase mentions the author's professional credentials; it also points out the importance of her book, which is appropriate to do in the case of a work as famous as Carson's *Silent Spring*.

Below is a fuller list of words and expressions that may be useful in the crafting of signal phrases:

according to ________,
acknowledges
adds
admits
advances
agrees
allows
argues
asserts
attests
believes
claims
comments
compares
concludes
confirms
contends
declares
demonstrates
denies
disputes
emphasizes
endorses
finds
grants
illustrates
implies
in the view of ________,
in the words of ________,
insists
intimates
notes
observes
points out
puts it
reasons
refutes
rejects
reports
responds
suggests
takes issue with
thinks
writes

3.3 Capitalization

• **capitalization**: Conventions concerning capitalization have been anything but fixed in the history of the English language. It was not until the late medieval period that capital letters began to be used consistently to begin sentences and proper names. From there the use of capitals became more and more common, until, during the eighteenth century, a great many common nouns were often capitalized. In particular, common nouns naming abstract qualities were capitalized frequently, but many writers would also capitalize without any great degree of consistency any noun or pronoun that they felt to be important. Here is a sample: ... *you may be Mine in the manner you now are for a much longer time, yet I at last may lose you, and one unlucky Moment destroy the Constancy of Ages.*

In the twenty-first century there has been a substantial resurgence of this eighteenth-century practice. Students and other writers—many of whom have not been taught at school the difference between a proper and a common noun—are reverting more and more frequently to the eighteenth-century practice of simply making a stab at what words should begin with a capital letter, without much sense of any rules governing the practice. The basis of those rules is very simple, but there are also a good many subtleties and gray areas.

needs checking In this Company we want to hire Managers who convey a strong sense of Authority.

revised In this company we want to hire managers who convey a strong sense of authority.

In English the fundamental principle on which the rules of capitalization are based is that proper nouns (naming specific persons, places, or things) should always be capitalized. Proper adjectives (adjectives formed from these proper nouns) are also always capitalized. Common nouns, however, are not normally capitalized. *Marx*, *California*, and *Spain*, are all proper nouns. *Marxist*, *Californian*, and *Spanish* are all proper adjectives. The nouns *sinker*, *state*, and *nation*, on the other hand, are all common nouns; they do not name *specific* persons, places, or things. Here are a number of other examples of proper and common nouns:

Proper	***Common***
June	summer
Parliament of Canada	in parliament
Mother (used as a name)	my mother
Memorial Day	as a memorial
National Gallery	a gallery
Director of Admissions	a director
Professor Smith	a professor
the Enlightenment	the eighteenth century
the Restoration (historical period in England)	the restoration (other uses of the word)

Proper	*Common*
the Renaissance (historical period)	renaissance (a revival)
God	a god
Catholic (belonging to that particular church)	catholic (meaning *wide-ranging* or *universal*)
a Liberal (belonging to the Liberal Party)	a liberal (holding liberal ideals)

Some categories frequently cause difficulty over the issue of capitalization. When should one write *professor* and when *Professor*, for example? Following are some more detailed guidelines.

Names of People
Maya Angelou, *Professor Smith*, *Samantha*.

Names of Places
Cleveland, *Asia*, *the North Pole*, *the White House*. Note here that all nouns in a name should be capitalized (*Central Park*, *the Statue of Liberty*).

Names of Days of the Week, Months, and Holidays
Monday, *January*, *Labor Day*, *Yom Kippur*. Note that the names of seasons are not capitalized.

• **Academic names**: All nouns in a formal name should be capitalized: *the University of Chicago*, *Camosun College*, *Philosophy 150*, *Economics 205*. Note that, when not describing a specific course, the names of academic subjects are not capitalized unless they are names of languages. In formal use, capitalize *the Physics Department*, *the Department of History*, etc.

needs checking	Most offices in the Philosophy department are located in the Arts Tower.
revised	Most offices in the Philosophy Department are located in the Arts Tower.
needs checking	She is studying Philosophy at the University of Michigan.
revised	She is studying philosophy at the University of Michigan.

On the Companion Website

Exercises on capitalization may be found at **sites.broadviewpress.com/grammar**. Click on **Exercises** and go to **"Punctuation and Other Conventions."**

• **institutional names**: All nouns in these names should be capitalized (*the University of Toronto, the Audit Committee, the Board of Directors, the Golden Financial Corporation, the Department of Justice*). Note that where a specific body is not being named, capitals should not be used.

needs checking Every large company must have an Audit Committee.
revised Every large company must have an audit committee.

• **occupational names**: When a title is used before a person's name, it must be capitalized: *Reverend Philips*; *President Biden*; *Professor Said*. When the title appears as a substitute for the name, capitalizing the title is optional. As always in such cases, be sure to be consistent.

worth checking The Prime Minister will deliver a speech this afternoon, and the president of Shell Oil will be speaking this evening.
revised The Prime Minister will deliver a speech this afternoon, and the President of Shell Oil will be speaking this evening.
or The prime minister will deliver a speech this afternoon, and the president of Shell Oil will be speaking this evening.

When titles follow a name, capitalization of the title is optional.

Sandra Mbeki, professor of German
or Sandra Mbeki, Professor of German
Frank Gibbs, president of Acme Tools
or Frank Gibbs, President of Acme Tools

Names of Major Historical Events, Movements, or Periods

It is not surprising that students and other writers often become confused over whether or not to capitalize historical references of this sort, since the names of centuries, decades, and so on are not normally capitalized. It is thus correct to refer to *the eighteenth century* in lower case, but *the Enlightenment* with a capital; to *the medieval period*, but to *the Middle Ages* with capitals; *the thirties*, to refer to the 1930s, but *the Depression* to refer to the economic condition that dominated the period. If we speak of the study of *Romantic literature* we are speaking of the study of the Romantic period (i.e., the late eighteenth and early nineteenth centuries), whereas if we speak of studying romantic literature we are referring to the study of any literary works with romantic themes. Here are a few more examples of major historical events, movements, or periods that are normally capitalized: *the Thirty Years' War, the Great Fire of London, World War II, the Big Bang, the Impressionists.*

Names of Religions, Deities, Religious Persons, Terms, or Texts
Nouns or adjectives of this sort are normally capitalized: *Buddhism, a Buddhist, Islam, a Muslim, Christian, Jewish, Holy Ghost, the Bible, the Qur'an.*

Names of Races, Groups, Nationalities, and Their Languages
Nouns or adjectives of this sort should be capitalized: *Mexican, Hispanic, the Yoruba, Nova Scotians, a Native American, Indigenous peoples of North America, European professor, Chinese, students learning Mandarin or French.*

Names of Geographical Areas
Depending on context, certain geographical words may denote either a direction or an area—or, indeed, more than one area. If, for example, we say *keep traveling west, and you will reach the sea*, the word *west* is a direction and should not be capitalized. If, however, we write that *in the West, American voters tend to be fiscally conservative*, when referring to the western portion of the United States, it is normal to capitalize *West*. In a different context we might write *in the West, capitalism took root in the seventeenth and eighteenth centuries*. In that context *the West* is a synonym for *the Western World*. Similar multiple meanings may attach to the words *south*, *north*, and *east* and *South*, *North*, and *East*.

• **literary titles:** Major words in titles should be capitalized. Articles, short prepositions, and conjunctions are normally not capitalized in titles.

needs checking Robert Boardman discusses *The Bridge On The River Kwai* extensively in his book.

revised Robert Boardman discusses *The Bridge on the River Kwai* extensively in his book.

Names of Teams or Clubs
Where a specific name is given it should be capitalized (*the Vancouver Canucks, Team USA, Manchester United*). Where a specific team or club

is mentioned but not given its formal name, no capitals should be used (*the national team, our bridge club*).

Names of Abstract Qualities

As in the eighteenth century, writers today are often inclined to capitalize the names of abstract qualities in order to signal their importance. These are common nouns, however, and should in almost all cases not be capitalized. An exception occurs if in the context the abstract quality is personified; in that case the noun may be regarded as a proper name (*if Chance is often blind, it is also often a powerful friend*).

needs checking Keats shared with writers of the Romantic period a strong interest in notions of Truth and Beauty.

revised Keats shared with writers of the Romantic period a strong interest in notions of truth and beauty.

Capitalization Following a Colon

Some style guides recommend capitalizing independent clauses that begin after a colon. Somewhat oddly, they do not similarly recommend capitalizing independent clauses that begin after a semicolon. In view of this inconsistency—and in view as well of the fact that the colon is often used for purposes other than separating independent clauses—it is probably wisest for students to refrain from any use of capitals following a colon.

3.4 Abbreviations

Abbreviations are a convenient way of presenting information in a smaller amount of space. This section discusses conventions for using abbreviations in formal writing.

Titles

Titles are normally abbreviated when used immediately before or after a person's full name.

Mr. Isaiah Thomas *Dr. Jane Phelps*
Sammy Davis Jr. *Marcia Gibbs, MD*

When using a title together with the last name only, the full title should be written out.

Prof. Marc Ereshefsky *Professor Ereshefsky*
Sen. Keith Davey *Senator Davey*

Academic and Business Terms

Common abbreviations are acceptable in formal writing so long as they are likely to be readily understood. Otherwise, the full name should be written out when first used and the abbreviation given in parentheses. Thereafter, the abbreviation may be used on its own, as shown in these examples:

- The Atomic Energy Commission (AEC) has broad-ranging regulatory authority.
- The American Philosophical Association (APA) holds three large regional meetings annually.

Latin abbreviations

Several abbreviations of Latin terms are common in formal academic writing:

cf.	*compare* (Latin *confer*)
e.g.	*for example* (Latin *exempli gratia*)
et al.	*and others* (Latin *et alia*)
etc.	*and so on* (Latin *et cetera*: *and the rest*)
ibid.	*in the same book or passage* (Latin *ibidem*: *in the same place*)
i.e.	*that is to say* (Latin *id est*)
NB	*note well* (Latin *nota bene*)

Numbers

Numbers of one or two words should be written out. Use figures for all other numbers.

needs checking The building is 72 stories tall.
revised The building is seventy-two stories tall.

The same principle applies for dollar figures (or figures in other currencies).

needs checking She lent her brother 10 dollars.
revised She lent her brother ten dollars.

It is acceptable to combine figures and words for very large numbers:

- The government is projecting a $200 billion deficit.

In general, figures should be used in addresses, in dates, to give percentages, and to report scores or statistics.

needs checking In the third game of the tournament, Sweden and Czechia tied three three.

revised In the third game of the tournament, Sweden and Czechia tied 3–3.

Italics

Italics serve several different functions. While short stories, poems, and other works are set off by quotation marks, longer works and the names of newspapers, magazines, and so on should appear in italics:

"The Dead"	*Dubliners*
"Burnt Norton"	*Four Quartets*
"Budget Controversy Continues"	*The Economist*
"Smells Like Teen Spirit"	*Nevermind*

Italics are also used for the names of paintings and sculptures, television series, and software. In addition, italics may be used for words or phrases from other languages in written English.

needs checking The play ends with an appearance of a deus ex machina.
revised The play ends with an appearance of a *deus ex machina.*

Either italics or quotation marks may be used to indicate that words are mentioned rather than used (see above, under "Quotation Marks"). Finally, italics are often used to provide special emphasis that is not otherwise clear from the context or the structure of the sentence.

3.5 Spelling

Spelling and Sound

The wittiest example of the illogic of English spelling remains Bernard Shaw's famous spelling of *fish* as *ghoti*. The *gh* sounds like the *gh* in *enough*; the *o* sounds like the *o* in *women* (once spelled *wimmen*, incidentally); and the *ti* sounds like the *ti* in *nation* or *station*. Shaw passionately advocated a rationalization of English spelling; it still has not happened, and probably never will. Perhaps the best way to learn correct spelling is to be tested by someone else, or to test yourself every week or so on a different group of words. For example, you might learn the words from the list below beginning with *a* and *b* one week, the words beginning with *c* and *d* the next week, and so on.

• **spell-check**: No computer can be a substitute for careful proofreading. Spell-check is wonderful, but it cannot tell if it is your friend or your fiend, or if you have signed off a letter with best wishes or beast wishes. Grammar check too makes plenty of errors. Very frequently, for example, it will flag as incorrect an entirely correct use of the subjunctive.

• **spelling and sound—a/an**: Authorities agree that an *n* should be added to the indefinite article when the following word begins with a vowel sound. This is a "rule," it should be noted, that is based entirely on euphony; the reason that *a egg* is not "good English" is simply that it is awkward to say. Thus it is that we use *an* not only before words that begin with a vowel, but also before words that are pronounced as if they began with a vowel (*an hour*, *an f-word*).

Something of a gray area exists with a small group of words that have a *his-* sound at the beginning, and in which the second syllable is stressed. No one would think of writing *an hiccup* or *an hellish day*, and nor are most people ever tempted to write *an history* or *an hysterectomy*. Many people, though, think that *an hysterical outburst* sounds better than *a hysterical outburst*, and that *an historical introduction* sounds better than *a historical introduction*. As the first sound in an unstressed syllable, the *h* in such words is softer than the *h* in such words as *history*, where a strong stress is placed on the first syllable. Some authorities ridicule this common practice; we sound the *h* in such words, goes the argument, and therefore we should use *a* rather than *an*. But what is the rationale for this "rule" in the first place? Again, purely what sounds better. And the fact is that many people find it easier to say *an historical introduction* than *a historical introduction*. So why the fuss? We may reasonably disagree as to which sounds better, but there is surely no justification for terming one correct and the other incorrect.

• **spelling and sound**: Many spelling mistakes result from similarities in the pronunciation of words with very different meanings. These are covered in the list below. Other words that cause spelling difficulties are listed separately.

absent (adjective)	absence (noun)
absorb	absorption
accept	except
access (*entry*)	excess (*too much*)
advice (noun)	advise (verb)
affect (verb)	effect (noun)
allowed (*permitted*)	aloud
alter (*change*)	altar (*in a church*)
appraise (*value*)	apprise (*inform*)
base (*foundation*)	bass (*in music*)
bath (noun)	bathe (verb)
berry (*fruit*)	bury (*the dead*)
beside (*by the side of*)	besides (*as well as*)

birth	berth (*bed*)
bitten	beaten
bizarre (*strange*)	bazaar (*market*)
bloc (political grouping)	block
breath (noun)	breathe (verb)
buoy (*in the water*)	boy
buy (*purchase*)	by
cash	cache (*hiding place*)
casual (*informal*)	causal (*to do with causes*)
cause	case
ceased (*stopped*)	seized (*grabbed*)
ceiling (*above you*)	sealing
chick	cheek/chic (*stylish*; pronounced *sheek*)
chose (past tense)	choose (present tense)
cite (*make reference to*)	sight/site
climatic (*climate*)	climactic (*climax*)
cloths (*fabric*)	clothes
colonel (*officer*)	colonial (*of colonies*)
coma (*unconscious*)	comma (*punctuation*)
compliment (*praise*)	complement (*make complete*)
conscious (*aware*)	conscience (*sense of right*)
contract	construct
conventional (*usual*)	convectional (*transfer of heat*)
conversation	conservation/concentration
convinced	convicted (*of a crime*)
cord (*rope*)	chord (*music*)
council (*group*)	counsel (*advice*)
course	coarse (*rough*)
credible (*believable*)	creditable (*deserving credit*)
critic (*one who criticizes*)	critique (*piece of criticism*)
defer (*show respect*)	differ
deference (*respect*)	difference
deprecate (*criticize*)	depreciate (*reduce in value*)
desert (*dry place*; also *what is deserved*)	dessert (*sweet*)
device (*thing*)	devise (*to plan*)
died/had died	dead/was dead/dyed (*colored*)
dissent (*protest*)	descent (*downward motion*)
distant (adjective)	distance (noun)
edition (*of a book*, etc.)	addition (*something added*)
emigrant	immigrant
entomology (*study of insects*)	etymology (*study of words*)
envelop (verb)	envelope (noun)
except	expect
exercise	exorcise (*remove*)
fear	fair/fare (*payment*)
feeling	filling
fell	feel/fill
flaunt (*display*)	flout (*disobey*)
formally	formerly (*previously*)

forth (*forward*)	fourth (*after third*)
forward	foreword (*in a book*)
foul	fowl (*birds*)
future	feature
genus (*biological type*)	genius (*creative intelligence*)
greet	great/grate (*scrape*)
guerrillas	gorillas
guided (*led*)	guarded (*protected*)
had	heard/head
heat	heart/hate
heir (*inheritor*)	air
human	humane (*kind*)
illicit (*not permitted*)	elicit (*bring forth*)
illusion (*unreal image*)	allusion (*reference*)
immigrate	emigrate
independent (adjective)	independence (noun)
inhabit (*live in*)	inhibit (*retard*)
instance (*occurrence*)	instants (*moments*)
intense (*concentrating*)	intents (*purposes*)
isle (*island*)	aisle (*to walk in*)
kernel	colonel
know	no/now
lack	lake
later	latter/letter
lath (*piece of wood*)	lathe (*machine*)
lead (*heavy element*)	led (*guided*)
leave	leaf
leave	live
leaving	living
lessen (*reduce*)	lesson
let	late
lightning (*from clouds*)	lightening (*becoming lighter*)
lose (*be unable to find*)	loose (*not tight*)
mad (*insane*)	maid (*servant*)
man	men
martial (*to do with fighting*)	marshal
mental	metal
merry	marry
met	meet/mate
minor (*underage*, or *lesser*)	miner (*underground*)
mist (*light fog*)	missed
moral (*ethical*)	morale (*spirit*)
mourning (*after death*)	morning
new	knew
of	off
on	own
ones	once
ordinance (*decree*)	ordnance (*guns*)
pain	pane (*of glass*)
patients (*sick people*)	patience (*ability to wait*)

peer (*look closely*)	pier (*wharf*)
perpetrate (*be guilty of*)	perpetuate (*cause to continue*)
perquisite (*privilege*)	prerequisite (*requirement*)
personal (*private*)	personnel (*employees*)
perspective (*vision*)	prospective (*anticipated*)
peruse (*study*)	pursue (*follow*)
poor	pour (*liquid*)/pore
precede (*go before*)	proceed (*continue*)
precedent	president
price (*cost*)	prize (*reward*)
prostate (*gland*)	prostrate (*lying down*)
quay (*wharf*; pronounced *key*)	key
quite	quiet (*not noisy*)
rein (*to control animals*)	rain/reign
release (*let go*)	realize (*discover*)
relieve (verb)	relief (noun)
residence (*place*)	residents (*people*)
response (noun)	responds (verb)
rid	ride
ridden	written
rise	rice
rite (*ritual*)	right/write
rod	rode/reared
rote (*repetition*)	wrote
saved	served
saw	seen
saw	so/sew
scene (*location*)	seen
seam (*in clothes*)	seem (*appear*)
secret	sacred (*holy*)
sell (verb)	sail (*boat*)/sale
senses	census (*population count*)
shed	shade
shone	shown
shot	short
sit	sat/set
smell	smile
snake	snack (*small meal*)
soar	sore (*hurt*)
sole (*single*, *a fish*, or *an undersurface*)	soul (*spirit*)
sort (*type or kind*)	sought (*looked for*)
steal (present tense)	stole (past tense)
straight (*not crooked*)	strait (*of water*)
striped (e.g., *a zebra*)	stripped (*uncovered*)
suite (*rooms* or *music*)	suit/sweet
super	supper (*meal*)
suppose	supposed to
sympathies (noun)	sympathize (verb)
tale (*story*)	tail

talk	took
tap	tape
than	then
they	there/their
thing	think
this	these
throw	threw (past tense)
tied	tired
urban (*in cities*)	urbane (*sophisticated*)
vanish (*disappear*)	varnish
vein (*to carry blood*)	vain
vicious (*brutal*)	viscous (*sticky*)
waist (*your middle*)	waste
wait	weight (*heaviness*)
waive (*give up*)	wave
wants	once
weak (*not strong*)	week
weather (*sunny*, *wet*, etc.)	whether (*or not*)
wedding	weeding
were	where
whole (*complete*)	hole (*empty space*)
wholly (*completely*)	holy (*sacred*)/holly
woman	women
won	worn
yoke (*for animals*)	yolk (*of an egg*)

- **English language spelling variations:** A number of words that cause spelling difficulties are spelled differently in different countries. In most cases Australians prefer British spellings. Either British or American is correct in Canada, so long as the writer is consistent.

American	British
behavior	behaviour
center	centre
color	colour
defense	defence
favor	favour
favorite	favourite
fiber	fibre
fulfill	fulfil
gray	grey
humor	humour
likable	likeable
maneuver	manoeuvre
marvelous	marvellous
meter (*measurement*)	metre
neighbor	neighbour
omelet	omelette
program	programme

Shakespearian	Shakespearean
skillful	skilful
skeptical	sceptical
theater	theatre
traveling	travelling

On the Companion Website

An exercise on spelling may be found at **sites.broadviewpress.com/grammar**. Click on **Exercises** and go to **3.**

Spelling: One Word or Two?

A number of very commonly used English words have over many years become accepted as one word because they are combined so often. Other similar combinations, however, should still be written as two words. In a few cases one can see English usage changing on this point right now. A generation ago, for example, *alright* as one word could not have been found in any dictionary. Now numerous authorities regard *alright* as acceptable, and perhaps in another generation or two it will have completely replaced *all right*. For the moment, though, it is best in formal writing to stick with *all right* rather than the more colloquial *alright*.

One word preferred

What has been written as two words should be one. Here are some common examples:

already:	one word when used as an adverb (*He has finished already.*)
altogether:	one word when used as an adverb to mean *completely* or *entirely* (*He is not altogether happy with the result.*)
another	
anybody	
anyone:	one word unless it is followed by *of*
anytime:	one word when used as an adverb (*You can come over anytime.*)
awhile:	one word when used as an adverb
bathroom	
bloodshed	
businessman	(but preferred usage is *business person* [or *executive*, or *entrepreneur*, etc.])
cannot:	*can not* is less common, but still acceptable

everybody

everyday: one word when used as an adjective (*Brushing your teeth should be part of your everyday routine*—here *everyday* is an adjective modifying the noun *routine*.)

needs checking Doctors perform procedures of this sort everyday.

revised Doctors perform procedures of this sort every day.

needs checking Doctors perform procedures of this sort as part of their every day routine.

revised Doctors perform procedures of this sort as part of their everyday routine.

everyone: one word unless it is followed by *of*

everything

forever

furthermore

indeed

intact

into: one word except in the relatively few cases where the senses of *in* and *to* are clearly separate (*She brought the craft in to land.*)

maybe: when used as an adverb meaning *perhaps* (*Maybe I will join you later*—here the verb is *will join* and *maybe* is an adverb.)

nearby

nobody

onto: see *into*

ourselves

somebody

someone

sometime: one word when used as an adverb (*I would love to see you sometime.*)

straightforward

themselves

wartime

whatever

whenever

Two words preferred

What has been written as one word should be two words. Here are some common examples:

a lot
all ready: two words when not used as an adverb (*We are all ready to go.*)
all right
all together: two words when not used as an adverb (*They were all together when I left them.*)
any time: two words when used in a sentence as noun preceded by modifier (*Is there any time next week when we could meet?*)
every day: two words when not used as an adjective (*We see each other every day.*)
every time
in fact
in front
in order
in spite of
may be: two words when used as a verb (*He may be here later tonight—may be* is the verb in the sentence.)
no one
some time: two words when used in a sentence as noun preceded by modifier (*Will you be able to take some time to study this?*)

Commonly Misspelled Words

Following is a list of some other commonly misspelled words:

abbreviation
absence
accelerator
accident
accidentally
accommodation
achieve
acknowledge
acquire
acquisition
acquit
acre
across
address
adjacent
advertisement
affidavit
aficionado
ambulance
ameba (also *amoeba*)
ammonia
among
amortize
amount
anachronism
analogous
analysis
anchor
androgynous
annihilate
antecedent
antisemitic
anxious
apocalypse
apparatus
apparently
appreciate
approach
architect
arguable
argument
arsonist
arteriosclerosis
artillery
asinine
atheist
author
auxiliary
awesome
awful
bacteria

basically
battery
beautiful
beginning
believe
boast
boastful
bouillon
breakfast
bulletin
burglar
burial
buried
business
candidate
capillary
cappuccino
Caribbean
carpentry
cautious
ceiling
chaise longue (or *chaise lounge*)
changeable
character
chilblain
chlorophyll
choir
cholesterol
chrome
chromosome
chronological
chrysalis
chrysanthemum
coincidence
colleague
colonel
colossal
column
commitment
committee
comparative
competition
competitor
complexion
conceive
condemn
conjunction
connoisseur
consensus
consistent
controller
convenience
cooperation
cooperative
courteous
courtesy
creator
creature
criticism
cyst
decisive
definite
delicious
description
desirable
despair
despise
destroy
develop
diesel
different
dilemma
dining
disappear
disappoint
disastrous
discrimination
disease
disintegrate
dissatisfied
dominate
dormitory
double
doubtful
drunkard
drunkenness
duchess
due
dyeing
dying
eclipse
eczema
effective
efficient
eighth
embarrass
employee
encourage
enemy
enmity
enormous
entertain
enthusiasm
entitle
entrepreneur
environment
enzyme
epidermis
epididymis
erroneous
esophagus
especially
espresso
essential
exaggerate
excessive
excite
exercise
exhilaration
existence
existent
experience
extraordinary
Fahrenheit
faithful
faithfully
farinaceous
fault
February
financial
foreigner
foretell
forty
fourth
gauge
gamete
germination
government
grammar
grateful
gruesome
guarantee
guerrillas
guilty
happened
happiest
harass
hatred
hectare
helpful
hyena
hypothesis
ichthyology
idiosyncratic
imaginary
imagine
immigration
immersible
impeccable
importance
impresario
inchoate
incomprehensible
indigenous
independent
indestructible
indispensable
ineffable
infinitesimal
inoculate
insufferable
intention
intentional
interrupt
irrelevant
irresponsible
isosceles
isthmus
itinerary
jealous
jeopardy
journalist
junction
kneel
knowledge
knowledgeable
laboratories
laboratory
language
lazy, laziness
ledger
leisure
liaise
liberation
library

license
lieutenant
liquid, liquefy
literature
lying
medicine
medieval
membrane
memento
merciful
mermaid
millennia
millennium
millionaire
mischief
mischievous
modern
naked
naughty
necessary
necessity
noticeable
nuclear
nucleus
obscene
obsolescent
obsolete
occasion
occasional
occupy
occur
occurred
occurrence
omit
ophthalmology
ourselves
paid
parallel
parliament
parliamentary
party
permissible
permission
perpendicular
perseverance
photosynthesis
playful
possess
possession
poultry
predictable
pregnancy
pregnant
prerogative
prescription
privilege
properly
psychiatric
psychological
punctuation
pursue
questionnaire
really
receipt
recommend
referee
reference
regret
repeat
repetition
replies
reply
residence (*place*)
residents (*people*)
restaurant
restaurateur
revolutionary
rheumatism
rhododendron
rhombus
rhubarb
rhyme
rhythm
saddest
sandals
scene
schedule
schizophrenic
science
scintillate
scissors
scream
scrumptious
search
seize
sense
separate
shining
shotgun
sigh
significant
simultaneous
sincerely
ski, skis, skied, skiing
slippery
slogan
smart
solemn
spaghetti
speech
spongy
sponsor
stale
stingy
stomach
stubborn
studious
studying
stupefy
stupid
subordinate
subpoena
substitute
subtle, subtlety
suburbs
succeed
success, successful
sue, suing
summary
supersede
surprised
surreptitious
surrounded
survive
symbol
synthesis
talkative
tarred
television
temperature
tendency
theoretical
theory
title
tough
tragedy
trophy
truly
unique
until
vacancy
vacillate
valuable
vegetable
vehicle
vicious
visitor
volume
voluntary
Wednesday
welcome
whisper
writer
writing
written
yield
zucchini

4 EAL: For Those Whose Native Language Is Not English

The fact that different languages have different grammatical and syntactical conventions creates particular problems for anyone learning a new language. That is a point that may seem obvious, but a large percentage of the population of North America, Britain, and Australia (a majority of whom are unilingual) remain unaware of it as a felt reality. It is a measure of the degree to which English-speaking North Americans are unaccustomed to learning other languages that ESL—English as a Second Language—remains a widely-used umbrella term. We prefer EAL—English as an Additional Language—a term that allows for the possibility that someone learning English may already know several other languages.

This section of *The Broadview Guide to Grammar, Usage, and Punctuation* focuses on some of the peculiarities of English that are most likely to present difficulties to those learning the language. More often than not, multilingual students who are not yet fully fluent in English have at least as good a grasp of the formal grammatical principles of the language as do those for whom English is their first language. If you are not familiar with these principles, however, Section 1 (pages 1–82) may be helpful.

Because of the differences in the ways that the structure of a student's own language may compare with English, students from different linguistic backgrounds are likely to want to focus on different aspects of English; what is particularly challenging for someone whose first language is Vietnamese may seem straightforward to someone whose first language is Spanish, and vice versa. For that reason the following guide may be helpful:

> Many speakers of languages such as Chinese (in its various forms), Japanese, and Vietnamese are likely, as a result of the ways in which those languages differ structurally from English, to have particular difficulty with topics treated under the following headings in this book: articles (4.1–2); plurals (4.5); infinitives (4.12); conjugation of verbs, especially in the simple present tense (1.4); word order (2.4, 4.17–18).

Many speakers of languages such as Russian, Polish, and Bulgarian are likely, as a result of the ways in which those languages differ structurally from English, to have particular difficulty with topics treated under the following headings in this book: articles (4.1–2); omission of the predicate (4.3); double negatives (4.9); the present perfect tense (1.4); word order (2.4, 4.17–18); possessives (4.7); relative pronouns such as *who* and *which* (4.6); countable and uncountable nouns and words such as *much*, *many*, *little*, and *few*.

Many speakers of languages such as French, Spanish, and Italian are likely, as a result of the ways in which those languages differ structurally from English, to have particular difficulty with topics treated under the following headings in this book: relative pronouns such as *who* and *which* (4.6); double negatives (4.9); comparatives and superlatives (4.10); progressive (or continuous) verb tenses (1.4, 4.14); word order (4.17–18).

4.1. **articles**: Articles are words used to introduce nouns. Unlike many other languages, English often requires the use of articles:

needs checking We are interested in house with garage.
revised We are interested in a house with a garage.

There are only three articles—*a*, *an*, and *the*. Articles show whether or not one is drawing attention to a particular person or thing. For example, we would say *I stood beside a house* if we did not want to draw attention to that particular house, but *I stood beside the house that the Taylors used to live in* if we wanted to draw attention to the particular house.

A (or *an* if the noun following begins with a vowel sound) is an indefinite article—used with singular nouns when you do not want to be definite or specific about which thing or person you are referring to. *The* is a definite article, used with singular or plural nouns when you *do* want to be definite or specific. Remember that, if you use *the*, you are suggesting that there can be only one or one group of what you are referring to.

In order to use articles properly in English it is important to understand the distinction English makes between nouns naming things that are countable (*houses*, *books*, *trees*, etc.) and nouns naming things that are not countable (*milk*, *confusion*, etc). *A* can be used with singular count nouns (*a radio*), *the* with singular and plural count nouns (*the carpet, the horses*). *The* should be used with a non-count noun when it is followed by a specifying phrase (*the furniture in my house*). Some non-count nouns name things that it does seem possible to count: *sugar, grass, furniture*, etc. In such cases counting must in English be done indirectly: *a grain of sugar, two grains of sugar, three blades of grass, four pieces of furniture*, and so on.

Distinguishing between count and non-count nouns is inevitably a challenge for those whose first language is not English. A dictionary such as *The Oxford Advanced Learner's Dictionary* can be very helpful; unlike most dictionaries it indicates whether or not each noun is a count noun.

needs checking They bought a nice furniture.
revised They bought a nice piece of furniture.

● *Frequently Used Non-count Nouns*

abstractions: advice, anger, beauty, confidence, courage, fun, happiness, hate, health, honesty, information, knowledge, love, poverty, truth, wealth, wisdom.

to eat and drink: bacon, beef, beer, bread, broccoli, butter, cabbage, candy, cauliflower, celery, cereal, cheese, chicken, chocolate, coffee, corn, cream, fish, flour, fruit, ice, ice cream, lettuce, margarine, meat, milk, oil, pasta, pepper, rice, salt, spinach, sugar, tea, water, wine, yogurt.

other substances: air, cement, clothing, coal, dirt, equipment, furniture, gas, gasoline, gold, grass, homework, jewelry, luggage, lumber, machinery, mail, metal, money, music, paper, petroleum, plastic, poetry, pollution, research, scenery, silver, snow, soap, steel, timber, traffic, transportation, violence, weather, wood, wool, work.

The plural of many of these non-count nouns may be employed when you want to denote more than one type of the substance. *Breads*, for example, refers to different sorts of bread; *coffees* refers to different types of coffee, *grasses* to different types of grass, and so on.

4.2. **dropping the article**: Articles are not used in English to the same extent that they are used in some other languages; nouns can frequently stand alone without any article, particularly when they are being used in a general, non-specific sense. When used in this way, non-count and plural-count nouns need no article.

needs checking If the English is to be spoken correctly, the good grammar is important.

revised If English is to be spoken correctly, good grammar is important.

needs checking The freedom is something everyone values.

revised Freedom is something everyone values.

In most cases no article is necessary before a noun that is capitalized:

needs checking They were strolling through the Stanley Park.

revised They were strolling through Stanley Park.

Unfortunately, there are many exceptions to this rule (e.g., *the Hebrides, the Netherlands, the Dominican Republic, the United Kingdom, the Soviet Union, the United States*). A dictionary such as *The Oxford Advanced Learner's Dictionary* should be consulted in any case where you are uncertain if an article is needed.

4.3. **omission of the subject or predicate**: Many languages allow the subject or the predicate to be assumed in certain situations, whereas (with the exception of imperative formations such as [*you*] *come here this instant!*) English requires that sentences include explicit subjects and predicates.

needs checking Is very hot this afternoon.

revised It is very hot this afternoon.

needs checking She doctor and her husband carpenter. They both like their jobs.

revised She is a doctor and her husband is a carpenter. They both like their jobs.

needs checking Is not possible to finish the job this week.

revised It is not possible to finish the job this week.

needs checking Most authorities agree that malaria is a disease that could be targeted for eradication because would be feasible and relatively inexpensive to develop and distribute effective vaccines.

revised Most authorities agree that malaria is a disease that could be targeted for eradication because it would be feasible and relatively inexpensive to develop and distribute effective vaccines.

needs checking By the end of the century, were almost one million more people in Houston than there had been in 1980.

revised By the end of the century, there were almost one million more people in Houston than there had been in 1980.

Note: In this sort of sentence construction English requires a "dummy" subject (such as *it* or *there*) before the verb *to be*;[1] by contrast, languages such as Spanish allow the subject to be assumed in similar circumstances.

4.4. **repetition of the subject**: Unlike many other languages, English does not permit the repetition of either the subject or the object within a single clause.

needs checking The body of water outside the hotel it is called Chesapeake Bay.

revised The body of water outside the hotel is called Chesapeake Bay.

needs checking The members of the cast loved the play that they were acting in it.

revised The members of the cast loved the play that they were acting in.

4.5: **plurals**: Since many languages do not form plural nouns differently from nouns in the singular, it is easy if your background is in one of those languages to omit the *s* in plural formations in English.

needs checking Many team play here every weekend.

revised Many teams play here every weekend.

4.6. **gendered words/neutered words**: In Romance languages such as French all nouns are masculine or feminine; for that reason many speakers of these languages use a masculine or feminine pronoun in English where the neuter pronoun is required.

needs checking When I first saw the lake he was as smooth as glass.

1 Also known as an "empty subject" or an "artificial subject."

revised When I first saw the lake it was as smooth as glass.

Most Romance languages and Slavic languages do not differentiate things from people in their relative pronouns. For that reason it is easy to forget to use *who* or *whom* rather than *that* or *which* in English.

needs checking I spent the weekend visiting my grandparents, which are both in their eighties.
revised I spent the weekend visiting my grandparents, who are both in their eighties.

4.7. **possessives**: Some languages make no distinction between possessive pronouns and possessive adjectives; in others possessive adjectives agree with what is possessed, not the possessor. In both cases English's different approach can cause difficulty.

needs checking I told him that the book was my.
revised I told him that the book was mine.
or I told him that it was my book.

needs checking As he sat in his office he looked out of her window at the moon.
revised As he sat in his office he looked out of his window at the moon.

Additional Material Online

Exercises specially designed for those whose native language is not English may be found at **sites.broadviewpress.com/grammar**. Click on **Exercises** and go to **"EAL."**

4.8. **negatives**: Whereas English uses auxiliaries to form standard negatives, many languages use particles. As a result of this difference, the correct formation of negatives in English can present difficulties.

needs checking In later life he not wanted to see his old friends.
revised In later life he did not want to see his old friends.
or In later life he never wanted to see his old friends.

4.9. **double negatives**: Languages in both the Slavic and Romance groups permit double negatives, thus making it difficult for those whose first language is from one of those groups to become habituated to the English prohibition against double negatives—and to grasp that words such as *without* can function as negatives.

needs checking	I never not like to be away from home very long.
revised	I never like to be away from home for long.
or	I do not like to be away from home for long.

needs checking	No one can survive in this society without no money.
revised	No one can survive in this society without money.
or	No one can survive in this society with no money.
or	No one can survive in this society without any money.

4.10. **comparatives and superlatives**: In many languages comparatives and superlatives must always include a word equivalent to *more* or *most*; there are no parallels for English formations such as *better*, *best* or *larger*, *largest*. Not surprisingly, many whose first language is not English find it difficult to get used to the English system of alternative forms of the comparative and superlative.

needs checking	I wanted to buy the more larger size.
revised	I wanted to buy the larger size.

4.11. **compound verb formations**: English has many verb tenses, and many compound verb forms, including compound negative forms; these cause particular difficulty for those who are used to a less heavily conjugated system of verb tenses.

needs checking	I waited for some time, but he not come.
revised	I waited for some time, but he did not come.

needs checking	She always working hard to help her family.
revised	She is always working hard to help her family.

4.12. **infinitives**: The infinitive form (*to go*, *to be*, *to do*, etc.) is not native to many languages, particularly many Far Eastern languages. For that reason it is sometimes given tense or person markers. In English the infinitive must always keep the same form.

needs checking	When she first met him she found it difficult to felt any sympathy for him.
revised	When she first met him she found it difficult to feel any sympathy for him.

4.13. **phrasal verbs**: A phrasal verb occurs when a word that would normally function as a preposition instead becomes part of a two-word verb. *Break in*, *take off*, *put on*, *pick up*, *give up*—these are all examples of phrasal verbs. In such combinations an adverb cannot intercede between the two.

needs checking	He put hurriedly on his clothes.
revised	He put on his clothes hurriedly.

4.14. **continuous verb tenses** (see also under 1.4 Verb Forms): In English the progressive (or continuous) tenses are not normally used with many verbs having to do with feelings, emotions, or senses. Some of these verbs are *to see*, *to hear*, *to understand*, *to believe*, *to hope*, *to know*, *to think* (meaning *believe*), *to trust*, *to comprehend*, *to mean*, *to doubt*, *to suppose*, *to wish*, *to want*, *to love*, *to desire*, *to prefer*, *to dislike*, *to hate*.

needs checking	He is not understanding what I mean.
revised	He does not understand what I mean.

needs checking	At that time he was believing that everything on Earth was created within one week.
revised	At that time he believed that everything on Earth was created within one week.

4.15. **infinitives and gerunds**: As discussed in the chapter on this topic earlier, there are no rules in English as to why some verbs must be followed by an infinitive and others by a gerund, while still others may take either. Some combinations are particularly odd from the point of view of anyone whose first language is not English. For example, *start to go* and *start going* may be used interchangeably in most circumstances, whereas *stop going* is the opposite of both; *stop to go* has a quite different meaning. Unfortunately, these combinations must be learned one by one. One helpful rule, however, is that an infinitive can never follow a preposition.

needs checking	They were planning for to go to New York for the holidays.
revised	They were planning to go to New York for the holidays.
or	They were planning on going to New York for the holidays.
or	They were planning a trip to New York for the holidays.

4.16. **prepositions**: As discussed in the chapter on preposition problems earlier, there are no overarching logical principles governing the use of prepositions in English. We say *angry with someone* rather than *angry to someone* or *angry against someone* purely as a matter of convention. In some cases general guidelines may be offered, however. For example, where place and time are concerned, *in* is used for larger expanses of space and larger durations of time; *at* is used for specific times and specific addresses; and *on* is used for street names (without precise addresses) and days of the week or the month (without precise times). *She lives in England, she lives on Downing St., she lives at 10 Downing St; she will meet you at 1 p.m.; she will see you sometime in December; she will see you on December 15.*

needs checking I live in 316 7th St. NW.
revised I live at 316 7th St. NW.
or I live on 7th St. NW.
or I live in the house at 316 7th St. NW.

4.17. **word order (subject/verb/object)**: The rules governing word order in English are much more rigid than those of many other languages. For one thing, the subject, verb, and object normally appear in that order. Many other languages permit far more freedom in the ordering of subject, object, and verb, and for that reason this basic structural element of English can be difficult to grasp.

needs checking Yoshiki opportunities always welcomes.
revised Yoshiki always welcomes opportunities.

(Note: Speakers of languages such as Japanese and Korean, in which the verb must always come last in a sentence, are particularly likely to experience this sort of difficulty with English.)

needs checking Opportunities welcomes Yevgeny always.
revised Yevgeny always welcomes opportunities.

(Note: Speakers of languages such as Russian, in which the object may appear before the subject, are particularly likely to experience this sort of difficulty with English.)

In most Romance languages object pronouns come before the verb. This often creates difficulties for native speakers of those languages with the word order required in English, where object pronouns normally follow the verb.

needs checking When we these give him, he will be very grateful.
revised When we give him these, he will be very grateful.

4.18. **word order (adjectives and adverbs)**: In English, adjectives generally precede the noun to which they refer, while adverbs generally follow the verb to which they refer. Moreover, there are rules governing the order of adjectives and adverbs—rules which native English speakers have absorbed unconsciously, but which otherwise must be learnt. Since it is common to use two or more adjectives to describe something, problems often arise.

The proper order of adjectives: determiners (*my*, *his*, *this*, *that*, etc.); adjectives concerning number or quantity (*first*, *many*, *some*, etc.); adjectives expressing a subjective opinion (*beautiful*, *sad*, *fascinating*, etc.); adjectives concerning size or shape (*large*, *small*, *straight*, *flat*, etc.); adjectives describing age or condition (*old*, *clean*, *sharp*, *wet*, etc.); adjectives describing color (*red*, *mauve*, *blue*, etc.); adjectives naming substances and adjectives that may also be used as nouns (*metal*, *woolen*, *English*, etc.); the noun.

needs checking They lived in a white lovely house near the sea.
revised They lived in a lovely white house near the sea.

APPENDIX: *Correction Key*

abbr	Abbreviation error (267–69)
adj	Adjective used improperly (5–7, 182–83)
adv	Adverb used improperly (7–8, 182–83)
agr	Agreement issue with subject & verb (40–42)
amb	Ambiguity (83–89, 130–32)
appr	Appropriateness of language issue (124–25, 127–29, 191–94)
awk	Awkward expression or construction
cap	Capitalization faulty (262–67)
⁀‿	Close up
dang	Dangling construction, dangling modifier (83–89)
ℓ	Delete
dict	Diction faulty
frag	Fragment (incomplete sentence) (22–23, 31–35)
^	Insert
ital	Italics
lc	Lowercase should be used (262–67)
¶	Paragraph: begin a new paragraph here
no ¶	Paragraph: do not begin a new paragraph here
//	Parallelism faulty or lacking (137–40)
pass	Passive voice (55–61)

p	Punctuation error (236–53)
❛	Apostrophe (or single quotation mark) needed (191–92, 249–51, 252–53, 259)
^,	Comma needed (144–45, 237–42)
⊙	Period needed (22–39, 236)
" "	Quotation marks needed (251–53)
pron	Pronoun reference error (8–10, 124–32)
rep	Repetition
run-on	Run-on sentence (fused sentence or comma splice) (22–31)
ss	Sentence structure faulty
sl	Slang or overly informal language (191–94)
#	Space should be added
sp	Spelling error (269–79)
t	Tense of verb wrong (39–53, 88–89, 100–05)
tr	Transition faulty or insufficient (36–38, 206–28)
∼	Transposed elements
v	Verb form wrong (39–53)
w	Wordiness (228–35)

INDEX

Entries in **bold** are to words, not topics.

Appendix / Index

Appendix / Index

Appendix / Index

The Authors

Doug Babington was for many years Director of the Writing Centre at Queen's University; he is co-author of *Writing Analytically with Readings* (2012) and also author of a book of bilingual poems, *News from the Recent Quake* (2015).

Corey Frost, an Associate Professor in the English Department at The City University of New Jersey, has published widely on poetry and poetics, orality, and digital pedagogy; his *A Prescription for Zombies: A Critical Approach to English Grammar and Usage* is forthcoming from Broadview Press.

Don LePan's other books include *The Broadview Pocket Glossary of Literary Terms* (2013), *Animals: A Novel* (2010), and *Lucy and Bonbon: A Novel* (2022); he is a general editor of *The Broadview Anthology of British Literature* and Co-Managing Editor of *The Broadview Anthology of American Literature*.

Maureen Okun, for many years a professor in both the English and the Liberal Studies Departments at Vancouver Island University, is the author, co-author, or editor of several books, among them Sir Thomas Malory's *Le Morte Darthur: Selections* (2014).

Nora Ruddock is co-author of *The Broadview Pocket Guide to Citation and Documentation* and co-editor of *The Broadview Anthology of Expository Prose* and of *Popular Culture: A Broadview Topics Reader*.

Karen Weingarten, Associate Chair of the English Department at Queens College, CUNY, is the author of *Abortion in the American Imagination: Before Life and Choice, 1880–1940* (2014), and of *Pregnancy Test* (2023), a volume in Bloomsbury's "Object Lessons" series.

About the Publisher

The word "broadview" expresses a good deal of the philosophy behind our company. Our focus is very much on the humanities and social sciences—especially literature, writing, and philosophy—but within these fields we are open to a broad range of academic approaches and political viewpoints. We strive in particular to produce high-quality, pedagogically useful books for higher education classrooms—anthologies, editions, sourcebooks, surveys of particular academic fields and sub-fields, and also course texts for subjects such as composition, business communication, and critical thinking. We welcome the perspectives of authors from marginalized and underrepresented groups, and we have a strong commitment to the environment. We publish English-language works and translations from many parts of the world, and our books are available world-wide; we also publish a select list of titles with a specifically Canadian emphasis.

broadview press

This book is made of paper from well-managed FSC® - certified forests, recycled materials, and other controlled sources.